FOUNDATIONS OF ETHICS

FOUNDATIONS OF
ETHICS

THE GIFFORD LECTURES
delivered in the
University of Aberdeen, 1935–6
by
SIR W. DAVID ROSS
Provost of Oriel College, Oxford
President of the British Academy

OXFORD
AT THE CLARENDON PRESS

Oxford University Press, Ely House, London W. 1

GLASGOW NEW YORK TORONTO MELBOURNE WELLINGTON
CAPE TOWN SALISBURY IBADAN NAIROBI LUSAKA ADDIS ABABA
BOMBAY CALCUTTA MADRAS KARACHI LAHORE DACCA
KUALA LUMPUR HONG KONG TOKYO

FIRST EDITION 1939

REPRINTED LITHOGRAPHICALLY IN GREAT BRITAIN
AT THE UNIVERSITY PRESS, OXFORD
FROM SHEETS OF THE FIRST EDITION
1949, 1951, 1960, 1963, 1968

CONTENTS

I. INTRODUCTORY

II. NATURALISTIC DEFINITIONS OF 'RIGHT'

III. THE NATURE OF RIGHTNESS AND OBLIGATION

IV. THEORIES ABOUT THE GROUND OF RIGHTNESS

CONTENTS

V. THE OBLIGATION TO FULFIL PROMISES

VI. THE GENERAL NATURE OF WHAT IS RIGHT: SOME THEORIES

VII. THE GENERAL NATURE OF WHAT IS RIGHT: POSITIVE CONSIDERATION OF THE QUESTION

VIII. THE KNOWLEDGE OF WHAT IS RIGHT

CONTENTS

IX. THE PSYCHOLOGY OF MORAL ACTION

CONTENTS

X. INDETERMINACY AND INDETERMINISM

XI. THE NATURE OF GOODNESS

mind, or, failing this, of the greater number and the most authoritative; for if we both refute the objections and leave the common opinions undisturbed, we shall have proved the case sufficiently.'[1] Again, Kant's method was the same. 'I have adopted in this work', he says in the Preface to the *Grundlegung*, 'the method which I think most suitable, proceeding analytically from common knowledge to the determination of its ultimate principle';[2] and to this 'common knowledge' he again and again returns, as to that on which his own theory is based and by comparison with which it must from time to time be tested.

I would add a further remark. Aristotle habitually takes as a starting-point a consideration of the opinions not only of the many but also of the wise. He is predisposed to think that in all the main theories, no less than in the views of the plain man, there is much that is true, and that even when theories are in broad opposition to each other, each is probably erring only by overstatement or mis-statement of something that is profoundly true. It would indeed be strange if any of the main theories of ethics were completely in error; it is far more likely that each has grasped something that is both true and important but has, not through blindness to moral values but by some apparently trivial logical error, claimed as the whole truth what is only one of a set of connected truths. I may illustrate the ideal which ethical theory should aim at, by an example taken from a different field. A physical object which has a certain shape, say the circular shape, when seen from different points of view presents a variety of apparent shapes, ranging from the circular through a whole series of elliptical shapes, which are explicable as the result of different perspectives. So too, if we could reach the truth about the essential problems of ethics, we should be able to recognize the varieties of common opinion and the varieties of philosophical view as being none of them wholly false, but all of them distortions of the truth due to the different perspectives in which men have looked at the pro-

---

[1] *Eth. Nic.* 1145^b 2–7.
[2] Akad. Ausgabe, iv. 392 (Abbott's translation, p. 9).

blems. Some slight contribution to this result is all that I would claim for the attempt which will follow.

The method of ethics is in this respect different from that of the physical sciences. In them it would be a great mistake to take as our starting-point either the opinions of the many or those of the wise. For in them we have a more direct avenue to truth; the appeal must always be from opinions to the facts of sense-perception; and natural science entered on its secure path of progress only when in the days of Galileo men began to make careful observations and experiments instead of relying on *a priori* assumptions that had hitherto prevailed. In ethics we have no such direct appeal. We must start with the opinions that are crystallized in ordinary language and ordinary ways of thinking, and our attempt must be to make these thoughts, little by little, more definite and distinct, and by comparing one with another to discover at what points each opinion must be purged of excess and mis-statement till it becomes harmonious with other opinions which have been purified in the same way.

In the complex fabric of common opinions about moral questions two main strands may be discovered. On the one hand, there is a group of opinions involving the closely connected ideas of duty, of right and wrong, of moral law or laws, of imperatives. On the other hand, there are opinions involving the idea of goods or ends to be aimed at. In the one case the ideal of human life is envisaged as obedience to laws, in the other as the progressive satisfaction of desire and attainment of ends. The one may be called the Hebrew, the other the Greek ideal. In the first way of thinking, the laws of human life were originally thought of not as grasped on their own merits by human thought but as having been authoritatively revealed on Mount Sinai as the will of God. But as ethics came to win for itself a status independent of religion, these laws or others like them came to be thought of as grasped by an intuitive act of human reason, as categorical imperatives directly apprehended as involved in the nature of the moral universe.

At the same time the plurality of the imperatives in the original code tended to be pruned down, as when Christ reduced the ten commandments to two, stating our duty to God and to man respectively, or as when Kant reduced the multiplicity of imperatives to the one imperative, 'act so that your act can be universalized'. But through all such varieties of view the thought remains in essence the same, that the essence of the good life is obedience to one or more principles. On the other hand, we have the whole variety of teleological systems of ethics, which start with the thought of certain things as good, and of the good life as essentially the attempt to bring these into existence. In the crudest form of this general type of theory, the individual's own pleasure is thought of as the supreme end. In the course of time, this view was modified in two directions. On the one hand, other elements than pleasure were recognized as elements in the end; as when Aristotle substituted for pleasure εὐδαιμονία, which he thought of as including pleasure indeed but as having for its main constituent good activity. On the other hand, the *general* pleasure came to be thought of as being, instead of his own pleasure, the proper object of each agent's activity. And finally, by a fusion of these two corrections of the original, crude view, we have the view of ideal Utilitarianism, that the supreme end is to secure, both for oneself and for others, a life which includes in it both good activity and pleasure.

The general antithesis between ethical systems in which duty is the central theme, and those in which goods or ends are the central theme, is clear enough. Yet it would be a mistake to suppose that there has ever been an ethics of duty which did not include a recognition of intrinsic goods, or an ethics of ends which did not include a recognition of duties. Kant's ethics has been perhaps the nearest approach to a pure ethics of duty; and he claims to evolve the whole duty of man by an analysis of the implications of the notion of duty, without introducing the thought of goods to be aimed at. But it has often been shown that when it comes to the point, he has to argue for the wrongness of certain acts on the ground of the badness of the results they bring. On the other hand, Aristotle's ethics would seem at first sight to be based entirely on the notion of a good or an end to be achieved; but in his discussion of the individual virtues he does not relate the virtuous act to the final goal of human life, but treats it as simply right in its own nature. Nor are these mere lapses on the part of Kant or Aristotle, due to lack of firmness of purpose. The facts have been too strong for them; both the notion of right and the notion of good are implied in the study of moral questions, and any one who tries to work with one only will sooner or later find himself forced to introduce the other.

The question remains whether either is more fundamental than the other, in the sense that the other can be defined by reference to it. Only a very careful attention to each of the two terms will justify us in giving any answer to this question, and we may find even after careful attention that we cannot give a simple answer.

The question what is the relation between the attributes goodness and rightness is, however, only part of a larger question or series of questions which can be asked about either of them. About each of them we can, to begin with, ask the question whether it is definable or indefinable. By this question I mean the question, with regard to 'right' and again with regard to 'good', whether that which we are thinking of when we use these terms can be fully expressed by using a complex expression of such a form as '*a* which is *b*' or '*m* in the relation *r* to *n*', in which none of the terms used is a synonym of the term about which we are asking the question. The question is, in fact, whether 'good' or 'right' can be elucidated without remainder in terms other than itself.

The various theories which offer definitions of ethical terms may be classified in various ways, by using a variety of different principles. It seems to me that it is on the whole best to divide them into two main classes. In one of these the term in question is defined by reference to the attitude of some being or other.

One would be holding a view of this kind if one defined a right act, or a good moral state, as one which God approves, or again as one which a majority of men approve. Here the rightness or goodness of that which is right or good is identified with God's having, or most men's having, a certain attitude towards that thing. In the other main type of view, the term in question is defined by reference to the total consequences of the act or moral state in question. One would be holding a view of this kind if one defined a right act as one which would produce a maximum of life, or as one which would produce a maximum of happiness.

This is not a logically perfect classification of the attempts to define ethical terms; for it is not based on an *a priori* disjunction. It is not possible to see *a priori* that any such attempt must be an attempt to define them either by reference to a mental attitude or by reference to total consequences, as it is possible to see that any angle must be right, acute, or obtuse. Nor do I see how this list of the types of theory could be added to so as to make a complete list of all the possible types of attempt to define ethical terms. What I think we can assure ourselves of by inspection is that in fact all or almost all the attempts to define them have conformed to one or other of these types.

There is another way of classifying them which cuts right across this classification, viz. Professor Moore's classification into naturalistic and non-naturalistic definitions. The former are definitions which claim to define an ethical term without using any other ethical term; the latter are attempts to define one ethical term by the aid of another. It is clear that mental-attitude theories may be of either of these types. If you define 'right' as meaning what is approved by the community, you are putting forward a naturalistic definition. If you define 'good' as meaning 'such that it *ought* to be desired', you are putting forward a non-naturalistic definition. Consequence theories also may be either naturalistic or non-naturalistic. If you define 'right' as 'productive of the greatest pleasure', you are putting forward a naturalistic definition. If you define it as 'productive of the greatest amount of *good*', you are putting forward a non-naturalistic definition.

We might adopt either of these classifications as our main classification, and use the other for purposes of subdivision. We may either use the scheme:

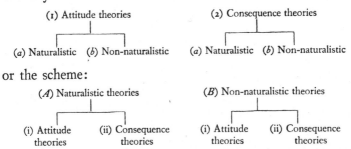

or the scheme:

From one point of view the former classification seems the more fundamental. It seems to bring together the theories that have most in common. Thus the definition of 'right' as 'productive of most pleasure' (2*a*) *seems* to have more in common with the definition of it as 'productive of most good' (2*b*) than with the definition of it as 'approved by society' (1*a*). And historically the two former are more closely connected; for theory (2*b*) has in fact been produced by reflection on the shortcomings of theory (2*a*), which has no historical connexion with theory (1*a*).

Yet in their general colouring, if I may put it so, all naturalistic theories have more in common than any of them has with any non-naturalistic theory. For all naturalistic theories amount to saying that all the statements in which we use either the predicate 'right' or the predicate 'good', and think that in doing so we are dealing with a very special kind of attribute, are really statements of ordinary matters of fact which can be discovered by mere observation. Whether a certain kind of act is commanded by society, or whether it produces more pleasure than any other possible act would, is a thing to be discovered (if at all) by ordinary observation; if that is all that 'ought' means, there is no need and no place for a special branch of study called ethics; for there are no ineradicably ethical terms. On the other hand, all non-naturalistic theories have more in common with one another than any of them has with any naturalistic theory; for while they define some ethical terms by reference to others, they preserve at least one ethical term as irreducibly different from any term expressive of ordinary matter of fact. And if, as we have seen, there have been historical connexions between certain naturalistic and certain non-naturalistic theories, there have also been historical connexions between attitude theories and consequence theories. The whole sociological school of ethics, while it is evolutionary in its origin, and therefore began by defining ethical terms by reference to the biological consequences of certain acts or states, shows a tendency to relapse into defining 'right' as 'commanded by the community'—a tendency most clear in the French sociologists, who claim to reduce ethics to the *science des mœurs*, the historical and comparative study of the codes current in different communities, and reject the notion that there is any absolute standard by which these codes can be judged to be higher or lower.

On the whole, then, the division into naturalistic and non-naturalistic theories is the more important, and I have had it always in the background of my mind, though I have not thought it necessary to discuss all the naturalistic theories consecutively and all the non-naturalistic theories consecutively.

It is not always clear at first sight to which type a well-known theory really belongs. At first sight Hedonism, in all its forms, whether egoistic or utilitarian, would seem to belong to the class of naturalistic theories about rightness, and it is often so described—described as 'reducing' rightness to the tendency to produce pleasure. But we must be careful to distinguish two possibilities. A hedonist may take the view that this is what rightness *is*, that this is its correct definition; and then he is offering a naturalistic theory. But he may be holding something quite different. He may be holding that rightness is something indefinable, and merely claiming that that which *makes* right acts right is their tendency to promote pleasure. Then he is holding that a non-ethical characteristic, a pyschological characteristic, is the ground of rightness but not its essence. And if so, the theory, whether right or wrong, is not a naturalistic theory; the specific quality of rightness is then still recognized as something not reducible to merely psychological terms.

The hedonists have not always been very clear which of the two things they meant. Bentham, for instance, *seems* to take the naturalistic view. I take leave to quote some sentences from an earlier book of my own.[1]

'He says[2] that "when thus interpreted" (i.e. as meaning "conformable to the principle of utility"), "the words *ought* and *right* ... and others of that stamp, have a meaning; when otherwise, they have none". And elsewhere[3] he says "admitting (what is not true) that the word *right* can have a meaning without reference to utility". Yet as Sidgwick points out,[4] "when Bentham explains (*Principles of Morals and Legislation*, chap. i, para. 1, note) that his fundamental principle 'states the greatest happiness of all those whose interest is in question as being the right and proper end of human action', we cannot understand him really to *mean* by the word 'right' 'conducive to the general happiness'; for the proposition that it is conducive to general happiness to take general happiness as an end of action, though not exactly a tautology, can hardly serve as the fundamental principle of a moral system." Bentham has evidently not made up his mind clearly whether he thinks that "right" *means* "productive of the general happiness", *or* that being productive of the general happiness is what makes right acts right; and would very likely have thought the difference unimportant. Mill does not, so far as I know, discuss the question whether right is definable. He states his creed in the form "actions are right in proportion as they tend to promote happiness",[5] where the claim that is made is

[1] *The Right and the Good,* 7–8.
[2] *Principles of Morals and Legislation,* chap. i, para. 10.
[3] Ibid., para. 14. 10.
[4] *Methods of Ethics,* ed. 7, 26 n.
[5] *Utilitarianism,* copyright eds., 9.

not that this is what "right" means, but that this is the other characteristic in virtue of which actions that are right are right. And Sidgwick says[1] that the meaning of "right" or "ought" "is too elementary to admit of any formal definition", and expressly repudiates[2] the view that "right" means "productive of any particular sort of result".'

It is impossible to know what the Egoism or the Utilitarianism of any particular thinker means, and to pass judgement on it, until we have decided which of the two things the writer in question means; and since different writers have meant different things, and the same writer has sometimes not known which of the two he meant, it is not possible to say that Egoism or again that Utilitarianism is the name of any one ethical theory. Each of the two names may stand for either of two theories which logically are quite different, though they unite in the general characteristic of laying great stress on pleasure in the discussion of ethical questions.

Up to now I have referred to these various views as views that may be taken about ethical characteristics in general. It is clear, however, that it is possible to hold one type of view about one ethical characteristic and another about another, to hold for instance a relational view about 'right' and a non-relational view about 'good'; and these views might be united in a single system. So that we cannot use this classification as a classification of ethical systems taken as a whole; though there will probably be a tendency for a thinker who holds one type of view about one ethical characteristic to hold a similar view about others. Again, it is possible that one type of view might be *true* about one characteristic and false about another. From this point onwards, we must consider the main ethical characteristics separately, and ask what kind of view is true about them. Now the two main ethical characteristics or groups of characteristics are those which are designated by such terms as 'right', 'obligatory', 'my duty' on the one hand, and by 'good', 'noble', 'valuable' on the other. A good many people

[1] *Methods of Ethics*, ed. 7, 32.   [2] Ibid. 25–6.

are disinclined to admit any clear-cut distinction between the two groups, and inclined to use 'good' and 'right', for instance, indifferently as applied to actions. ·And I should be the last to claim that in all our ordinary use of language we draw a clear distinction between the two words. What I would claim, and I think the claim is very important if we want to think clearly about ethics, is that there are two quite different characteristics, which, once we have grasped the difference between them, we see it to be proper to designate by different words, even if we do not always in ordinary speech so designate them; and I suggest 'right' as on the whole the most convenient word for designating the one, and 'good' as the most convenient term for designating the other. That the characteristics are different I hope to show later.[1]

[1] Cf. pp. 165–7.

II

NATURALISTIC DEFINITIONS OF 'RIGHT'

I WILL first discuss the meaning of 'right', and I will begin by some discussion of the evolutionary type of view. On historical grounds it is justifiable to treat this school as a whole, though it has in fact not limited itself to one type of definition of ethical terms. It has at times tended to define 'right' by reference to consequences—to the promotion of life—and at times to define it by reference to the approval of the community; and at times it has tended to define it in yet a third way, which does not belong either to the attitude type or to the consequence type—to define right conduct as evolved conduct.

The evolutionary and sociological school of thought has on the whole shown little if any awareness of the distinction between two questions which are logically entirely different. One is the question as to the *meaning* of such terms as 'right' or 'obligatory', as to what it is that we intend to say about conduct when we describe it as right or obligatory. The other is the question what is the other characteristic, or what are the other characteristics, in virtue of which we describe conduct as having the characteristic of being right or obligatory. The method usually followed by this school is to pass under review a variety of types of act that are commonly called right; to find, or argue, that they have some characteristic in common, e.g. that of being comparatively highly evolved; and then to assume that that is what 'right' or 'obligatory' means. But it is clear that, assuming the review of instances to be adequate, and the discovery of a common characteristic to be correct, two possibilities remain. The common characteristic thus discovered may be what we mean by 'right'; or it may be a characteristic on which rightness is consequent but which is itself different from rightness; not the essence of rightness, but its ground.

Now what we are considering at present is views as to the *meaning* of rightness, and it is surely obvious that the supposition that 'right' *means* 'comparatively evolved' is not one that can be seriously entertained. If we ask ourselves what 'more evolved' means, we shall find in it, I think, two main elements: (1) that conduct so described comes, in time, after a process of evolution of more or less duration, and (2) that it has a characteristic which usually emerges in the course of evolution, that of being complex, in comparison with the simple activities which appear in an early stage of evolution. And it is surely clear that neither temporal posteriority nor complexity, nor the union of the two, is that which we mean to refer to when we use the term 'right' or 'obligatory'. Even if it be true that there is a perfect correspondence between the characteristic of being right and that of being more evolved, such that neither is ever found without the other, there is really no resemblance between the characteristic which we have in mind when we say 'right' or 'obligatory' and that which we have in mind when we say 'more evolved'. The claim to have found the *meaning* of rightness must be completely rejected. We are left, however, with two possibilities as to the underlying intention of those who carelessly claim in this way to have discovered the meaning of rightness. (1) They may be thinking that some actions genuinely have the characteristic of rightness, and that they have discovered another quality or characteristic on which this always depends. In this case theirs will not be at bottom a naturalistic account of rightness, and there will be nothing in their view which on *general* grounds need be rejected by those who hold that rightness is an indefinable characteristic which certain actions have and others have not. It will simply be a matter for inquiry in detail whether the characteristic of evolvedness is in fact that whose presence in an action renders the action right. Now to a large extent the coincidence between evolvedness and rightness which is claimed to exist may be admitted to exist. Let me anticipate the view I will later put forward, so far as to say that one of the main grounds on which we regard actions as right is their presumed tendency to bring as much good as is possible into being for all men, or for all sentient beings. Let us accept the general truth of the evolutionary account which describes man as having evolved from the condition of an animal seeking food and safety for itself and for its offspring, but without any interest in any wider community, to his present condition, in which many men consciously seek the good of their whole class or community, and some consciously seek the good of the whole human race. If this be true, then there will be a tendency for the acts that come later in the course of evolution to envisage and to promote a wider good than those that come earlier. And if 'more evolved' means, not merely coming later in the course of evolution, but sharing in the general characteristics that accompany the coursë of evolution, the more evolved acts will tend to have, in comparison with the less evolved, the characteristic of promoting a wider range of goods, and will on that account tend more to be right acts.

But even if we admit that the characteristics of being highly evolved, of tending to promote the maximum good, and of being right tend to a large extent to go together, we must surely recognize a closer relation between the last two characteristics than between the first and the third. It will be not because of the merely historical fact that they come later in the course of evolution, but because they share in a characteristic common to the later stages of evolution, the characteristic of being promotive of a wider good, that acts will tend to be right. The evolutionary account will be encouraging, in so far as it gives us reason to believe that, as time has gone on, actions envisaging a wider good have tended to become commoner, and that the same process may be expected to continue; but it will not have thrown any light on the question what makes right acts right, any more than on the question what rightness is. No particular position in the temporal process, be it late or early, has as such any tendency to make an act right.

(2) So far I have been dealing with one of two alternatives, that the evolutionary account recognizes the existence of the attribute of rightness and is looking for its ground. But another alternative remains. May the upshot of the evolutionary account be, not that obligatoriness just means evolvedness, nor that evolvedness is the ground of obligatoriness, but that there is no such thing as obligatoriness; that there is *nothing* in reality answering to the meaning which we have in mind when we use the word obligatory, the only distinction that remains being that between less and more evolved acts? This was certainly not Herbert Spencer's intention; there never was a more serious moralist, one more persuaded that there is an objective difference between right and wrong. Nor again was it the intention of Huxley, who in his famous Romanes Lecture urged that we are under an obligation to reverse to a large extent the tendency of the evolutionary process. Yet there is no doubt that in many minds the study of evolutionary science has tended to produce scepticism about the difference between right and wrong. That has come about in this way. Before the evolutionary theory had been put forward, the question as to the origin of the idea of obligation had hardly arisen. So long as man was thought to be a species standing in no historical continuity with the lower animals, it was possible to regard the idea of obligation as an original and permanent endowment of the human race. But we cannot now refuse to accept the view that the human race *is* historically continuous with lower animal species, which we cannot credit with having had any idea of obligation. The question of the origin of the idea becomes a pressing one, and the position is often adopted that either the idea of obligation must be a complex one, a sort of amalgam put together by a sort of mental chemistry out of simpler elements which we *can* ascribe to our animal ancestors, or that if it is not this, it is a fanciful and illegitimate invention belonging to a fairly late stage in evolution.

To this the answer has often been made, that the question of origin has no logical connexion with that of validity, and

that in particular the validity of the idea of obligation cannot
be impaired by any problem as to how the idea arose. This
answer I cannot accept in its entirety. I venture to quote again
from my earlier book.

'An inquiry into the origin of a judgement may have the effect
of establishing its validity. Take, for instance, the judgement that
the angles of a triangle are equal to two right angles. We find that
the historical origin of this judgement lies in certain pre-existing
judgements which are its premisses, plus the exercise of a certain
activity of inferring. Now if we find that these pre-existing judgements were really instances of knowing, and that the inferring was
also really knowing—was the apprehension of a necessary connexion—our inquiry into the origin of the judgement in question
will have established its validity. On the other hand, if any one can
show that A holds actions of type B to be wrong simply because
(for instance) he knows such actions to be forbidden by the society
he lives in, he shows that A has no real reason for believing that
such actions have the specific quality of wrongness, since between
being forbidden by the community and being wrong there is no
necessary connexion. He does not, indeed, show the belief to be
untrue, but he shows that A has no sufficient reason for holding it
true; and in this sense he undermines its validity.'[1]

The question is, whether evolutionary theories have done
this. Now the solid fact with which we start is that we now
have the thought that certain acts are right and others wrong.
And it seems clear—I will attempt to argue for this in more
detail later[2]—that by right and wrong we do not mean 'commanded, or forbidden, by the community'. The question then
is, how did we come by this thought? Two answers may be
given. One is that by an exercise of fancy we came to believe,
without justification, that certain actions have this character.
The other is that, having up to a certain time recognized only
naturalistic characteristics of actions, such as that they conduced to survival or that they were commanded by the community, the human mind, when it had reached a certain degree

---

[1] *The Right and the Good*, 14.   [2] pp. 24–5.

of maturity, became able to detect in actions the non-naturalistic characteristic of rightness. Whichever account is given, we are crediting the human mind with having made at some time a new departure—either the fanciful invention of a new idea, the idea of rightness, or the detection of a hitherto undetected characteristic of actions. In either case a breach of continuity is involved, and that involved in the former case is certainly no more easy to understand than that involved in the latter. We are perfectly familiar with the fact that within the limits of a single life a mind may pass from a state in which it is quite incapable of forming certain ideas or of making certain judgements, to one in which it is capable of doing this, and we do not doubt the truth of our mature judgements because we were earlier incapable of making them; we do not for that reason treat them as mere plays of fancy. We recognize that the truths in question—say, mathematical truths—were there all the time to be apprehended, but that a certain degree of mental maturity was necessary for their apprehension. And if this be so within the limits of a single life, it is only natural to suppose that the growth and ripening of mind from generation to generation which has taken place in the history of evolution was similarly the necessary condition for the apprehension of certain truths which were there all the time to be apprehended.

There is, however, another way in which the work of the evolutionary school tends to produce in some minds a scepticism about moral principles. The studies of the comparative sociologists have revealed very clearly the great variety of views on moral questions that exists in different societies, and this sometimes leads to the belief that there are no objective moral principles, but only a variety of codes adopted by various communities. And this scepticism is reinforced by the fact that even within the same society and as between people of approximately the same degree of mental development very different views are often held on moral questions. This might seem to make the position about moral truth very different from that with regard to mathematical truth. Mathematical truths are accepted unanimously by those who have reached sufficient mental maturity; but mental maturity is no sufficient guarantee of agreement on moral questions.

Yet on examination the diversity of opinion on moral questions is found to rest not on disagreement about fundamental moral principles, but partly on differences in the circumstances of different societies, and partly on different views which people hold, not on moral questions but on questions of fact. Professor Taylor has pointed out[1] that the approval of the blood-feud by some societies and its condemnation by others is explicable by the simple fact that in an early and unsettled state of society, where there is no proper provision for the public punishment of murderers, private vengeance is the only way of securing respect for life, while in a more settled state of society this is better left to the arm of the law. That is an example of the fact that an actual change of circumstances may make that wrong which once was right (or at least more wrong that which was less wrong), without any variety of fundamental moral principles being involved. Or again, where there is no variation in the outward circumstances, there may be a difference of view on some non-moral question which leads to a difference of view on a secondary moral question, while the same fundamental moral principle may be accepted by both parties. To quote two more of Professor Taylor's examples,[2] the difference between those who think vaccination right and those who think it wrong turns largely on a difference of opinion on the question of fact whether vaccination does or does not prevent smallpox, while both parties accept the principle that parents should try to save their children from disease. And the difference of opinion between fox-hunters and those who condemn fox-hunting turns largely on a difference of view as to the comparative intensity of the pain of the fox and the enjoyment of his hunters.

The more we examine differences of opinion on the *media*

[1] *Mind*, xxxv (1926), 289.
[2] Ibid. 287–8.

axiomata of morals, the more we shall find them not to depend on divergence on fundamental moral questions, but either on the different circumstances of the differing parties or on the different opinions they hold on ordinary matters of fact. Now where a difference of circumstances causes one type of act to be judged right in one state of society and another in another, no doubt is cast on either moral judgement by the fact that if they are stated abstractly, without reference to the difference of circumstances, they contradict one another. And where different acts are judged right owing to a difference of opinion on a question of fact, it is not on the fundamental moral judgement that is accepted by both parties, but on the opinions about ordinary fact which form their minor premisses, that doubt is cast.

Yet it would be a mistake to regard the differences of opinion on moral questions as due entirely to these two causes. For while all men are probably at bottom agreed in thinking we ought to produce as much that is good as we can, and agreed also as to the goodness of certain things—virtue, intelligent thought, and happiness—there is a real difference of opinion as to the comparative worth of different goods; and this is a difference not on an ordinary matter of fact but on a moral question. It is in this region—in the *comparative* valuation of things that are agreed to be valuable—that the source of many of our differences of moral opinion is to be found.

Yet even if we admit the existence of great differences of opinion in this region, that does not really justify the conclusion that in this region there is not an objective truth to be known, any more than difference of opinion about ordinary matters of fact or about scientific questions justifies the conclusion that there there is no objective truth. The very fact of difference of opinion is itself evidence of the persisting confidence of all of us that there is an objective truth. To find a difference of opinion between ourselves and others, or between our own ages and previous ages, should weaken perhaps our confidence in our own opinions, but not weaken our confidence that there is some opinion that would be true. And I think we can go farther than this. We may feel doubt about many scientific doctrines which hold the field at any given moment. We may think that a new theory may for a time displace an older theory which was nearer the truth. But we do not really doubt that, in the main, science progresses towards a truer and truer view of the nature of the physical universe. We do not seriously question that we are nearer the truth about the physical universe than were the Greeks, or the men of the Middle Ages, or indeed the men of any century previous to our own. Individual vagaries of opinion may for a time prevail, but there is going on all the time the steady work of men whose purpose is to discover the truth, and the truth is there to be discovered. It is only natural then that mankind should, though with many set-backs, progress in the main steadily towards truer views. The same is in a measure true of moral questions. There is going on all the time a steady devotion, on the part of many people, to the task of discovering moral truth. Individual interests may often draw us aside from the truth, to over-estimate goods that will be enjoyed by ourselves or our class or our country, and to under-estimate those that will be enjoyed by other individuals or classes or countries. Probably the search for moral truth has been more affected by selfish interests than the search for scientific truth. But the moral facts are there, and disinterested thinking about them is always going on; and in the end the facts tend to prevail and to win our assent. And this progress goes on not only within individual lives. Each individual does not start where his predecessors started. He absorbs the new discoveries that have been made in the previous generation. Nor is the progress always gradual. Every now and then there arises in the course of history a genius who discovers some great moral truth which only needs to be proclaimed to be generally recognized; and all who come under his influence find their whole moral insight lifted to a higher plane. In the main, then, we need not doubt that man progresses fairly steadily towards moral truth as he does towards scientific.

There occur, also, periods in which mankind appears to sink to a lower moral plane, in which old moral standards are given up and moral lawlessness sets in. But these need not disquiet us too much. What is questioned in such periods is not, as a rule, the fundamental principles of morality but the *media axiomata*, the rules for which no *a priori* evidence can be claimed but which rest partly on circumstances that have ceased to exist, and partly on opinions about ordinary fact that have been given up. No doubt many people whose nature it is to escape from all moral restrictions will turn such a period of questioning to their own account. But the questioning itself is often perfectly sincere, and springs from a desire to get down to bedrock in morality; and this is all to the good. Moral codes that will not survive such questioning do not deserve to survive it, and those that do deserve to survive it will do so. *Magna est veritas et praevalet.* Acquiescence in moral codes merely because they are accepted by the society in which one lives spells death to progress in moral insight. The honest questioning of old rules, when it has led to their abandonment, has led to the discovery of new ones which have usually been much more rigorous, demanding an inner morality which is harder to practise than outward conformity to a code. Thus the periods in which the old tables of the law are broken form no real exception to the general progress in moral insight which we are justified in believing to have taken place.

These considerations have led us rather far afield from the study of evolutionary theories of morality, though they arose legitimately out of it. I return to repeat that evolutionary theories do not seem to have offered us anything that can be accepted as a definition of 'right' or 'obligatory'.

From this short study of evolutionary attempts at defining the meaning of 'right', I will turn to the group of theories which attempt to define the rightness of action by reference to the attitude adopted towards the action by some mind or minds. As we have seen, some evolutionary moralists have themselves tended to adopt such a theory; they have identified 'right' with 'approved by the community'. But it will be well to examine this view, apart from its connexion with evolutionary studies, as one among the group of mental-attitude theories.

Professor Broad divides attitude theories into the two varieties of private and public. 'If, e.g., a man holds that a "right" action means an action which evokes in *him* a certain kind of emotion when *he* contemplates it, he is a Private Psychological Naturalist. If he holds that a "right" action means one which evokes a certain kind of emotion in all or most men, or in all or most Englishmen, or in all or most Etonians, he is a Public Psychological Naturalist.'[1] These are clearly two possible forms of psychological naturalism. But it seems to me clear that they do not exhaust the possible varieties of such a view. For, suppose we confine ourselves to views which define rightness by some feeling or emotion roused by the contemplation of a given act; a third possibility besides the two recognized by Professor Broad remains. I might hold that I mean by a right act not one which arouses approval in me when I contemplate it, or one which arouses approval in all or most of some class of beings, but one which arouses in the agent, when he contemplates *himself* as doing it, a certain specific emotion, the kind of emotion which we certainly in fact feel when we think ourselves bound to do an act. This view will be neither private nor public in Professor Broad's sense; not private because the person to whose emotion reference is made is not the judger but the agent; not public, because no reference is made to the whole or the majority of any class of beings.

Let us consider first what may be called the private reaction view. This is the view that by calling an act right I mean that it awakes in me the emotion of approval. The theory has some plausibility, because the thought that an action is right and the feeling of approval always go together. We never judge an action right without experiencing the feeling of approval, nor

[1] *Five Types of Ethical Theory*, 259.

vice versa. But the theory is open to serious objections. For
(1) to begin with, 'approval' is much too wide a term. We
approve of many things to which we do not ascribe the character of being obligatory or morally right—e.g. works of art.
We shall have to equate rightness not with being an object
of approval, but with being an object of a specific kind of
approval, which we feel towards right actions but do not feel
towards, for instance, works of art. Now I do not doubt that
such a feeling exists, that our emotional reaction towards a
right action is different from our emotional reaction towards
anything else. But when I consider this emotion, it appears to
me that it is not just a feeling which arises in us, we know not
why, when we contemplate a right action. It seems to presuppose some insight into the nature of the action, as, for
instance, that it is an action likely to redound to the general
good, or a fulfilment of promise. It seems to be an intellectual
emotion, presupposing the thought that the action is right, and
right as being of a certain recognized character. And if this
contention is correct, if the emotion of moral approval presupposes the thought that the action is right, it follows that we
cannot mean by calling the action right that it awakes this
emotion, since in order to have the emotion we must already
be thinking of the action as right.

(2) Is it not clear that when we call an action right we mean
essentially that it stands in a certain relation not to a spectator
considered as capable of emotion in contemplating it, but to
an agent considered as an agent? An action is never obligatory
in the abstract; it is obligatory on a particular person in particular circumstances. To say that an act is obligatory is only
another way of saying that a particular person ought to behave
in a particular way. It is surely quite clear that what we have
in mind when we call another person's action right is not any
relation which it has to *us* as emotional beings, but a relation
which it has to *him* as an active being.

(3) Another objection appears as soon as we consider the
question of time. If I judge that Brutus did wrong in assassi-

nating Caesar, I certainly do not think that his act first acquired its wrongness when I began to experience disapproval of it, or will cease to be wrong when I have ceased to do so.

And (4) this view does away with the possibility of difference of opinion on the rightness of acts. If all I mean when I say 'action A is right' is 'I have a feeling of approval towards it', and all you mean when you say 'it is wrong' is that you have a feeling of disapproval towards it, then we are not disagreeing; for what you say is perfectly compatible with what I say. I may well be approving and you disapproving of the same act. But it is surely perfectly clear that when I say an action is right and you say it is wrong we mean to be making incompatible statements about it. We might try to get over the objection by supposing that I am judging it to be right in certain respects, and that you are judging it to be wrong in certain other respects; and if this is all we are doing, our statements are of course compatible. But if I am judging it to be right on the whole and you are judging it to be wrong on the whole, we are certainly making statements each of which means to contradict the other. And this they could not do if each only stated the personal reaction of an individual to the act. We should then no more be contradicting one another than we do if you say you like jazz music and I say I don't.

In view of these fatal objections to the private view, shall we take refuge in a public reaction view? Shall we say that when we pronounce an action to be right, what we mean is that all or most men, or all or most members of some class of men, react to the act with a feeling of approval?

The first three of the objections to the private reaction view apply equally to the public reaction view. The feeling of approval presupposes the judgement of rightness; rightness evidently stands for the relation of an act not to *any* man or body of men as emotional reagents, but for the relation of it to a possible doer; and rightness is not held to belong to an act only *when* some man or body of men is having any sort of reaction to it. The fourth objection will *not* apply. If I say 'all or most so-and-so's have a feeling of approval towards this act', and if you say 'all or most so-and-so's have a feeling of disapproval towards it', we certainly are contradicting one another, and a real place is left for difference of opinion on the rightness of acts. But then a new objection (4a) makes its appearance, from which the private reaction view was free. I never judge an action right except when I have the feeling of approval towards it, but I obviously may judge it right when I am not thinking that the whole or a majority of any set of people have such a feeling. Indeed, I may judge an act right when I think no one but myself approves of it, or wrong when I think no one but myself disapproves of it. That is, in fact, what happens with every moral reformer when he enunciates a new moral principle or denies an old one. Are we to suppose that when Wilberforce began to denounce the slave-trade as wrong, what he meant was that a majority of Englishmen or even a majority of the Clapham sect had a feeling of disapproval towards it? The first alternative he could not have thought true, and the second was equally certainly not what he meant to assert. What he meant to assert was that the slave-trade was wrong, however any body of men reacted to it.

But we still have on our hands the third reaction view. According to this, to say that an action is obligatory on so-and-so means 'so-and-so has a certain feeling in face of it'. Here we seem in one respect to be nearer to the truth; for, an obligation being an obligation resting on an individual agent, the state of his mind is much more likely to be relevant to a particular act's being obligatory on him than the state of mind of any observer or body of observers. We may later[1] see grounds for believing, not indeed that rightness *consists* in the arousal of any state in his mind, but that the state of his opinion about the facts of the case, rather than the actual facts of the case, is what *makes* a particular act right for him. But this is very different from saying that the presence of the emotion of obligation in him *is* the rightness of the act. And a little

[1] ch. 7.

consideration will show that this cannot be so. For as of moral approval, so of the emotion of obligation, we must say that it is not a blind feeling that arises in us, we know not why, on contemplating a possible act. It is an intellectual emotion which arises only when we judge the act to have a certain character, say that of producing a maximum of good, and to be on that account obligatory. And if the emotion of obligation presupposes the judgement that we are obliged, our being obliged cannot consist in our having the emotion of obligation. It is surely quite plain that the thought that I am obliged to do a certain act is not the thought that the contemplation of a certain possible act affects me in a certain way as an emotional being, but the thought that the act itself is related to me in a certain way as an active being.

We have now fairly considered all the reaction views, and have found that none of them gives even a plausible account of the essence of obligation. Are the causal views in any better position? One of them is the view that for an act to be right means just that it is, of all the acts possible for an agent at a certain time, that which will procure for him most pleasure. This is one form of egoistic Hedonism. It is not the only possible form; for an egoistic hedonist might quite well hold right to be an indefinable notion, or one definable in some other way, but hold that what *makes* acts to have the characteristic of rightness is their having the other characteristic of tending to produce most pleasure for the agent. With *that* variety of Hedonism we are not at present concerned. One consideration will sufficiently refute the view we *are* considering. No one will have the slightest difficulty in remembering instances in which he has thought of some act as his duty, without in the least thinking of it as likely to bring him more pleasure than any other would. And if the two thoughts are not even necessarily found together, still less can it be pretended that they are but one thought.

The suggestion that right means 'such as to produce most

pleasure *for all human beings*' is in one respect not so remote from the truth as the view last considered. The thought of an action as contributing to the pleasure of others is far more closely associated with the thought of its rightness, than is the thought of it as contributing to the agent's own pleasure. But it must surely be admitted that there are other things than pleasure which we think it our duty to promote for other people—the improvement of their character and of their intelligence; and even if this were not so, even if pleasure were the only thing we deemed it our duty to produce, it is clear that the proposition, 'right action is that which produces most pleasure for humanity', is not an analytic proposition in which we unfold what we *mean* by 'right', but a synthetic proposition in which we express the view that the characteristic in actions which entails their having the characteristic of rightness is their tendency to produce a maximum of pleasure.

I have dealt rather summarily with these theories of the meaning of right, partly because the subject has been treated very fully and well by Professor Moore, partly because I suspect that the issue is not a very live one. It requires only a very little attention to what is in our minds when we use the word 'right', to see that none of these suggested meanings is really in our minds. To each of the theories I have discussed there corresponds a pair of views, each of which is more plausible than the views I have considered. Take any of the characteristics that have been put forward as giving the essence of rightness. It would, in the first place, be more plausible to say it must be granted that the mention of this characteristic does not state the *meaning* of right. Right is perhaps to be defined otherwise, or perhaps it is indefinable. But this is the characteristic that *makes* right acts right.' It would be, for instance, far more plausible to say that contribution to the general happiness is what makes an act right, than to say that it is its being right. And in fact the clearest-headed of the hedonists have defined their view thus. Sidgwick, for example, regards rightness as an indefinable notion, and there are indications

that Mill did the same.[1] And any one can see that this is much
more plausible than the alternative. Thus, answering to each
of the psychological theories as to the *essence* of rightness,
there will be a view as to the *ground* of rightness. And these
views we shall have to consider when we come to that part of
our inquiry.[2]

There is, however, another possibility. It may be said, 'Let
us grant that none of these psychological characteristics is what
we mean by rightness. These characteristics, however, are
those which the actions we call right really have. Rightness
is only a characteristic which we *fancy* some actions to have;
and so is wrongness.' I have already, in dealing with evolutionary views, indicated the main reasons which have led some
people to adopt this type of view, and shown, I hope, their
insufficiency.[3] But to point out the insufficiency of the reasons
which have led people to adopt a view is not to prove the view
untrue. One can urge that one has oneself a clear conviction
that certain acts are right and others wrong; and if we believe
in the fundamental identity of human nature in all men, it is
very hard to suppose that any sane person is totally without
such a conviction, which it is clear that *nearly* all men have.
But if any one denies that he has it, I cannot prove to him that
he is wrong in his denial. As a rule, however, he will betray
himself in one way. He is quite likely, when blamed for some
act, to say that he is convinced that there is no such thing as
right or wrong. But when his interests are attacked or threat-
ened by some one else, his reaction usually convinces one that
he thinks there are things that *other* people ought not to do;
and if so he can hardly refuse to admit that there are things
that he himself ought not to do. The denial of any distinction
between right and wrong can usually be seen to be a dis-
ingenuous excuse for doing as one pleases. But if any one is
prepared to exempt others as well as himself from moral
obligation, I do not think he can be argued out of his view.

In fact, however, such an attitude is extremely uncommon,

---

[1] Cf. pp. 9–10.   [2] ch. 4.   [3] pp. 15–21.

and much that passes for it is not really of this nature. It is not unusual to deplore the present age as one in which the sense of moral distinctions is weakening, possibly to its final disappearance. I do not for a moment believe this to be true. Whether the *practice* of morality is weakening is a different question, with which I am not at present concerned; though there, too, one may be allowed to express the opinion that we are at least as much better in some respects than our ancestors, as in others we are worse. What I am concerned with is the question whether the recognition that there *is* a right and a wrong is weakening. Take, for instance, one particular question about which the complaint is often made—the relations between the sexes. Undoubtedly there has been a growth of opinion in favour of a relaxation of the code which has hitherto governed Christian countries. But the advocates of relaxation are just as much moralists as their opponents. Both alike think that there is *some* right way of arranging the relations between the sexes. And even if some go so far as to say that all rules for individual behaviour in this matter ought to be abolished, they say they *ought* to be abolished, i.e. that legislators *ought* to abolish certain laws and that public opinion *ought* not to visit certain acts with its displeasure. No one says 'it does not matter what we do about the question; there is no right or wrong about it at all'. In fact the difference that divides us is not a difference on the question whether there is a right and a wrong, but a difference on the questions, 'What are the characteristics of acts which make them right or wrong?' and 'How far do certain types of act in fact possess these characteristics?' The first is a question for ethics, and is probably its main problem. The second is a question for applied ethics or casuistry.

It is on our finding of the true answers to these two types of question that our attainment of a true solution of the problem of the sexes depends. Much will depend, obviously, on the nature of our answer to the first question. If, for instance, the only characteristic that makes acts right is their tendency to

produce pleasure, that might point to one solution of the
sex question; if a tendency to promote certain qualities of
personality is also a ground of rightness, and still more if it
is a more important ground, that might point to quite a
different solution. But again, even if it were to be agreed that
Hedonism is wrong and that there are other goods than
pleasure, we should still have to ask what kind of relation
between the sexes best tends to promote those qualities of
personality. It is by showing that a strict code of sexual
behaviour in fact secures for actions the characteristics which
in fact make actions right, that a strict code is to be defended;
and I do not think that it need fear the results of such an
inquiry.

Before leaving the naturalistic attempts to define ethical
terms, I ought to take some account of a way of thinking which
has affinities with these attepmts, which has come rather rapidly
to the front in the last few years. It has not, I think, made as
yet any wide popular appeal, but it has attracted many of our
younger philosophers, and bids fair to attract more. This is
the way of thinking represented by the Vienna school of
positivists, who found their inspiration in the teaching of
Mr. Wittgenstein but have developed and modified his views.
I take as representatives of the school Mr. Carnap and Mr. Ayer
—the *Philosophy and Logical Syntax* of the former, and the
Language, Truth, and Logic of the latter.

Their original inspiration goes a good deal farther back than
Wittgenstein; in fact they may be regarded as having reverted
to the views of Hume. Mr. Carnap[1] quotes with approval
Hume's famous words:[2]

'It seems to me, that the only objects of the abstract sciences or
of demonstration are quantity and number. . . . All other enquiries
of men regard only matter of fact and existence; and these are
evidently incapable of demonstration. . . . When we run over

---

[1] p. 35; cf. Ayer, p. 56.
[2] *Enquiry concerning Human Understanding, ad fin.*

libraries, persuaded of these principles, what havoc must we make? If we take in our hand any volume; of divinity or school meta-physics, for instance; let us ask, *Does it contain any abstract reasoning concerning quantity or number?* No. *Does it contain any experimental reasoning concerning matter of fact and existence?* No. Commit it then to the flames: for it can contain nothing but sophistry and illusion.'

'We agree', says Mr. Carnap,[1] 'with this view of Hume, which says—translated into our terminology—that only the propositions of mathematics and empirical science have sense, and that all other propositions are without sense.'

Stated more definitely, the view is that all significant pro-positions are either *a priori*, in which case they are purely tautologous, or else are empirical hypotheses reached by reasoning from observation and having a meaning only because they can be tested by further observation. It has long been matter of agreement among philosophers that at least the vast majority of the propositions of the natural sciences are empirical hypotheses, not known to be true but rendered probable by experience and capable of being rendered more, or less, pro-bable by further experience. Furthermore, the positivists, if I may take Mr. Ayer as typical, adopt the more sensible of two possible views with regard to the testability by further experience which is required in order to make an empirical proposition significant. He sees that no empirical general pro-position can ever be *completely* tested by further experience, in the sense of being completely proved, and adopts therefore the more temperate view that the sort of testing of which an empirical proposition must be capable, if it is to have sense, is a testing which will render the proposition more or less *probable*.

Mr. Ayer sees that ethical judgements in which we pro-nounce something to be good or bad, or right or wrong, offer at first sight a difficulty to the positivist's theory that 'all syn-thetic propositions are empirical hypotheses'. Ethical judge-

[1] p. 36.

ments seem to be synthetic, but 'they cannot with any show of justice be represented as hypotheses, which are used to predict the course of our sensations'.[1] He rejects two well-known attempts that have been made to exhibit ethical judgements as empirical hypotheses—viz. the subjectivist theory which defines the rightness of actions, and the goodness of ends, in terms of the feeling of approval which a certain person, or group of people, has towards them, and the utilitarian theory, which defines rightness and goodness in terms of pleasure. These he rejects on grounds similar to some of those on which I have already rejected them;[2] and it is unnecessary to repeat these. He is careful to point out that he is not 'denying that it is possible to invent a language in which all ethical symbols are definable in non-ethical terms, or even that it is desirable to invent such a language and adopt it in place of our own; what we are denying is that the suggested reduction of ethical to non-ethical statements is consistent with the conventions of our actual language'.[3] Clearly, then, his own theory, which he offers in place of Subjectivism and Utilitarianism, is meant to *be* consistent with the conventions of our actual language, i.e. to be an account not of what we ought to be saying, but of what we mean when we actually do say that so-and-so is right, or is good.

If Subjectivism and Utilitarianism are rejected, as they are by the positivists, it might seem that the conclusion to be drawn is that 'right' and 'good', and their opposites, are terms which cannot be defined naturalistically, and that judgements in which we use them as predicates are *a priori* judgements, judgements in which we express not the results of observation but a direct insight. But the positivists cannot accept this view, since they have committed themselves to the view that all *a priori* judgements are pure tautologies and that only empirical hypotheses have factual content, and since, as they admit, it is clear that when we say that something is right or good, we are not uttering a tautology. Holding, then, that all judgements that

[1] p. 149.   [2] *Supra,* ch. 2.   [3] p. 154.

have meaning are either empirical hypotheses or tautologies, and that ethical judgements do not belong to either of these types, what are they to say about them? The positivists cut the knot by saying that ethical judgements, or rather, those most important ethical judgements whose predicate is 'right' or 'good', are not judgements at all, that in them nothing whatever is asserted. There is a minor difference between the positivists as to what such 'pseudo-judgements' are. Mr. Carnap[1] says roundly that they are all commands—that to say 'so-and-so is right, or good' is to say 'do so-and-so'; Mr. Ayer[2] distinguishes 'actual ethical judgements' from 'exhortations to moral virtue', i.e. from commands.

The theory that all judgements with the predicate 'right' or 'good' are commands has evidently very little plausibility. The only moral judgements of which it could with any plausibility be maintained that they are commands are those in which one person says to another 'you ought to do so-and-so'. A command is an attempt to induce some one to behave as one wishes him to behave, either by the mere use of authoritative or vehement language, or by this coupled with the intimation that disobedience will be punished. And there is no doubt that such words as 'you ought to do so-and-so' may be used as one means of so inducing a person to behave in a certain way. But if we are to do justice to the meaning of 'right' or 'ought', we must take account also of such modes of speech as 'he ought to do so-and-so', 'you ought to have done so-and-so', 'if this and that had been the case, you ought to have done so-and-so', 'if this and that were the case, you ought to do so-and-so', 'I ought to do so-and-so'. Where the judgement of obligation has reference either to a third person, not the person addressed, or to the past, or to an unfulfilled past condition, or to a future treated as merely possible, or to the speaker himself, there is no plausibility in describing the judgement as a command. But it is easy to see that 'ought' means the same in all these cases, and that if in some of them it does not express a command,

---

[1] p. 24.   [2] p. 150.

it does not do so in any. And if the form of words 'you ought to do so-and-so' may be used as a way of inducing the person addressed to behave in a particular way, that does not in the least imply that the apparent statement is really not a statement, but a command. What distinguishes its meaning from that of the genuine 'do so-and-so' is that one is suggesting to the person addressed a *reason* for doing so-and-so, viz. that it is right. The attempt to induce the person addressed to behave in a particular way is a separable accompaniment of the thought that the act is right, and cannot for a moment be accepted as the meaning of the words 'you ought to do so-and-so'.

While Mr. Ayer avoids the crude view that all ethical judgements are really commands, he agrees with Mr. Carnap that, whereas all judgements proper have two characteristics—that of expressing a state of mind and that of asserting something,[1] ethical judgements assert nothing, and are mere expressions of a state of mind in which we are liking certain kinds of conduct and wishing others to behave accordingly. Mr. Ayer's choice of an example is rather unfortunate. 'If I say to some one', he remarks,[2] ' "You acted wrongly in stealing that money", I am not stating anything more than if I had simply said, "You stole that money".' There is some plausibility in this, simply because the word 'steal' already connotes wrongful action, and therefore the addition of the word 'wrongly' may at least plausibly be said to add nothing. But let us avoid the use of a question-begging term. Let us take the example, 'In saying that which you did not believe you acted wrongly'. It cannot, I am sure, with any plausibility be maintained that, in saying that, I am asserting no more than that you have said that which you did not believe. I am quite definitely meaning to characterize your action further in a certain way. The judgement, we are told, merely expresses my personal dislike and disapproval of the action; but when this is said it is forgotten that whatever be true of dislike, it is impossible to disapprove without thinking that what you disapprove is *worthy of disapproval.*

[1] Cf. pp. 254–5, *infra.*   [2] Ayer, op cit., 158.

This denial that when we use such terms as 'right' or 'good' we mean (as opposed to expressing) anything at all is not, I think, the product of disinterested reflection on such judgements. It is the product of a preconceived theory about judgements in general, viz. of the theory that judgements which are both synthetic and *a priori*, i.e. are neither tautologous nor empirical, are impossible. For that thesis no genuine proof is ever offered by its supporters; we are simply told repeatedly that it is manifestly true. In considering whether it is true or not, it may be useful to consider the straits to which its supporters are reduced in dealing with certain classes of judgements. I will take first judgements in which we appear to make universal synthetic *a priori* statements. The instance Mr. Ayer takes[1] is the judgement 'a material thing cannot be in two places at once'. This, says Mr. Ayer, is not a statement expressing any knowledge about the nature of things, but a statement about the use of language. 'It is necessary only because we happen to use the relevant words in a particular way. There is no logical reason why we should not so alter our definitions that the sentence "A thing cannot be in two places at once" comes to express a self-contradiction instead of a necessary truth.' There is, of course, a truth at the bottom of this contention. There is no necessary connexion between any of our words and the meanings in which we use them. The meaning which we express by 'can' might have been expressed by 'cannot' (if 'cannot' had not already come to have the meaning which it in fact has); and if in saying 'a thing cannot be in two places at once' we had meant what we do mean by saying 'a thing can be in two places at once', our statement would have been as obviously untrue as, with the existing usage of 'cannot', it is obviously true. Before we can discuss the meaning of any proposition, we must be satisfied that we are using our words in the same sense; but when we have satisfied ourselves of that, the question remains whether the things we are talking about have the connexions which they are

[1] p. 63.

alleged to have; and the fact that with different conventional meanings of words the statement 'a material thing cannot be in two places at once' might have been untrue throws no light on the question whether with the existing meanings of words it is not both true and necessary and synthetic.

I will take as a second example the positivistic view of statements about the past. Mr. Ayer thinks, in accordance with his general view that all non-tautologous propositions are empirical hypotheses stating what experiences may be expected in the future, that statements which are expressed as statements about the past are really 'rules for the prediction of those "historical" experiences which are commonly said to verify them';[1] i.e. the statement that the battle of Hastings was fought in 1066 is really the statement that any one who makes the necessary investigation will get certain experiences which will satisfy him that the battle was fought in that year. As against this it seems to me sufficient to say that a statement about the past *is* a statement about the past and not about the future—though no doubt a statement about the past may involve consequences about the future, and a statement about the future may involve consequences about the past. Mr. Ayer claims that those he is criticizing are assuming that the past is objectively there to be corresponded to, an assumption which he regards as objectionable. But it is surely clear that, if his opponents' view involved that, his own theory would equally involve that the *future* is objectively there to be corresponded to, and that is open to at least as much objection. There are reasons for thinking that only the present and neither the past nor the future are real, and reasons for thinking that only the present and the past are real,[2] but it is difficult to think of any ground on which it could be maintained that the present and the future are real, but not the past.

The positivistic theory simply falls into a confusion, amounting to an explicit identification, between what a statement means to assert and the evidence which would lead one to believe in

---

[1] p. 147.   [2] Cf. Broad, *Scientific Thought*, 66.

its truth. And this confusion is very far-reaching in its effect on the views of the positivists. Their objection to recognizing ethical judgements as genuine assertions arises from the *fact*, long known to moral philosophers, that ethical judgements cannot be verified by any sensible experience, coupled with the *view* of the positivists that the only synthetic judgements that have meaning, i.e. that are genuine judgements, are those that *are* verifiable. Sometimes, indeed, they go so far as to say that the meaning of a synthetic judgement *is* its verification. Now the verification, or partial verification, of a general statement may be achieved in either of two ways. If the proposition states that every A has the attribute B, we may effect a partial verification by producing, one after another, instances in which, by the use of the senses, particular A's are perceived to have the attribute B. And in this case the facts which form the evidence for the proposition are the very facts which (and others like them) are summed up in the proposition itself. In this case the meaning of the proposition may loosely be identified with the facts which verify it. But even then there must from the nature of things be some difference between that *which* is verified and that *by which* it is verified; and there is in fact a difference between the general statement that all A's are B, and the sum of the particular statements 'this A is B', 'this second A is B', and so on.

It may, however, well be the case that we cannot by the use of the senses perceive directly that *any* A is B. In such a case we may be able to verify the statement by discovering by sensuous experience A's which have the attribute C, which we already know to imply B. In such a case the facts which verify the proposition are *entirely* distinct from the meaning of the proposition. Instances in which statements about the past are verified can obviously be only of the latter order. And the existence of this type of case shows that statements can have a meaning completely different from the facts which verify them.

Sometimes, however, the positivists adopt a view less crude

than that which identifies the meaning of a statement with its verification, and content themselves with saying that no statement can have meaning unless it is verifiable, or at least partly verifiable. As against this form of the theory it seems to me enough to refer to Dr. Ewing's convincing refutation of it.[1] He shows *inter alia* that the positivists could not 'establish the truth of their view even in a single case merely by sense-experience. For how can we ever know by sense-experience that there is not a part of the meaning of a statement that we cannot verify? The fact that we do not have any sense-experience of such a part proves nothing, since the point at issue is whether there is something in what we mean beyond sense-experience; and how can we know by sense-experience that there is not?'[2]

If it cannot be verified by sense-experience that even the meaning of a single statement is entirely exhausted by what can be verified by sense-experience, still less, of course, can the general theory that all statements are meaningless unless they are thus verifiable be itself verified. Thus if the theory is true, the sentence which states the theory must be meaningless, since it is an unverifiable statement. 'But a sentence cannot possibly be true and meaningless. Therefore the sentence in question cannot' (i.e. cannot, on the basis of the theory itself) 'be true, but must be either meaningless or false.'[3]

I conclude, then, that the latest attempt to discredit ethics is not successful. Indeed, there is one of the arguments put forward by the positivists which seems to me to provide, when reflected on, an argument in favour not only of the view that our ethical judgements are genuine judgements, but of the view that there are fundamental ethical judgements for which general agreement may be claimed. Mr. Ayer remarks[4] that, while his theory escapes many of the objections brought against subjectivistic theories in ethics, there is one which it does not escape. This is the argument[5] that such theories would make

[1] *Mind*, xlvi (1937), 347–64.   [2] Ibid. 349.   [3] Ibid. 349.
[4] p. 163.   [5] Professor Moore's argument, in *Philosophical Studies*, 333–4.

it impossible to argue about questions of value, which never-theless we undoubtedly do. He admits that his own theory also would make it impossible to argue about questions of value; as he holds that such sentences as 'thrift is a virtue' and 'thrift is a vice' do not express propositions at all, he clearly cannot hold that they express incompatible propositions. If, then, he is to resist the argument in question, he must simply deny that in fact we ever do dispute about questions of value; for if we did dispute about things which on his theory we cannot dispute about, his theory would clearly be untrue. He boldly adopts the course to which he is logically forced, and denies that we ever do dispute about questions of value. And he justifies this by saying that apparent disputes about questions of value are really disputes about questions of fact.

'When some one disagrees with us about the moral value of a certain action or type of action, we do admittedly resort to argu-ment in order to win him over to our way of thinking. But we do not attempt to show by our arguments that he has the "wrong" ethical feeling towards a situation whose nature he has correctly apprehended. What we attempt to show is that he is mistaken about the facts of the case. We argue that he has misconceived the agent's motive: or that he has misjudged the effects of the action, or its probable effects in view of the agent's knowledge; or that he has failed to take into account the special circumstances in which the agent was placed. . . . We do this in the hope that we have only to get our opponent to agree with us about the nature of the empirical facts for him to adopt the same moral attitude towards them as we do. And as the people with whom we argue have generally received the same moral education as ourselves, and live in the same social order, our expectation is usually justified. But if our opponent happens to have undergone a different process of moral "conditioning" from ourselves, so that, even when he acknowledges all the facts, he still disagrees with us about the moral value of the actions under discussion, then we abandon the attempt to convince him by argument. We say that it is impossible to argue with him because he has a distorted or undeveloped moral sense; which signifies merely that he employs a different set of values from

our own. .... It is because argument fails us when we come to deal
with pure questions of value, as distinct from questions of fact,
that we finally resort to mere abuse.'[1]

It is perfectly true that, when we differ on a question of right
or wrong, or of goodness or badness, it is by consideration of
questions of fact—of the precise nature of the consequences or
of the probable consequences, or of the motives involved—
that we try to remove the difference of opinion on the moral
question. And in doing so we betray the conviction that if we
could get down to agreement about the facts of the case, we
should find ourselves in agreement on the moral question; or
in other words, that though we may differ in our moral judgements on some complicated case, we agree in our fundamental
judgements as to what kinds of consequences ought to be aimed
at and what kinds of motive are good. The more Mr. Ayer
emphasizes this element in our discussion of moral questions,
the more he pays tribute to the strength of this conviction; for
unless we thought that if we could agree on the factual nature
of the act we should probably agree on its rightness or wrongness, there would be no point in trying to reach agreement
about its factual nature. And in the great majority of cases we
find this confidence confirmed, by finding that we agree in our
moral judgements when we agree about the facts. But no doubt
we sometimes fail to find agreement even then. We do not
find, however, as Mr. Ayer claims, that no subject of dispute
remains. We find, indeed, that there is no room for further
argument; when we have come to some premiss which to us
seems axiomatic, and which the other person denies, we can
argue no further. But we do not find that all *difference of
opinion* has vanished, and that we are left only with different
feelings, one liking certain consequences or motives and
another disliking them. We find ourselves still saying 'this is
good', and the person with whom we are speaking still saying
'this is bad'. And it is not by showing that *argument* ceases,

[1] pp. 165–6.

but by showing that *difference of opinion* ceases, that Mr. Ayer could escape from Professor Moore's argument.

But indeed our adoption of the very practice which Mr. Ayer here describes is enough to refute his account of the nature of what are commonly called ethical judgements. He denies that they are judgements; he says they are mere expressions of liking or dislike. If that were all they are, why argue at all? What should we be trying to prove? Is *A* arguing to prove that he likes the given act, and *B* to prove that he dislikes it? Clearly not. *A* does not doubt that *B* dislikes it, nor *B* that *A* likes it; and if they did doubt, they would adopt quite different means of convincing one another, e.g. *A* by consistently seeking to do similar acts and *B* by consistently avoiding them. What they are attempting to do by the process Mr. Ayer describes is to convince each other that the liking, or the dislike, is justified, in other words that the act has a character that *deserves* to be liked or disliked, is good or is bad.

III

THE NATURE OF RIGHTNESS AND OBLIGATION

I PASS now to consider whether any *non*-naturalistic attempt to define 'right' or 'obligatory' can be accepted. By a non-naturalistic attempt I mean one that defines 'right' by a definition which includes a reference to some distinctively ethical term other than 'right'. Of such attempts I know only one, viz. Professor Moore's theory in *Principia Ethica* that right means 'productive of the greatest possible amount of good'. And I am bound to say that this seems just as little a true account of the meaning we have in mind when we use the word *right*, as are the naturalistic attempts we have been considering. Is it not clear that when a plain man says 'it is right to fulfil promises' he is not necessarily thinking of the total consequences of such an act, still less thinking that the total consequences are always the best possible or are even likely to be so? And if some one says 'it is right to do that which will produce the best consequences', he does not think he is elucidating the *meaning* of the word 'right', but that he is stating the characteristic, the possession of which by an act entails its having the characteristic of rightness. I need not elaborate the point, because, as I have shown elsewhere,[1] Professor Moore seems to have given up this view when he wrote his later book, *Ethics*, and to have adopted the view that tendency to produce the best consequences is not the essence of rightness but the ground of rightness. I think almost every one would admit that this is a far more plausible view.

I think, too, that, since in his later work Professor Moore makes no attempt to define rightness, he has presumably come to adopt the view that right is an indefinable notion. And this is the conclusion to which I am myself led by the break-down of the attempts to define rightness which we have considered.

[1] *The Right and the Good,* 10–11.

I believe I have passed under review all the main attempts at defining 'right' or 'obligatory'. That they have broken down does not prove that every attempt must break down, but it creates a presumption that it will. And, indeed, the more we think of the term 'right', the more convinced we are likely to be that it is an indefinable term, and that when one attempts to define it one will either name something plainly different from it, or use a term which is a mere synonym of it.

The word 'right', when used in a context of moral thought, seems to me to mean very nearly, but not quite, the same as 'obligatory' or 'what is my duty'. The first point of difference may, I think, be stated thus: In most situations that occur in life, there are a variety of claims upon me that I can by my action either satisfy or fail to satisfy. There are, or at least there may be, cases in which any one of two or more acts would completely satisfy these claims, or would satisfy them to an equal extent and to the greatest extent possible. Let there be two such acts, A and B. Then we should agree that in doing either of them we should have done a right act. But we should not in doing either of them have done an obligatory act; for I cannot be obliged to do act A if act B would equally well satisfy the claims upon me, nor can I be obliged to do act B if act A would equally well satisfy the claims upon me. My obligation in this case is not to do act A nor to do act B, but to do either act A or act B. In any situation in which there are any claims upon me, there is either one act which satisfies these claims more completely than any other would; then this act is both obligatory and right: or there are two or more acts which would fulfil the claims equally, and better than any other act open to me would; then all of these are right and none of them is obligatory, but it is obligatory to do one or other of them.

Thus it seems that both the question 'What is the right act for me to do?' and the question 'What is the act which it is my duty to do?' are wrong questions; the first because there may be more than one act that is right; the second because there may be none that is obligatory, the only obligation being to do one or other of certain acts.

Some would deny the correctness of this distinction. They would maintain that when there are two or more acts, one or other of which, as we say, we ought to do (it not being our duty to do one rather than any of the rest), the truth is that these are simply alternative ways of producing a single result, and that what is right is, strictly, not to do any of these acts, and what is obligatory is not to do 'one or other' of them; what is right and what is obligatory being to produce the result. This answer might, I think, fairly apply to many cases, in which it *is* the production of a single result that we think obligatory, the means being optional; e.g. to a case in which it is our duty to convey information to some one, but morally immaterial whether we do so verbally or in writing. But in principle, at any rate, there may be other cases in which it is our duty to produce one or other of two or more *different* states of affairs, without its being our duty to produce one of them rather than another; in such a case each of these acts will be right, and none of them will be obligatory.

In maintaining that an act may be right without being obligatory it might seem that I have reduced 'right act' to meaning 'act which it is not my duty not to do'. So to reduce it would not be correct. For there may be cases in which none of the acts open to me will be in any respect a fulfilment of claims, and in such a case we should not call such acts right, but indifferent. I have not, however, so reduced the meaning of 'right act'; for I have described it as including two moments —(a) that there is no other act that would more completely fulfil the moral claims on us, but also (b) that any act which is right is itself a fulfilment of at least one claim upon us.

I have pointed out this distinction between 'right' and 'obligatory' because it is, I think, clearly implied in the way in which we use the two terms; but it does not seem to me very important. The difference is a simple one, akin to that between 'first' and 'second to none', of which the former is applicable to any competitor who beats all his rivals, while the latter is applicable to any competitor who, while he may be equal with some, is not inferior to any. Or again, the difference might be expressed by saying that in calling an action obligatory we are implying not only that it is right, but that any other in the circumstances would be wrong.

I propose next to consider Professor Broad's discussion of the meaning of 'ought' and 'right', which I have found very suggestive. He begins his discussion[1] by distinguishing a wider and a narrower *sense* of 'ought'. 'In its narrower sense', he says, 'it applies only to actions which an agent could do if he willed. But there is a wider sense in which there is no such implication. We can say that sorrow ought to have been felt by a certain man at the death of a certain relation, though it was not in his power to feel sorrow at will. And we can say that virtue ought to be rewarded.'

On this I would comment as follows. I should agree that we often use 'ought' in this wider sense. But I should maintain that such a use is not strict. *Can* we *seriously* say that sorrow ought to have been felt by some one at the death of a relation? Only, it seems to me, (*a*) if we think that it was possible for him (and I agree with Professor Broad in holding this to be impossible) then and there to summon up a feeling of sorrow, or (*b*) if we think that by acting differently in the past he could have so modified his character that he would now have felt sorrow; and in the latter case the proper application of 'ought' is to say 'he ought to have so acted in the past', not 'he ought to have felt sorrow now'. Apart from such a thought, all we are entitled to say is, not that he ought to have felt sorrow now, but that his not feeling it is a bad thing, a manifestation of a bad character. The wider use of 'ought' is really an improper use of it, one which we could not seriously defend. Or again, take the saying that virtue ought to be rewarded. We can say this properly only if we think that some being or

[1] *Five Types of Ethical Theory*, 161.

beings, God or men, can and ought so to act that virtue will be rewarded. Unless we think this, all we are justified in saying is that an arrangement of human affairs in which virtue is not rewarded is a bad one; the specific justification required for saying 'virtue *ought* to be rewarded' is absent.

Professor Broad next,[1] following Sidgwick, distinguishes three *applications* of the word 'ought'. Some people, he says, judge that there are certain types of action that ought to be done in all or in certain types of situation, regardless of the goodness or badness of the probable consequences. This he calls the *deontological* application. Secondly, there are people who deny that they ever make such judgements as these, but nevertheless judge that every one ought to aim at certain ends, without any ulterior motive, e.g. at his own greatest happiness or at the greatest happiness of all sentient beings. This he calls the *teleological* application. Lastly, there may be people who deny that there are any types of action that are obligatory irrespective of their consequences, and also that there are any ends which every one ought to aim at, but who would admit a third application of 'ought'. They would say that if a man in fact takes a certain end as ultimate, he ought to adopt such means as will bring it into being, and not do things which he believes will be inconsistent with its realization. This Professor Broad calls the *logical* application of 'ought'.

He next asks how these three different *applications* are related to the wider and the narrower *meaning* of 'ought' which he has already distinguished. He points out that 'ought', when used in its teleological application, is used in its wider sense. For it is plain that we cannot desire a certain end at will, any more than we can at will feel sorrow at the death of a particular person, or love a particular person. Secondly, he argues that 'ought', when used in its logical application, is used in its *narrower* sense. For, since we believe that it is within the power of any sane person to be consistent if he tries, we believe that if he desires a certain end he can, if he tries, adopt the appropriate

[1] *Five Types of Ethical Theory*, 162–3.

means to it. The logical 'ought' is thus a special case of the deontological 'ought'. Finally, it is obvious that the deontological application of 'ought' involves the use of 'ought' in its narrower sense. Thus the three applications involve no new *sense* of 'ought' but only the two previously recognized.

Now if we have been right in saying that the wider sense of the word 'ought' is a loose and improper sense of it, and one in which we should not persist in using it when the implications of such a use have been pointed out, and if, as Professor Broad correctly says, the teleological application of it involves the wider sense, it will follow that the teleological application of it is an improper application, since it is an application of the word in an improper sense. And further, the logical application is also an improper application. It is true that in this case *one* of the conditions involved in the proper use of the word 'ought' is fulfilled, namely that we *can* be consistent if we choose, that we can will the means if we desire the end. But the *other* condition of the proper use of 'ought' is not fulfilled. For no one really thinks that the fact that a person desires a certain end makes it obligatory on him to will the means to it; if we think the end is a bad one (or that his desiring it is bad), we think that in spite of his desiring the end he ought *not* to adopt the means. Thus the logical application of 'ought', also, is an improper application of it, and we are left with but one proper application, as we are left with but one proper sense; viz. the application to acts within the agent's power to do if he chooses, and imposed on him by the moral law. In other words the categorical imperative is the only true imperative. When some one uses 'ought' in the teleological application he is emptying 'ought' of its real meaning, and all that he has a right to say is that it would be *good* if people aimed at certain ends; and when he uses it in its logical application he is equally emptying it of its proper meaning, and all that he is entitled to say is that a man who desires certain ends can hope to get them only if he adopts certain means. In neither of these statements does the distinctive meaning of 'ought' appear at all.

Professor Broad now proceeds to the relation between 'right' and 'ought'.[1] He points out (1) the distinction I have already pointed out, viz. that there may be cases in which several alternative acts are right and none of them is obligatory. (2) He holds that in a further respect the meaning of 'ought' is more restricted than that of 'right'. For he holds that we tend to confine the word 'ought' to cases where we believe that there are motives and inclinations against doing the rightest action open to the agent. He quotes with approval Sidgwick's remark that we should hardly say of an ordinary healthy man that he ought, in the narrower sense of 'ought', to take adequate nourishment; though we might say this of an invalid with a disinclination to take food, or of a miser.

Sidgwick's example is ill-chosen. We may know (or rather, have strong reasons for thinking) that a certain man has a natural liking for food, and that he never has an antipathy to food as such. Yet we know that in ordinary human nature, and therefore probably in his, there are many other desires which may incidentally conflict with desire for food (such as dislike of the particular food that is available, or of the company in which it would have to be eaten). And, knowing the possibilities of such conflict, I think we should not hesitate to say of such a man that he ought to take the food that he needs in order to keep him fit. And similarly, though we may know that a woman's natural love for her child is strong, we should not hesitate on that ground to say that she ought to look after her child's welfare; for we know that, however strong maternal love may be, there are many other desires with which it will often come into conflict. In principle it seems that, however much we know that an agent has a natural inclination to do a certain right act, we can never know that he has not some other inclination which might incidentally conflict with that inclination; and therefore that we never need hesitate on this

---

[1] *Five Types of Ethical Theory*, 164.

ground to describe the right act as obligatory. Some one might, however, try to restate Sidgwick's view in such a way as to avoid this objection. He might say 'Granted that we never can *know* this; yet suppose that in fact a man had an inclination to do the act which is right, and no inclination leading him towards any alternative act; would not this act then be (although we could not know it to be) right without being obligatory?' In support of this he might plead the assumption which we commonly make that what a man is morally obliged to do must be something that he can either do or refrain from doing, and add that in the case supposed the agent *could not* refrain from doing the act which is right.

The assumption that psychical necessity excludes obligation is one that should not be lightly made. For in the long run we must admit[1] that what a man does he does by a psychical necessity, and if the assumption is added to this admission, the conclusion can only be that obligation does not exist. We may perhaps get some light on the question by considering on what grounds, in a particular situation, we should reject certain things as not being our duty, however suitable they might be. We should reject (1) any act which would involve a metaphysical impossibility. When we have done a wrong, perhaps the most suitable thing, if it were possible, would be to undo our own act; but this we reject because from the nature of things it is impossible to undo the past. We should reject (2) any act which would involve a control over matter which we are convinced our mind does not possess. If the only way we could help some one we had wronged was by performing an impossible feat of endurance, we should reject that. We should reject (3) anything which would involve an impossible control over the state of our own mind. If we hate some one, then however right it would be that we should forthwith love him as intensely as we now hate him, we know that we cannot by a decision effect that result here and now, and we do not (or should not) think it our duty to love him now, though we

---

[1] Cf. ch. 10.

should think it our duty to try to mould our character so as to love him in time. But (4) if there is any act which we think we could do if we desired sufficiently strongly to do it, as in fact any act of self-exertion[1] can be done if we desire sufficiently strongly to do it, then we do not ask whether we in fact desire it sufficiently strongly to enable us to perform the act of self-exertion. The very fact that we recognize that the act would be right involves *some* attraction toward it, and we do not ask whether this is strong enough, for the excellent reason that it is only by our success or failure to do the act that we can discover whether the desire was strong enough. Even if there is a necessity to do the right act, or a necessity to do the wrong act, we never know there is, and therefore there is nothing to prevent us from thinking of the right act as obligatory.

But some one might reply, 'Will not your failure to do the act show that there was a psychical necessity to do otherwise and therefore no obligation to do that act? and will not your success, if you succeed, show that there was a psychical necessity to do the act, and therefore no obligation?' The fact, however, seems to be that even if the occurrence of either act implies that we were under a psychical necessity to do it, that does not prevent our continuing to recognize that we were under an obligation to do the one act and not the other. And if that be so, it implies that the sort of freedom involved in the recognition of an obligation is not freedom of indifference to choose to do or not to do the act, but only freedom in the milder sense of capacity to do the right act if we desire sufficiently strongly to do it.

Further, it seems clear that in trying to discover whether it is our duty to do a certain act, we regard as irrelevant the state of our inclination towards or against the doing of the act; and if this be so, the absence of a contrary inclination cannot prevent that from being our duty, which otherwise would be our duty. The notion of duty or obligation undoubtedly carries with it the idea of restriction; but the nature of the restriction is not

---

[1] As distinct from the effecting of a result; cf. pp. 153–4, 160–1.

that our duty is something that we ought to do though we have a contrary inclination, but that it is something that we ought to do irrespective of the state of our inclination.

Professor Broad next proceeds to state his view of the meaning of 'right'.

'It seems to me', he says, 'that, when I speak of anything as "right", I am always thinking of it as a factor in a certain wider total situation, and that I mean that it is "appropriately" or "fittingly" related to the rest of the situation. When I speak of anything as "wrong" I am thinking of it as "inappropriately" or "unfittingly" related to the rest of the situation. This is quite explicit when we say that love is the right emotion to feel to one's parents, or that pity and help are the right kinds of emotion and action in presence of undeserved suffering. This relational character of rightness and wrongness tends to be disguised by the fact that some types of action are commonly thought to be wrong absolutely; but this, I think, means only that they are held to be unfitting to *all* situations.'[1]

This account has the great merit of connecting the ethical sense of right and wrong with other uses of the words. It is plain that when we speak of 'the right road' or 'the right key' we are thinking of the road or key as fitting a particular situation in which some one is placed. The right road is that the taking of which fits into a situation of which the other element is his desire to get from A to B; the right key is that his using of which fits into a situation of which the other element is his wish to unlock a particular lock. It is worth while in this connexion to contrast the meaning of 'the right road' with that of a 'good road'. Goodness is an attribute which belongs permanently to the road or key, so long as it remains unchanged in its other characteristics; rightness is an attribute which they have only relatively to a particular situation and a particular need. A good road need not be the right road, and a bad road may be the right road, if the one does not and the other does meet the requirements of the particular situation.

[1] *Five Types of Ethical Theory*, 164–5.

A similar distinction between goodness and rightness in their moral applications may be noted. When we examine certain emotions, for instance, such as benevolence, we can merely by examining their intrinsic nature see that they are good. There are others which cannot in virtue of their intrinsic nature be called either good or bad, but can be judged to be right in certain situations, and wrong in others; e.g. sorrow is right when one contemplates the death of a friend, and wrong when one contemplates the success of a rival.

But if rightness in its ethical application shares with rightness in other connexions the characteristic of being relational, in *another* respect ethical rightness is quite different from any other kind of rightness. What we mean by calling a road or a key right can be explained purely in terms of desire and of causation. The right road or the right key is that the use of which by us will have a certain desired effect, that of taking us to a definite place or of opening a definite door. Moral rightness cannot, we may say in the light of our previous argument,[1] be thus explained in terms of any non-moral relation. As Professor Broad remarks, 'the kind of appropriateness and inappropriateness which is implied in the notions of "right" and "wrong" ' (i.e. in their ethical use) 'is, so far as I can see, specific and unanalysable'.[2]

The thought of rightness as being fitness, in a certain specific and unanalysable way, to a certain situation, is one that plays a large part in Samuel Clarke's moral philosophy,[3] and forms one of the main merits of that not sufficiently regarded philosopher.

It is possible to state more exactly the relation between moral suitability and rightness. Suppose we take a case in which a man has to choose between two actions each of which would bring some good and some evil into existence, and that action *A* would produce a greater balance of good than action *B*. Then action *B* will be morally suitable to a certain degree, and

---

[1] In ch. 2.   [2] *Five Types of Ethical Theory*, 165.
[3] Cf. for instance L. A. Selby-Bigge, *British Moralists*, paras. 482, 483.

in a certain respect, because it will produce some good; but we should not call it a right action. Not any and every degree of moral suitability will make an action right. On the other hand, *complete* suitability is not needed in order to make an action right; for action *A* will be right although in view of the fact that it will produce some evil it is not *completely* suitable morally. Rightness can be identified, then, neither with any and every degree of suitability, nor with complete suitability, but only with the greatest amount of suitability possible in the circumstances.

The same result emerges if we consider a case in which a man has made two promises, and can fulfil either only by breaking the other. If we decide that he ought to keep promise *A* rather than promise *B*, each of the actions will have *some* suitability because each will be the fulfilling of a promise; neither will have *complete* suitability, because each will be the breaking of a promise. We call right that act which is the most suitable of those possible in the circumstances. The other act cannot be called right, but only right in a certain respect.

One has, of course, to consider the question whether suitability is a genuine genus of which moral rightness is one species, or whether we are being taken in by a mere ambiguity in the term 'suitable', the utilitarian suitability of a road or a key having nothing whatever in common with the moral suitability of an action or an emotion. Are the two suitabilities related to each other as the 'colourness' of red is related to the 'colourness' of blue, or as the 'ploughness' of a certain agricultural instrument is related to the 'ploughness' of a failure in an examination? We surely must say of the two suitabilities, as Aristotle says of the different meanings of 'good', that they are not an instance of *mere* accidental ambiguity of a word; yet it is hard to find any element of real identity. The most obvious suggestion that arises in one's mind is that moral suitability is, after all, an example of utilitarian suitability—that to say of an act that it is right is to say that it serves a human purpose, or that it serves human purposes better than any other act possible in the circumstances. Yet I think we have only to examine carefully whether that is what we mean when we call an act right, to feel assured that it is not so.[1]

I am inclined to think that all that is common to these two suitabilities is that both are relations to which we feel a favourable reaction. There is some faint element of likeness in the two *reactions*, in that both are favourable; but we err if we therefore think there is an element of identity between utilitarian suitability and moral suitability, just as we err if we think that because we never call any thing good unless we have a favourable reaction to it, there is therefore a common element in the goodness of all the things we call good.

But if there is no real identity between moral suitability and utilitarian suitability, there seems to be another form of suitability which *has* an affinity with moral suitability, viz. aesthetic suitability. There seems to be something not altogether different in the way in which a situation calls for a certain act, and the way in which one part of a beautiful whole calls for the other parts. Here, as in the case of a right act, there is no question of subserving an extraneous purpose; there is a direct harmony between the parts of the composition, as there is between a moral situation and the act which completes it. The harmony is not of the same kind—rightness is not beauty; but there seems to be a genuine affinity, which justified the Greeks in their application of the word καλόν to both.

If Professor Broad's view is correct, as I think it is, moral rightness is a complex characteristic. It includes in it the generic quality of suitability, which it shares with the rightness of an element in a beautiful whole. And it includes in it the differentia which distinguishes it from every form of rightness but itself. It is a complex characteristic, just as redness is a complex characteristic, including in it a generic and a differential element. Now redness, though complex, is not definable; we can begin

---

[1] R. Price followed Clarke in making considerable use of the notion that rightness is 'fitness' of action to situation. But he is careful to point out that this is quite different from utilitarian fitness and is indefinable; cf. Selby-Bigge, *British Moralists*, para. 670.

to define it, when we say it is a form of colour, but we cannot complete the definition, since if we try to state what distinguishes it from other forms of colour we can only say that it is the being redness that does so. In the same way we can begin to define moral rightness, because we can say it is a form of suitability; but we cannot complete the definition, since if we ask what kind of suitability it is we can only say that it is the kind of suitability that is rightness. Professor Broad seems to me to be right in considering that no further analysis of it is possible.

Now it is to be noted that, whereas we cannot seriously say of any one that he ought to have a certain emotion, because we do not think it is in his power to acquire it forthwith, there is no such limitation to the use of the word 'right'. We can still call grief the right or fitting emotion in certain situations, for instance, even if we do not suppose the person we are thinking about has it in his power to feel grief in those circumstances. Its fittingness depends solely on the nature of the circumstances and not at all on his capacity or incapacity. Thus, while we had to reject the wider use of 'ought' (that in which it is used when the capacity to act or feel in the way in question is not believed to be present) as being a loose use, it is the wider use of 'right' that is the proper use of it; although it must be granted that when we use 'right' of acts, as opposed to emotions, we usually think of them as being in the agent's power to do or to forbear from doing. Our common use of the word 'right' is so fluid that, although what it naturally conveys is simply the notion of fitness or correctness, without implying either that there is only one act or emotion that fits the situation, or that it is in the agent's power to produce the act or emotion in question, yet by usage 'right' is very often treated as equivalent to 'obligatory'. This is clearly so in the common phrases 'the right act,' 'the right thing to do', where the use of the definite article shows the first of these implications to be present, and the second is in fact also present.

I have spoken of acts as being obligatory, and this language is often convenient, for brevity. But it is not strictly correct. For consider the situation when an obligation really exists, viz. before the act in question, or any alternative act, has been done. We cannot then, strictly speaking, say 'such and such an act is obligatory', for the act is not there, to be either obligatory or anything else. Nor, again, can we say 'such and such an act would be obligatory if it were done'; for clearly its obligatoriness, if it has any, does not depend on its being done. The only strict language which we can use in the circumstances is 'so and so is obliged to act in such and such a way'. In fact, obligatoriness is not a characteristic that attaches to acts; obligation is something that attaches to persons.[1]

[1] This point has been forcibly made by Professor Prichard in *Duty and Ignorance of Fact*; cf. pp. 155–6, *infra*.

IV

THEORIES ABOUT THE GROUND OF RIGHTNESS

FROM the question whether the characteristics right and obligatory are definable I turn to the question what are the grounds of rightness and of obligatoriness. As I have already pointed out,[1] to any theory which says 'so-and-so is the essence of rightness' there will correspond a possible theory that that same thing is the ground of rightness, rightness itself being treated as indefinable, or definable in some other way. And the example of Bentham[2] is enough to show that it is very easy to fail to distinguish between the two views. Logically, the two views are entirely different; but in their ethical consequences they will be the same. Whether you say 'so-and-so is the essence of rightness' or 'so-and-so is the ground of rightness', you will be led to the same ethical judgements on any act or type of acts; it will be in virtue of their possession or non-possession of the characteristic 'so-and-so' that you will judge of the rightness or wrongness of acts.

I remarked before[3] that the theories which specify this or that as the ground of rightness are in general more plausible than those which specify this or that as the essence of rightness. And in one respect this is so. For when such a characteristic as 'conducing to life' or 'being approved by the individual judger' or 'being approved by the majority of some body of men' is put forward as the essence of rightness, we have only to examine what is in our mind when we say such and such an act is right, to see that, however closely the characteristic in question may be connected with rightness, it is not the very meaning we have in mind when we assert the rightness of an act. From another point of view, some at least of the ground-theories are *less* plausible than the essence-theories. For, while, until we begin to reflect carefully on our meaning when we

[1] pp. 27–8.   [2] Cf. p. 9.   [3] p. 27.

predicate rightness, it may seem plausible to say that rightness
is just the being generally approved, for instance, it is very
unplausible to say that the being approved is the ground of an
action's having a quite different characteristic, a characteristic
of its own, that of being right.

But we had better consider the ground-theories methodic-
ally, as we considered the essence-theories. And first we may
consider the evolutionary or biological theories. An easily
detected characteristic of them is their instability, their tendency to turn, on examination, into theories of a different type
from that to which they appear to belong. Take, for instance,
Spencer's chapter on good and bad conduct, which he does not
distinguish from right and wrong conduct. In fact I think it is
clear that he means rather right and wrong than good and bad
conduct. For he entirely ignores motive as a source of goodness and badness; but I think almost every one must agree
that motive is at least the main factor in making action morally
good or bad, while opinions differ on whether it has anything
to do with making action right or wrong. Now Spencer's first
answer to the question what makes action right is that it is its
being relatively more evolved,[1] and 'most evolved' he explains
as meaning simultaneously achieving 'the greatest totality of
life in self, in offspring, and in fellow men'.[2] This, so far, is
a purely biological view. 'Right' is defined by reference not to
any psychological state but simply to life. But Spencer immediately goes on to ask, 'Is there any postulate involved in
these judgements on conduct? Is there any assumption made
in calling good the acts conducive to life, in self or others, and
bad those which directly or indirectly tend towards death,
special or general? Yes; an assumption of extreme significance
has been made—an assumption underlying all moral esti-
mates.... Yes, there is one postulate in which pessimists and
optimists agree. Both their arguments assume it to be self-
evident that life is good or bad, according as it does, or does
not, bring a surplus of agreeable feeling.'[3] He expressly says

---

[1] *Data of Ethics* (cheap edition), 25.　　[2] Ibid. 26.　　[3] Ibid. 26, 27.

that 'by those who think life is not a benefit but a misfortune, conduct which prolongs it is to be blamed rather than praised'.[1] And he sums up by saying 'if we call good the conduct conducive to life, we can do so only with the implication that it is conducive to a surplus of pleasures over pains'.[2] Spencer's position, then, is this: action which conduced as much as possible to the increase of life would not be right unless it conduced as much as possible to the increase of pleasure; action which conduced as much as possible to the increase of pleasure would be right whether or not it conduced as much as possible to the increase of life. Clearly it is conduciveness to pleasure that is for him the real ground of rightness. This is his fundamental ethical theory. But he holds, on grounds with which we need not concern ourselves, that life always contains a surplus of pleasure over pain, and that conduciveness to life and conduciveness to pleasure always go together, so that he can say right action is always that which conduces to life, though he does not really think that it is this that makes it right. His fundamental theory turns out to be universalistic Hedonism, or Utilitarianism; the apparently biological theory turns out to be really a psychological theory. And I believe this to be in the long run true of evolutionary ethics in general, so that it need not be examined as a separate form of theory regarding the ground of rightness.

We turn then to the psychological theories. The psychological theories about the *essence* of rightness we divided into the reaction (or attitude) theories and the causal theories; we may consider the psychological theories about the *ground* of rightness under the same two heads. The reaction theories we may divide into those that rest rightness on the reaction of the individual judger, those that rest it on the reaction of a majority of men or of some class of men, and those that rest it on the reaction of the agent (who may or may not be identical with the judger). The first of these theories will be the theory that

[1] Ibid. 26.　　　　　　　　　　　[2] Ibid. 45.

because an individual contemplating an act reacts to it with the emotion of approval, therefore the act in itself has the characteristic of rightness. This theory is open to at least three objections, any one of which is fatal. (1) In the first place, suppose that an act is contemplated by two observers one of whom reacts with approval and the other with disapproval. Then, since the act itself is the same act, we can only suppose either that they are not, both of them, grasping the whole nature of the act (e.g. one may be contemplating it simply as an act of promise-breaking and the other as an act productive of great pleasure), or that while both are grasping its whole nature, idiosyncrasies of the two men cause them to react in different ways to it. In other words, their reaction is due not directly to the nature of the act, but to two things in them, their opinions about the constitutive nature of the act, and the idiosyncrasies which lead them as a result of these opinions to react with approval or disapproval. And it is surely impossible that any quality of the act itself can be founded on a reaction which is itself founded not directly on the nature of the act but on the opinions and idiosyncrasies of individual contemplators of it.

(2) If an act is right because it is approved by A and wrong because it is disapproved by B, the same act will be in fact right and wrong. But while we might agree that the same act may be in some respects right and in others wrong, we do not suppose that the same act can be in fact right on the whole and wrong on the whole. To think this would be to put an end to all ethical judgement. The corresponding essence-theory of rightness put an end to ethical discussion because it implied that two men who respectively call an act right and wrong are not contradicting one another.[1] The ground-theory puts an end to discussion because it implies that the two men are contradicting one another but nevertheless both are right.

(3) I have not so far urged that the emotion of approval presupposes a judgement that the act is right, but merely that it presupposes an opinion about it in its constitutive character,

[1] Cf. p. 24.

e.g. that it is an act of promise-keeping or that it is an act productive of great pleasure. But I think that in fact the emotion of approval presupposes a judgement that the act is right. About this there is perhaps room for difference of opinion. Some may think that the emotion comes first and the judgement second. I am willing to admit that there may be cases in which our first reaction to an act is not an ethical opinion about it, but a non-ethical emotion of disgust, perhaps simply due to its foreignness to our habitual ways of acting and thinking, and that this may through lack of reflection lead to the opinion that the act is wrong. But it seems to me clear that a genuine emotion of ethical disapproval presupposes a judgement that the act is wrong, and not the other way about. If this be so, the situation we are asked to believe in is this: 'A spectator forms a certain view of the constitutive character of the act. In consequence of that he judges it to be wrong. In consequence of that he feels the emotion of disapproval. And in consequence of his doing this the act really is wrong.' Thus his opinion that it is wrong is made indirectly the ground of its *being* wrong. But it is surely clear that if his opinion is incorrect the act is not wrong; and if his opinion is correct, it is correct because the act is wrong already; the act is not wrong because he has the opinion that it is.

If, on the other hand, it be suggested that the vital thing is not an emotion of ethical disapproval presupposing the opinion that the act is wrong, but merely an unfavourable emotion of disgust, it would be absurd to hold that in consequence of this the act has the ethical quality of wrongness. The only natural conclusion would be that acts are not right or wrong, but that some of them happen to disgust us and others do not. And if any one is willing to adopt this view, I do not think that he can be reasoned out of it. But apparently very few people are willing to adopt this view. Those who do not think wrong the things that most people think wrong, at least think wrong the things that most people think *right*.

The next theory to be examined is that an act is right because the *majority* of men, or of some class of men, feel the emotion of approval towards it. This 'public' theory is exposed to the first and the third objection which I raised to the corresponding 'private' theory—the objections arising from the difficulty that there is in supposing that any act can have an objective character of rightness in consequence of the reaction of individuals to it; to this difficulty the fact that many individuals and not one are involved makes no difference. The reaction of the many is just as much coloured by their idiosyncrasies as is the reaction of one individual by his. But in addition this view is exposed to the further difficulty that we often judge an action to be right when we do not for a moment suppose that there is a majority which either is actually approving of it, or would approve of it if it contemplated it. A moral pioneer, or a man who is being generally blamed for an act which he regards as justifiable, no doubt thinks that most people, if they knew all the circumstances and judged truly of them, would agree with him. But if he does, he does not think that his act is right because they would do so, but that they would do so because his act is in fact right.

We come now to the third reaction-theory—that an act is right because the *doer* of it approves of it. Those who hold this view are, I think, more likely to mean by approval the doer's thinking the act right, than his having a mere emotion of satisfaction not presupposing this thought. The question then comes to be, Is an act made right by the agent's thinking it right? On general grounds there would seem to be a fatal objection to this suggestion; it appears perfectly impossible that anything can be necessitated to have any attribute merely by being thought to have it;[1] it does not seem possible that an act could have the characteristic of rightness by being thought to have it, any more than anything else could have any other characteristic by being thought to have it. We may, however,

---

[1] The opinion that *A* has the attribute *B* may in certain circumstances *cause* it to have that attribute; e.g. *possunt quia posse videntur*. But simultaneous necessitation is of course something quite different from causation.

be faced with the indignant protest 'Can it really be right for a man to do what he thinks wrong, or wrong for him to do what he thinks right?' The view underlying such a protest must be one or other of two views; it must either be the view that the being thought by the agent to be right is the sole condition of an act's being right, or the view that in addition to having the other conditions of being right an act must, in order to be right, be thought by the agent to be so. On reflection it can be seen that neither of these contentions can be true. We must adhere to the general principle that a thing's being thought to have a certain characteristic cannot be either the sole condition or one of the conditions of its having that characteristic. To assure ourselves of this, we need only consider the fact that opinion must be either true or false. Now if the opinion that an act is right is false, the act is plainly not right and therefore cannot be right in virtue either of being thought to be so or of anything else. And if the opinion is true, it is true because the act is already right independently of our opinion about it.

It might however reasonably be suggested that the characteristic of being thought to be right confers on an act *another* characteristic; that, for instance, the character of being thought to be objectively right confers on an act the characteristic of being subjectively right, to use language which Sidgwick has used before us.[1] This suggestion escapes the general objection which has been drawn above from the relation between opinion and fact. A thing may perhaps have one characteristic by being thought to have another. For instance, an imagined future state of affairs may have the characteristic of attractiveness by being thought to be such that it will yield a great balance of pleasure to the agent; it is plain that its attractiveness depends not on the characteristics it will actually have, but on those which it is thought that it will have.

It is plain, however, that if the being thought to be objectively right is made the ground of an action's being subjectively right, 'subjectively right' must be given a meaning

[1] *Methods of Ethics*, ed. 7, 207.

other than the being thought to be objectively right; whether such a sense can be found, I will inquire later.[1]

I used to think that the protest I have imagined to be made could be effectively met by the distinction which should be drawn between the rightness of an act and its moral goodness. If we are asked 'can it be right to do what you think wrong?', our answer, it seemed to me, should be 'yes, it can be right, since that cannot be affected by your thinking it to be so or not; but it cannot be morally good, since moral goodness depends[2] on the goodness of the motive, and your motive in doing what you think wrong cannot be good. And similarly it can be wrong to do what you think right, but when it is, it may nevertheless be morally good, and will be so if you not only do what you think right but do it because you think it right. To say that when we fail to do what we think right our action is not morally good, and that when we do what we think right, because we think it right, our action *is* morally good, covers all the truth that lies behind the loosely worded protest "It cannot be right to do what you think wrong, or wrong to do what you think right".'

Now, however, I am inclined to think that in saying this I was not paying enough attention to the strong persuasion which we have that a man who does what he thinks is his duty, really does his duty. This persuasion cannot be right as it stands, for nothing can have any characteristic merely by being thought to have it. But we should try to come to terms more closely with this persuasion, and this I will try to do later.[3]

From the reaction theories I turn to the causal theories. The only naturalistic[4] causal theory that has ever found much favour is the hedonistic one which says that what makes acts right is their tendency to produce either pleasure for the agent, or pleasure for mankind or for all sentient beings (the latter difference being one of detail, and not affecting the general

---

[1] pp. 159-65.   [2] Mainly, at least; but cf. pp. 306-8.   [3] pp. 159-68.
[4] Or rather, apparently naturalistic. See pp. 65-7.

character of the theory, while the former affects it profoundly). I have already remarked[1] that this form of Hedonism, in which productivity of pleasure is made the *ground* of rightness, is far more plausible than the form previously considered, in which productivity of pleasure is put forward as the *essence* of rightness. But I do not propose to examine Hedonism in detail, and that for various reasons. In the first place, I do not think that Hedonism has much vitality to-day. Egoistic Hedonism is put out of court by the fact which stares us in the face, that it is consideration for the rights or interests of others, far more often (to state the matter very mildly) than consideration for our own interests or rights, that makes us think it our duty to behave in a certain way. Whether consideration of our own rights or interests ever gives rise to the thought that we *ought* to behave in a certain way, in distinction from the thought that it would be prudent or sensible to behave in a certain way, is a question to which I hope to come later.[2] But that it is the sole consideration which gives rise to the thought of duty is too palpably untrue to need serious discussion. Universalistic Hedonism, again, seems to me to have been put effectively out of court, by (*inter alia*) Professor Moore's arguments to show that there are other things, notably virtuous action, which we regard as good in their own right, independently of their tendency to produce pleasure. To flog Hedonism is, I believe, to flog a dead or dying horse. That many people behave in a great many of their actions as if they believed in Hedonism is true enough, but as a theory of morals it has very little if any serious claim to our attention. I do not propose therefore to join in the easy game of exposing its fallacies.

There is a further reason why I may excuse myself this task. I believe that no one holds the hedonistic creed unless he believes two things: (1) that what makes acts right is their being productive of the greatest good, and (2) that pleasure is the only thing good in itself. Mill, for instance, describes the theory of life on which Utilitarianism is grounded as being the theory

---

[1] pp. 27-8.   [2] See pp. 272-4.

'that pleasure, and freedom from pain, are the only things desirable as ends'.[1] But it is plain that this is not in itself sufficient ground for the theory that productivity of pleasure is the sole ground of rightness; there is needed also the major premiss that productivity of what is desirable as an end is the sole ground of rightness. This premiss Mill nowhere, I think, seeks to prove; he assumes it silently. But it is just as much needed for the proof of utilitarianism as is the premiss which he takes some pains to prove. However much it might be true that pleasure is the only good, it would not follow that productivity of pleasure is the sole ground of rightness, unless it were also true that productivity of *good* is the sole ground of rightness. The ground of the rightness of acts is rooted, according to Utilitarianism, in the goodness of their results; and goodness is a genuinely ethical notion, not a naturalistic one.

It is true that the only reason Mill gives for the view that pleasure is the only good is at first sight a naturalistic one, viz. the psychological fact, as he holds it to be, that pleasure is the only thing that is desired.[2] But it is plain that here again a further premiss is needed. That pleasure is the only thing that is desirable, or good, can follow from the fact that pleasure is the only thing that is desired, only in virtue of the further premiss that the only thing which is desired must be the only thing which is desirable, or good, and in this the non-naturalistic notion of desirable or good is already present. Thus not only does Mill's view that productivity of pleasure is the only ground of rightness rest on the non-naturalistic premiss that only pleasure is good, but this in turn rests on the naturalistic premiss that only pleasure is desired + the non-naturalistic premiss that the only thing that is desired is the only thing that is desirable.

Similarly, Sidgwick devotes a whole chapter[3] to showing that ultimate good consists solely of pleasant consciousness. And

---

[1] *Utilitarianism*, copyright eds., 10.
[2] Ibid. 52–3.
[3] *Methods of Ethics*, ed. 7, iii. 14.

this would be irrelevant to his main contention, that productivity of pleasure is the ground of rightness, unless he were
assuming as self-evident that productivity of ultimate good is
the ground of rightness. He is clear-sighted enough to reject
the reason which Mill gives for regarding pleasure alone as
ultimately good, viz. that it alone is desired, and candid enough
to admit, or indeed contend, that pleasure is not the only thing
that is desired for its own sake. But he is at one with Mill in
accepting the two premisses: (1) that only productivity of good
is what makes acts right, and (2) that only pleasure is ultimately good, premisses of which the subject of the first and the
predicate of the second involve the non-naturalistic notion
'good'.

The position then is this. There is a certain widely held
view, which we may call Utilitarianism, that productivity of
good is the only thing that makes acts right. There is one form
of this view, hedonistic Utilitarianism, which adds the premiss
that only pleasure is good. There is another form of the view,
with which the writings of Professor Moore and Dr. Rashdall
have made us familiar, which holds that other things besides
pleasure are good. This is non-hedonistic Utilitarianism.
Hedonistic Utilitarianism cannot be true unless Utilitarianism
is true, but may be untrue even if Utilitarianism is true.
Thinking as I do, then, that Utilitarianism in general is an
untrue view, I am not much interested in the question whether,
if it were true, the hedonistic or the non-hedonistic variety of
it would be the true one; and if I can persuade any one that
Utilitarianism is untrue, he will not wish me to discuss the
other question. Yet even if Utilitarianism is not true, it is still
the case that it is *one* of our main responsibilities to produce
as much good as we can, so that the question whether pleasure
is the only good remains a very important question. But it will
belong to a later stage of our discussion.

It is Utilitarianism in its general form, the view that our sole
duty is to produce as much good as possible, that we have now
to discuss. If we could persuade ourselves that right just *means*

'calculated to produce the greatest good', the matter would be simple. But we have seen, I hope,[1] that that contention is not at all plausible. If productivity of good is different from rightness but is the universal ground of rightness, how do we know this? There are, I think, only three possibilities. Either it is known by an immediate intuition, or it is established deductively, or it is established inductively. I do not know of any attempt to establish it deductively, and I cannot think of any middle term which could with any plausibility be used to connect the two terms in question. The effective alternatives appear to be intuition and induction. I will first ask whether the proposition has been established inductively. I take leave to quote some sentences from *The Right and the Good*.

'Such an enquiry, to be conclusive, would have to be very thorough and extensive. We should have to take a large variety of the acts which we, to the best of our ability, judge to be right. We should have to trace as far as possible their consequences, not only for the persons directly affected but also for those indirectly affected; and to these no limit can be set. To make our inquiry thoroughly conclusive, we should have to do what we cannot do, viz. trace these consequences into an unending future. And even to make it reasonably conclusive, we should have to trace them far into the future. It is clear that the most we could possibly say is that a large variety of typical acts that are judged right appear, so far as we can trace their consequences, to produce more good than any other acts possible to the agents in the circumstances. And such a result is far short of proving the constant connexion of the two attributes. But it is surely clear that no inductive inquiry justifying even this result has ever been carried through. The advocates of utilitarian systems have been so much persuaded either of the identity or of the self-evident connexion of the attributes "right" and "optimific" (or "felicific") that they have not attempted even such an inductive inquiry as is possible.'[2]

It is clear, too, that even if we could establish inductively that all optimific acts are right and all right acts optimific, that would not establish that their being optimific is the *ground* of

---

[1] Cf. p. 42.   [2] *The Right and the Good*, 36.

their rightness, which is the proposition we are inquiring into. If we have only proved that the two attributes always go together, that is not enough. We should have to show that all right acts not only are optimific but are right *because* they are optimific. I do not mean to insist that it should be shown that unreflective people always reach their judgement that an act is right because they first judge it to be optimific. To this demand the utilitarian would have a perfectly proper answer. He would say, 'Certain types of act have been in practice found to be optimific, and have in consequence been judged to be right; and so, for plain men, the character of rightness has come to seem to belong to such acts directly, in virtue of their being, e.g. fulfilments of promise, and the middle term which established their rightness has come to be forgotten. *Media axiomata* such as "men should keep their promises" have come to be accepted as if they were self-evidently true, and people habitually judge acts to be right on the strength of the *media axiomata*, forgetting the method by which the *media axiomata* have themselves been established'. That is a fair answer. The test I would prefer to impose is a different one, viz. this: when we reflect, do we really come to the conclusion that such an act as promise-keeping owes its rightness to its tendency to produce maximum good, *or* to its being an act of promise-keeping?

It seems clear that Utilitarianism has not established inductively that being optimific is always the ground of rightness, and as a rule utilitarians have not attempted to do so. The reason is simple: it is because it has seemed to them self-evident that this is the only possible ground of rightness. Professor Moore definitely says that for him the principle is self-evident.[1] For my part, I can find no self-evidence about it. And I think I can point to several facts which tell against its truth, and to some which tell against there being even a constant correspondence between the two attributes, optimificness and rightness.

(1) Professor Broad has pointed out one such difficulty.

[1] *Ethics*, 168–9.

Utilitarians hold that pleasure is either the only good, or is at least a good; and in the latter assertion most people would be, with certain qualifications, in agreement with them. Then, if any other consequences that an act may have be abstracted from, utilitarians are bound to say that an act which produces the greatest possible amount of pleasure is the right or obligatory act. Now, Professor Broad points out,

'among the things which we can to some extent influence by our actions is the number of minds which shall exist, or, to be more cautious, which shall be embodied at a given time. It would be possible to increase the total amount of happiness in a community by increasing the numbers of that community even though one thereby reduced the total happiness of each member of it. If Utilitarianism be true it would be one's duty to try to increase the numbers of a community, even though one reduced the average total happiness of the members, so long as the total happiness in the community would be in the least increased. It seems perfectly plain to me that this kind of action, so far from being a duty, would quite certainly be wrong.'[1]

His criticism appears to be clearly justified. We should not merely not judge that such action was right because it was optimific; we should judge that it was wrong although it was optimific. It already begins to become clear that it is not our duty to increase to the utmost the total happiness, irrespective of how the happiness is distributed.

Professor Broad does not apply his argument to any other good than pleasure; for it is hedonistic Utilitarianism that he is criticizing. But the same argument will apply to any other form of good, say virtuous action or intelligent thought. The utilitarian doctrine involves that all goods are commensurable —that, for instance, in any two virtuous acts there must be different quantities of good which are in a certain ratio to each other, even if we cannot detect the ratio. And a utilitarian should maintain that it is self-evident that if we had to choose between promoting the existence of a certain amount of virtue

---

[1] *Five Types of Ethical Theory*, 249–50.

and intelligence spread out very thin among a certain population, and a slightly smaller amount concentrated in a much
smaller population (whose average virtue and intelligence
would therefore be greater), we ought to choose the former.
But it is clear to me that this is far from self-evident.

Thus we have already a principle which theoretically at any
rate is capable of coming into conflict with the principle of
producing the greatest total amount of good, viz. the principle
which bids us concentrate good in a population of high average
virtue and intelligence, rather than spread it out over a population of low average virtue and intelligence, if the choice ever
lay between these alternatives.

(2) Consider now a case in which the size of the population
is not assumed to be alterable by anything we can do. If the
essential utilitarian principle is true, that productivity of
maximum good is the sole ground of rightness, it ought to be
quite indifferent how an 'extra dose'[1] of happiness should be
distributed among the population, provided the total amount
of the dose is unaltered. It would be morally just the same
whether A is made very happy and B only very slightly happy,
or whether A and B are both made rather happy, provided that
the net gain in happiness for A and B taken together were
equal in both cases. Now if A and B are people of equal
moral worth, we do not really think that it would be right to
distribute happiness unequally between them. Sidgwick, while
criticizing some of our supposed intuitions of justice, has the
candour to admit that there is one principle of justice that is
axiomatic, viz. that of impartiality in the application of general
rules.[2] This, in its application to the case we are considering,
can only mean that it is *not* morally indifferent how we divide
an extra dose of happiness between two individuals, but that
in the absence of some relevant difference between them it
should be equally divided between them. But though Sidgwick
recognizes the 'principle of justice' alongside of the 'principle
of rational benevolence' (that which commands us to produce

---

[1] Ibid. 251.　　　　　　　　[2] *Methods of Ethics*, ed. 7, 380.

the maximum of good), he seems to assign to it a subordinate position. He would still, I think, say that if we can produce a greater total extra dose of happiness by giving much to A and little to B, than by giving the same amount to both, we ought to do so. This, however, is a half-way house at which we cannot stop. The principle of justice in the distribution of happiness can in no way be derived from the principle bidding us produce the greatest *total* of happiness. If it is true, as Sidgwick holds, then it is independent of the greatest happiness principle; and if it is independent of it, it is capable of coming into conflict with it. And where it does, I believe we should all judge that it would be rather our duty to produce a smaller increase of total happiness, fairly divided between individuals, than a slightly larger increase, very unfairly divided. Furthermore, I think we should judge not only that there is an independent moral principle bidding us divide happiness equally between people of equal moral worth, but also that the same principle bids us divide it, so far as we can, unequally between people of unequal moral worth. This appears to me just as axiomatic as the principle which bids us promote the general happiness, or (more widely) the general good.

(3) A further difficulty for utilitarians arises when we consider the distribution of pleasure between the agent and any one else. For utilitarians, it is always a duty for me to produce a greater pleasure for myself rather than a smaller pleasure for another (except of course where the ulterior consequences of the two acts would weigh the balance in favour of the latter act —but we can ignore this complication). Now the plain truth seems to be that we never judge so in fact. It seems to me that if we are honest with ourselves, which in a matter affecting us so closely it is hard to be, we shall find that we never really think ourselves morally bound to do an act which will increase our own pleasure, except for some ulterior reason, e.g. where we think that the pleasurable experience will fit us to do our work better, or that the relinquishing it to another person will tend to have a bad effect on his character.

Of these three difficulties for utilitarianism, arising out of the distribution of good, the first two may be dealt with in either of two ways. We may say (*a*) that quite apart from the duty to produce as much good as possible, there is an independent duty to produce a concentration of good in a smaller number of persons rather than a distribution of an equal amount of it among a larger number, and another independent duty to distribute happiness in proportion to merit. Or we may say (*b*) that the concentration of good in a smaller number of persons is itself a good, a good of higher order,[1] as it were, than the good (consisting, say, of virtuous action, intelligent thought, and pleasure) which is thus concentrated; and similarly that the enjoyment of happiness in proportion to merit is itself a good of higher order than the happiness and the merit themselves. In this case the duty to produce such concentrations or such distributions will fall under the general duty of producing good; and our criticism of Utilitarianism will be, so far, less radical than in the other case. We shall not have established a duty other than the duty of producing good. We shall simply have shown that Utilitarianism in naming virtuous action, intelligent thought, and pleasure as the things that are good has overlooked two important goods of higher order.

It is difficult to choose between these two views. On the whole I incline towards the latter. It seems to me that the existence of a greater concentration of good is not only something in which we should in fact take greater satisfaction than in the wider and thinner distribution of the same total amount of good, but something in which it is *reasonable* to take satisfaction, i.e. is a greater good.[2] And similarly I think it is reasonable to take satisfaction in a distribution of happiness in proportion to merit rather than in a distribution not in proportion to merit. If we had before us in imagination two communities in which the total amounts of virtue and of happiness were equal, but in one the good were happy and the bad wretched, and in

[1] In a mathematical, not in a moral sense.
[2] For this sense of good cf. pp. 275–6, 278–9.

the other the bad were happy and the good were wretched, I think it would be reasonable to say that the state of the first community is a better state than that of the second, and one which on that ground we ought to do our best to bring about rather than the other.

In answer to the third objection also, a utilitarian might be tempted to say that a good of higher order is involved. He might say that the enjoyment of pleasure by a man as a result of another man's action is a good of higher order, while the enjoyment of pleasure by a man as a result of his own action is not such a good. It is clear, however, that this is not true. Suppose that *A*, desiring to produce pleasure for *B*, produces it for himself, and that *B*, desiring to produce pleasure for himself, produces it for *A*. No one thinks *A*'s enjoyment in the first case less of a good than his enjoyment in the second, though in the first it has been produced by himself and in the second by *B*.

The utilitarian might then seek to amend his suggestion by saying 'the enjoyment of pleasure by a man as a result of another man's action *directed to that end* is a good of higher order, while the enjoyment of pleasure by a man as a result of his own action directed to that end is not such a good, and that is why it is a duty to produce pleasure for others and not a duty to produce it for oneself'. But he is not entitled to make this amendment. For on his own showing the duty of doing an act depends on the results produced, or (according to a different form of the theory) on the results intended; and he is not entitled to reckon a difference between the two *motives* as a difference in the results produced or intended.

Yet here also our argument does not necessarily point to a duty quite distinct from that of producing a maximum of good. For, while for a third person the enjoyment of pleasure by *A* is the same kind of thing as its enjoyment by *B*, *A*'s own pleasure stands in quite a different relation to *A* from that in which *B*'s pleasure stands to *A*. There is at least some ground for thinking that for *A* they may be good only in quite different senses of 'good', *B*'s pleasure being for *A* a morally suitable object of satisfaction, and A's pleasure being for A only an *inevitable* object of satisfaction, having nothing morally suitable or unsuitable about it.[1] If this be the true account, the hard fact (one of the most certain facts in morals) that we have a duty to produce pleasure for others, and have not a duty to produce it for ourselves, will involve us in admitting that it is only things that are good in the sense of being morally suitable objects of satisfaction, and not those that are good in the sense[2] of being inevitable but morally neutral objects of satisfaction, that we have a duty to produce.

I pass now to an objection connected not with the distribution of pleasure but with the fact that we may by our action produce pleasure for some people and pain for others. On the utilitarian view, to each dose of pleasure there is some dose of pain that is exactly equal. The one may be represented by $+x$, the other by $-x$. Now for a utilitarian it is morally indifferent whether by your act you produce x units of pleasure for A and inflict y units of pain on B, or confer $x-y$ units of pleasure on one of them, since in each case you produce a net increment of $x-y$ units of pleasure. But we should in fact, I think, always judge that the infliction of pain on any person is justified only by the conferment not of an equal but of a substantially greater amount of pleasure on some one else (assuming the persons to be of equal worth). We do not, in fact, think that persons other than ourselves are simply so many pawns in the game of producing the maximum of pleasure, or good. We think they have definite rights, or at least claims, not to be made means to the giving of pleasure to others; and claims that ought to be respected unless the net pleasure, or good, to be gained for the community by other action is very considerable. We think the principle 'do evil to no one' more pressing than the principle 'do good to every one', except when the evil is very substantially outweighed by the good. This consideration seems to be perfectly clear, and it is strange that it has been overlooked by the utilitarians.

---

[1] Cf. pp. 272-9.   [2] If this *is* a legitimate sense of 'good' at all; cf. pp. 284-5.

I pass next to a group of difficulties for Utilitarianism arising from our sense of special duties towards individuals, based on special relations between them and the agent. These seem to fall under three general heads. There is first the sense which we all possess that we have a special duty to make compensation to any one for any wrong we have done him. When I have wronged some one, he has ceased to be merely what Utilitarianism regards him as being, one out of many possible recipients or receptacles of good, between whom the choice is to be made simply on the basis of the question how the maximum good is to be achieved. He has become some one with a *special* claim on my effort, over and above the claim which all men have to my beneficence.

There is similarly the claim which those have from whom we have accepted benefits in the past. This again is a claim which, in fact, I believe every one recognizes, and it is evident that it is on it that our special duty to parents and friends in the main depends.

These two responsibilities—the responsibility for compensation and for rendering good for good—arise incidentally from past actions having another purpose. But, thirdly, there are obligations arising from acts whose express object was to create them. Our name for these acts is 'promises'; a promise is just the voluntary making of something obligatory on us which would not, or need not, have been obligatory before. To make this clear, we must in the first place distinguish (as we do, more or less clearly, in ordinary life) between the making of a promise and the announcement of an intention. There are cases in which it is difficult to know whether some one is making a promise or is merely announcing an intention; but that does not affect the fact that the two things are in principle quite different. As Sidgwick remarks, 'If I merely assert my intention of abstaining from alcohol for a year, and then after a week take some, I am (at worst) ridiculed as inconsistent; but if I have pledged myself to abstain, I am blamed as untrustworthy.'[1]

[1] *Methods of Ethics*, 304.

The announcement of an intention is merely a statement about one's present state of mind; a promise is a statement about the future. But, secondly, not every statement about one's own behaviour in the future is a promise. If I merely say incidentally in conversation with some one that I shall be at a certain place at a certain time, that does not constitute a promise to be there. To make a promise, there must be a more or less clear intimation to another person that he can *rely* upon me to do something which he, at least, regards as a service to him. The difference between this and a mere statement about the future can be seen from the fact that when I have merely made a statement about the future, what he relies upon, if he expects me to fulfil it, is my unchangeability, while, when I make a promise, what he relies upon is my sense of duty.

A promise being this, an intentional intimation to some one else that he can rely upon me to behave in a certain way, it appears to me perfectly clear, that, quite apart from any question of the greatness of the benefits to be produced for him or for society by the fulfilment of the promise, a promise gives rise to a moral claim on his part that the promise be fulfilled. This claim will be enhanced if there are great benefits that will arise from the fulfilment of the promise in contrast to its violation; or it may be overridden if the fulfilment of the promise is likely to do much more harm than good. But through all such variations it remains as a solid fact in the moral situation; and it arises solely from the fact that a promise has been made, and not from the consequences of its fulfilment. I would go so far as to say that the existence of an obligation arising from the making of a promise is so axiomatic that no moral universe can be imagined in which it would not exist.

These seem to me to be the main difficulties in the way of accepting Utilitarianism as a complete ethical creed; these are the principles of duty which seem to emerge as distinct from the principle 'promote the maximum good'.

I may be allowed to reinforce these criticisms of Utilitarianism by quoting some words from the most sagacious, if not the most consistent or systematic, of the British Moralists. In his ripest work on ethics, the *Dissertation on the Nature of Virtue*,[1] Butler indicates more clearly than in the *Sermons* his distrust of the view which treats zeal for the general good as the only virtue.

'Without inquiring', he says, 'how far, and in what sense, virtue is resolvable into benevolence, and vice into the want of it; it may be proper to observe, that benevolence, and the want of it, singly considered, are in no sort the whole of virtue and vice. For if this were the case, in the review of one's own character, or that of others, our moral understanding and moral sense would be indifferent to every thing, but the degrees in which benevolence prevailed, and the degrees in which it was wanting. That is, we should neither approve of benevolence to some persons rather than to others, nor disapprove injustice and falsehood upon any other account, than merely as an overbalance of happiness was foreseen likely to be produced by the first, and of misery by the second. But now, on the contrary, suppose two men competitors for any thing whatever, which would be of equal advantage to each of them: though nothing indeed would be more impertinent, than for a stranger to busy himself to get one of them preferred to the other; yet such endeavour would be virtue, in behalf of a friend or benefactor, abstracted from all consideration of distant consequences: as that examples of gratitude, and the cultivation of friendship, would be of general good to the world. Again, suppose one man should, by fraud or violence, take from another the fruit of his labour, with intent to give it to a third, who he thought would have as much pleasure from it as would balance the pleasure which the first possessor would have had in the enjoyment, and his vexation in the loss of it; suppose also that no bad consequences would follow; yet such an action would surely be vicious. Nay, farther, were treachery, violence and injustice, no otherwise vicious, than as foreseen likely to produce an overbalance of misery to society; then, if in any case a man could procure to himself as great advantage by an act of injustice, as the whole foreseen inconvenience, likely to be brought upon others by it, would amount to; such a piece of injustice would not be faulty or vicious at all: because it would be no more than, in any other case, for a man to prefer his own satisfaction to another's in equal degrees.

---

[1] *The Works of Joseph Butler* (Gladstone's edition), i. 334–7.

'The fact then appears to be, that we are constituted so as to condemn falsehood, unprovoked violence, injustice, and to approve of benevolence to some preferably to others, abstracted from all consideration, which conduct is likeliest to produce an overbalance of happiness or misery. And therefore, were the Author of nature to propose nothing to himself as an end but the production of happiness, were his moral character merely that of benevolence; yet ours is not so. . . . The happiness of the world is the concern of him, who is the Lord and the Proprietor of it: nor do we know what we are about, when we endeavour to promote the good of mankind in any ways, but those which he has directed; that is indeed in all ways not contrary to veracity and justice.'

These weighty words of Butler's answer better to what we really think on moral questions, than a theory which makes the production of good at all costs the only duty.

The fact is that Utilitarianism is a product of the craving for a simple creed, and that the facts of the moral life are too complex to fit into its scheme. If the root idea of rightness is suitability to the situation, there is not the slightest reason to anticipate that the only way in which an act can be right, i.e. fit a situation, is by being likely to amend it to the greatest possible extent; it may fit it no less by harmonizing with existing features of the situation, such as the existence of a claim to the fulfilment of a promise.

I must discuss at this point Professor Broad's view on this matter. He is dissatisfied, as I am, both with Utilitarianism (whether hedonistic or agathistic) and with out-and-out Intuitionism. He sees that such an act as the fulfilling of a promise has a tendency to be right which does not arise from a tendency to promote the general good, but from the fact that a promise has been made. He sees, on the other hand, that it cannot be maintained, with out-and-out Intuitionism, that all promises should be kept irrespectively of the consequences. He therefore puts forward the following analysis:

'We have to distinguish two quite different ethical features of the action x, viz., its fittingness or unfittingness to the total course of events as modified by it, and its utility or disutility. . . . Fittingness or unfittingness is a direct ethical relation between an action or emotion and the total course of events in which it takes place. As this course of events consists of a number of successive phases, it is possible that a certain action may be fitting to some of the phases and unfitting to others. In particular it might be "immediately fitting", i.e. it might be appropriate to the initial phase F_1, but it might be unfitting to some or all of the later modified phases F_2^x, etc. Again, since each phase is itself complex, the action might be fitting to certain factors of a certain phase but unfitting to other factors of that phase. It is quite easy to give examples. If I am asked a certain question and answer it in a certain way I may be answering that question truly but my answer may lead to subsequent false inferences. It might then be said that this answer was fitting to the initial phase, but was unfitting to subsequent phases in the course of events as modified by it. It would then become a question whether a true answer, or a lie, or silence was the most fitting action on the whole, given the initial phase. The second complication may be illustrated as follows. I may be an elector to an office, and one of the candidates may have done me a service. To prefer him to a better qualified candidate would fit one aspect of the situation, since it would be rewarding a benefactor; but it would be unfitting to other factors in the situation, since it would be an act of bad faith to the institution which was employing me as an elector and an act of injustice to the other candidates. The statement that "x is more fitting to be done in the situation F_1 than y is" means that x is more fitting to the whole course of events $F_1 F_2^x \ldots F_n^x$ than y is to the whole course of events $F_1 F_2^y \ldots F_n^y$. The fittingness of an act to a whole course of events will be a function of its fittingness or unfittingness to each phase in the series, and its fittingness to any phase in the series will be a function of its fittingness or unfittingness to each factor or aspect of that phase.'[1]

Having explained the fittingness of an action, he proceeds to consider its utility, and defines it thus:

'The statement that "x is more useful to be done than y in the situation F_1" means that, apart from all reference to fittingness

---

[1] *Five Types of Ethical Theory*, 218–20.

and unfittingness, the course of events $F_1 F_2^x \ldots F_n^x$ is on the whole intrinsically better than the course of events $F_1 F_2^y \ldots F_n^y$.'[1]

He adds that

'the rightness or wrongness of an action in a given initial situation is a function of its fittingness in that situation and its utility in that situation. The pure Deontologist would deny that its utility or dis-utility was relevant to its rightness or wrongness. The pure Teleo-logist would deny that there is such a relation as direct fittingness or unfittingness, and would make its rightness or wrongness depend entirely on its utility or disutility. Both these extremes seem to me to be wrong, and to be in flagrant conflict with common sense.'[2]

On this I have two comments to make. (1) Professor Broad has already described rightness as a certain unique mode of fittingness of an act to a situation[3]—what we may call moral fittingness. Now if this be what rightness is, we cannot make rightness depend on a combination or balance of fittingness and utility. Unless the utility has a tendency to make the act fitting, it cannot have a tendency to make it right, if rightness is a kind of fittingness. It seems to me then that he should make right-ness depend not on a joint consideration of fittingness and utility, but on a joint consideration of fittingness arising from utility and fittingness arising from other sources, such as that a promise has been made. I feel, myself, no difficulty in recog-nizing, in the tendency which an act has to amend the situation in the best possible way, i.e. to produce the maximum good, something in virtue of which that act tends to be fitting to the situation.

(2) I find a difficulty in Professor Broad's conception of an act as fitting the later phases in a process modified by its own occurrence. It seems to me clear that the situation which an act must fit if it is to be right is the situation that exists when, or just before, the act is done, not the situation as it will develop if modified by the act. Take the example that he takes, a true statement which may lead in the future to the formation of false opinions by the person to whom I speak or by some one

else. It seems to me clear that any tendency that my statement may have, to lead to the formation of false opinions later, must be considered under the heading of disutility and not under the heading of what Professor Broad calls direct unfittingness. For if the duty to tell the truth be one of the duties that stand outside the utilitarian scheme, if it springs not from the badness of the total consequences of a lying statement but from the special nature of one special consequence, viz. that the statement leads directly to the formation of a false opinion on the subject-matter of my statement, then so far as that goes any opinion that any one may in the future form on *other* subject-matters falls outside of the 'direct unfittingness' of the act and must come under the heading of unfittingness arising from disutility.

These are differences of detail. In the main, Professor Broad's view is just that which I wish to advocate, viz. that among the features of a situation which tend to make an act right there are some which are independent of the tendency of the act to bring about a maximum of good. To say this is to hold an intuitionistic view of one kind. It has, of course, often been pointed out that every ethical system admits intuition at some point. Utilitarianism in the general form represented by Professor Moore's ethical writings admits the supposed intuition that only what is productive of the greatest good is right. Hedonistic Utilitarianism adds to this the supposed intuition that only pleasure is intrinsically good. Sidgwick's form of hedonistic Utilitarianism adds to these intuitions two that contradict the essential principle of Utilitarianism, the 'axiom of rational self-love' and the 'axiom of justice'. The objection that many people feel to Intuitionism can hardly be an objection to the admission of intuition; for without that no theory can get going. The objection rather is that Intuitionism admits too many intuitions, and further that it admits intuitions that in practice contradict one another. These objections must be considered separately.

(1) The view which admits only one intuition—that only

the production of maximum good is right—gratifies our natural wish to reach unity and simplicity in our moral theory. We have a natural wish to reach a single principle from which the rightness or wrongness of all actions can be deduced. But it is more important that a theory be true than that it be simple; and I have tried to show that a system which admits only this one intuition is false to what we all really think about what makes acts right or wrong. After all, there is no more justification for expecting a single ground of rightness than for expecting a single ground of goodness, and agathistic or generalized Utilitarianism recognizes a variety of goods without succeeding in finding, or even feeling any need to find, a single ground of the goodness of them all. It is, to my mind, a mistake in principle to think that there is any presumption in favour of the truth of a monistic against a pluralistic theory in morals, or, for that matter, in metaphysics either. When we are faced with two or more ostensible grounds of rightness, it is proper to examine them to find whether they have a single character in common; but if we cannot find one we have no reason to assume that our failure is due to the weakness of our thought and not to the nature of the facts. Just so in metaphysics; where we find two types of entity that are *prima facie* quite different, as bodies and minds are, it is proper to ask whether they are not two forms of one kind of entity; but there is no reason for assuming that they necessarily are; and if on examination we can find no unity of nature in them, it is wiser to accept this result than to assume that there must be a unity that we have not discovered. There is no reason why all the substances in the world should be modifications of a single pattern.

(2) But it may be argued that the plurality of moral intuitions is disproved by the fact that the supposed intuitions in practice contradict one another; that often we cannot obey one without disobeying another; that sometimes we cannot obey the principle of telling the truth without disobeying the principle of not causing needless pain, or the principle of keeping

promises without disobeying the principle of producing the maximum good. This objection is to be met by care in stating the content of the principles for which we claim an axiomatic character. Moral intuitions are not principles by the immediate application of which our duty in particular circumstances can be deduced. They state what I have elsewhere[1] called *prima facie* obligations. This way of describing them is, I think, in two ways useful. In the first place, it brings out the fact that when we approach the question, what should I do in these particular circumstances, it is the fitness or unfitness of an imagined act *in certain respects* that first catches our attention. Any possible act has many sides to it which are relevant to its rightness or wrongness; it will bring pleasure to some people, pain to others; it will be the keeping of a promise to one person, at the cost of being a breach of confidence to another, and so on. We are quite incapable of pronouncing straight off on its rightness or wrongness in the totality of these aspects; it is only by recognizing these different features one by one that we can approach the forming of a judgement on the totality of its nature; our first look reveals these features in isolation, one by one; they are what appears *prima facie*. And secondly, they are, *prima facie, obligations*. It is easy to be so impressed by the rightness of an act in one respect that we suppose it to be therefore necessarily the act that we are bound to do. But an act may be right in one respect and wrong in more important respects, and therefore not, in the totality of its aspects, the most right of the acts open to us, and then we are not obliged to do it; and another act may be wrong in some respect and yet in its totality the most right of all the acts open to us, and then we *are* bound to do it. *Prima facie* obligation depends on some one aspect of the act; obligation or disobligation attaches to it in virtue of the totality of its aspects.

Yet the phrase '*prima facie* obligation' does not do full justice to the facts. It says at the same time too much and too little. It says too much; it seems to say that *prima facie* obliga-

---

[1] *The Right and the Good*, 19.

tions are one kind of obligation, while they are in fact something different; for we are *not* obliged to do that which is only *prima facie* obligatory. We are only bound to do that act whose *prima facie* obligatoriness in those respects in which it is *prima facie* obligatory most outweighs its *prima facie* disobligatoriness in those respects in which it is *prima facie* disobligatory.

In another way it says too little. If we dismiss the wrong suggestion just pointed out, the phrase may then suggest that the whole character of the things we are speaking of is to *appear to be obligations*. But on general grounds we may say that it cannot be the whole character of anything to seem to be something. There must be something which it is, as well as something which it seems to be. And in particular, if we are mistaken when we suppose these things to be obligations, that is not the whole truth about them. They are not illusions which we dispense with when we view the act in its totality and see it to be really obligatory or really disobligatory. It remains hard fact that an act of promise-breaking is morally unsuitable in so far as it is an act of promise-breaking, even when we decide that in spite of this it is the act that we ought to do.

We want an expression, then, which shall state what these things are which we have so far described by reference to what they seem to be. Professor Prichard has suggested that the word 'claims' may supply the need. But it has the inconvenience of stating the matter from the point of view of the persons to be affected by the action; we want also a word to express the matter from the point of view of the agent. And, further, the expression 'claim' seems to be completely suitable only to cases where our duty is duty to another person or persons. But there are duties besides these—the duties of improving our own character and our own intellect; and it is only metaphorical to describe our own character or intellect as having a claim on us. Mr. Carritt has suggested the word *'responsibility'* as escaping both these objections;[1] and I gladly accept the suggestion.

[1] *Morals and Politics*, 185.

When we try to formulate laws of nature, we find that if we are to state them in a universal form which admits of no exception, we must state them not as laws of actual operation but as laws of tendency. We cannot say, for instance, that a certain force impinging on a body of a certain mass will always cause it to move with a certain velocity in the line of the force; for if the body is acted on by an equal and opposite force, it actually remains at rest; and if it is acted on by a force operating in some third direction, it will move in a line which is oblique to the lines of both forces. We can only say that any force *tends* to make the body move in the line of the force. Thus alone do we get a perfectly universal law. In the same way if we want to formulate universal moral laws, we can only formulate them as laws of *prima facie* obligation, laws stating the tendencies of actions to be obligatory in virtue of this characteristic or of that. It is the overlooking of the distinction between obligations and responsibilities, between actual obligatoriness and the tendency to be obligatory, that leads to the apparent problem of conflict of duties, and it is by drawing the distinction that we solve the problem, or rather show it to be non-existent. For while an act may well be *prima facie* obligatory in respect of one character and *prima facie* forbidden in virtue of another, it becomes obligatory or forbidden only in virtue of the totality of its ethically relevant characteristics. We are perfectly familiar with this way of thinking when we are face to face with actual problems of conduct, but in theories of ethics responsibilities have often been overstated as being absolute obligations admitting of no exception, and the unreal problem of conflict of duties has thus been supposed to exist.

V

THE OBLIGATION TO FULFIL PROMISES

PERHAPS the severest criticism with which the view I am maintaining has met is that which is passed on it by Mr. W. A. Pickard-Cambridge. I quote a passage which shows the general nature of his criticism.

'It is evident at once that a theory which hides the process which it professes to defend, at the most critical point, in a cloud of negations, is not easy to attack convincingly. Anyone who maintains that we decide what is our duty by comparing together *prima facie* obligations and picking out one of them as the more stringent by inspection only, and on no principle at all, puts himself at a double advantage.

'It is very difficult to subvert or to prove inappropriate any method which rejoices in working on no constant principle—as difficult as it is to confute a man who does not mind how much he contradicts himself. Such a man retains a power to strike at his opponent who does believe in some constant, universal principle of judgment, if he can only find a single case where the latter is inconsistent in his principles. On the other hand, he robs the opponent of any chance to strike at him with a like charge of inconsistency, because inconsistency of principle is, in his view, the normal and natural feature of all moral judgment. It is impossible to correct him at any point (as it is often easy to correct anyone who admits the existence of some one universal ground or character of our duties) by reference to his own judgment or to the principles he has employed elsewhere. He can always get out of the net by saying "I know that principle B on which I act to-day not only does not support but actually collides with principle A on which I acted yesterday: but that is as it should be, because an unprincipled intuition makes me of opinion" (or, in shorter American phrase, "I guess") "that to-day B has the stronger claim". Or again, if such order of priority between certain kinds of *prima facie* duty as the theory claims to be self-evident is ever reversed on any particular occasion (e.g. if ever it is believed to be right to give a present rather than pay a debt, when both cannot be done) the defender of the theory can always here again say that his intuition leads him in this case to this conclusion, and that that for him is sufficient. By thus professing to discard any consistent principle of judgment save to abide by his intuition at the moment, he puts himself outside the reach of any appeal to maintain any consistent principle of conduct—a form of appeal which is usually accepted and predominant in moral as in all other discussions. Argument, then, on these lines is impossible. The need for consistency in one form, indeed, he readily admits, viz. for consistency in judgment between different people. If he judges truly at any point, then anyone else ought to judge the same. If they disagree, one must be in error, and he will admit that the error may be his: his opinions on all such matters are "highly fallible", never more than "probable". This candid admission saves his judgments from the fate, to which the total disclaimer of consistency in *any* form would expose him, of being the expressions of pure caprice and so totally insignificant. But it still affords no possible basis for argument, nor opens any way to an agreement between the parties (except, of course, by a spontaneous and equally unprincipled change of opinion on one side or the other) upon the question which of them is in error and which not.'[1]

I find it difficult to seize what is the precise point of my theory which is here being attacked. But perhaps the most definite statement made is that in my view inconsistency of principle is the normal and natural feature of moral judgement. It is true that what distinguishes my view from Mr. Pickard-Cambridge's is that I believe in a plurality of moral principles, while he believes in but one, that we should always do the act which seems likely, and do it because it seems likely, to produce most good. This appears to me to be clearly not the only principle which we recognize. But why should recognition of a plurality of principles be thought to involve inconsistency of principle? That will depend on the nature of the principles. If my principles were, for instance, 'I should always keep a promise' and 'I should always do that which seems likely to produce most good', these principles, while not formally

---

[1] *Mind*, xli (1932), 150–1.

inconsistent in themselves, would sometimes involve inconsistent consequences; for sometimes the keeping of a promise does not seem likely to produce most good, and then the one principle would lead to the consequence 'I ought to keep the promise' and the other to the consequence 'I ought to break it'. This is precisely the difficulty into which a view like Kant's falls. But I have tried to avoid this objection, by stating the two principles quite differently—the one in the form 'an act, in so far as it is the fulfilling of a promise, *tends* to be right', the other in the form 'an act, in so far as it is the act which seems likely to produce most good, tends to be right'. And neither these principles, nor any consequences to which they lead, are inconsistent. What, then, is the justification for representing me as saying 'I know that principle B on which I act to-day not only does not support but actually collides with principle A on which I acted yesterday: but that is as it should be, because an unprincipled intuition makes me of opinion . . . that to-day B has the stronger claim'? Surely Mr. Pickard-Cambridge himself must admit on his own principles the existence of conflicting tendencies in the same act. An act which seems likely to do good to A and harm to B tends to be right in the first respect and wrong in the second. And there would be no inconsistency in his saying that though one act which does good to A and harm to B is on balance right, another which, while doing an equal good to A, did *more* harm to B may be wrong. And similarly there is no inconsistency in saying that though an act which keeps a promise to A and does harm to B is right, an act which keeps a promise to A and does *more* harm to B may be wrong.

Next, I must examine Mr. Pickard-Cambridge's claim[1] that the ideal utilitarian method is, compared with the intuitionistic, one which it is *easy to apply* in order to ascertain our duty. To this I would make two answers. (1) The claim seems to me to be justified as regards some moral situations, and unjustified as regards others. (*a*) Consider first a case in which

[1] Ibid. 330–40.

we are really in doubt whether we ought to fulfil a particular promise, or to do an act which seems on the face of it likely to bring more good into the world. In such a case I believe the utilitarian method is one which it is easier to apply. For my view involves me in saying that in such a case we have to take account, just as a utilitarian would say we must take account, of the goodness and badness of the various consequences of either act. We are alike involved in this difficult evaluation. And, in addition, I am involved in the further problem of evaluating the *prima facie* obligatoriness of the one act *qua* fulfilment of promise with that of the other act *qua* productive of good; and this is in border-line cases a very real further difficulty. But (*b*) life is not full of such border-line cases. When we ask ourselves whether we ought in a given case to keep a promise, then if we hold as I do that there is a strong *prima facie* obligatoriness attaching to the fulfilling of a promise, which therefore no *slight* preponderance of good to be effected by an alternative act can prevent from being my duty, I am saved from the task of narrowly scrutinizing the situation to see whether there might not be some slight preponderance of good effected by breaking my promise. Accordingly, in perhaps nine out of ten cases in which I have given a promise, I have no difficulty at all in seeing that I ought to fulfil it; while the opposite view would involve me in anxious scrutiny of *every* case in which I have made a promise, before I could know that I ought to fulfil it. Putting it briefly, the utilitarian method is the easier to apply in difficult cases; but in return, utilitarianism would make practically all cases in which a promise is to be kept or broken seem difficult cases—even those which our natural moral consciousness informs us not to be so.

My main answer, however, would be a different one, viz. (2) that any appeal to the ease of applying the one view or the other is beside the mark. It is not the business of moral philosophy to provide us with a theory which is easy to apply. Its business, or the part of its business with which we are at present concerned, is to say on what the rightness or wrongness of actions in fact depends. The fact that it would be easier to recognize our duty if it depended on factor a only than it would be if it depended on factors a, b, and c has no tendency whatever to prove that in fact it depends on a alone. The kind of argument which Mr. Pickard-Cambridge turns against me could equally well be turned against him by a hedonist. A hedonist could fairly say that his own theory, which recognizes in pleasure the only intrinsic good, is easier to apply than one which recognizes, as Mr. Pickard-Cambridge's does, other types of good as well, and requires us to evaluate goods of different types against one another. To him Mr. Pickard-Cambridge would rightly reply: 'That may be so, but the fact is that we think other things than pleasure good, and it is our business to take account of the facts and not to adopt a relatively easily applied theory because it is relatively easily applied.' And similarly I would reply to Mr. Pickard-Cambridge: 'The fact is that we recognize other grounds of rightness than productivity of good results, and the theory which points this out is the true theory, even if it is in many cases harder than the rival theory is to apply to the question what I should do here and now.'

We must, however, see whether his system *will* square with the facts of the moral consciousness. In particular, we must consider further the question of promise-keeping. Mr. Pickard-Cambridge of course admits that, in general, promises should be kept. He gives his reason for this by pointing out various goods which are produced, and evils that are avoided, by the keeping of promises. His analysis is as follows:—We may start with the evils produced by the breach of promise, viz.:

1. The loss by the promisee of the promised benefit.
2. The disappointment caused to him by the breach of promise.
3. The damage to the promiser's reputation, and therefore to his power to co-operate with others, and therefore to his power to do good.
4. The damage to society caused by his weakening the general confidence that promises will be kept.

If the promise is kept, on the other hand, the following goods will be produced:

1. The gaining by the promisee of the promised benefit.
2. The pleasure caused to him by the fulfilment of his expectation.
3. The heightening of the promiser's reputation for trustworthiness, with the greater power to do good which this will bring in its train.
4. The benefit to society caused by his increasing the general confidence that promises will be kept.

It is quite clear that the preservation of general mutual confidence between man and man is a source of very great good to a society. If men could not generally rely on others' keeping their promises, commercial credit, for instance, would break down, and society would be conducted at a great disadvantage. Utilitarians, therefore, have naturally laid great stress on this, and have put forward, as perhaps the main reason why an individual promise should be kept, the fact that every breach tends to weaken this general confidence. I ventured to say elsewhere[1] that 'it may be suspected . . . that the effect of a single keeping or breaking of a promise in strengthening or weakening the fabric of mutual confidence is greatly exaggerated by the theory we are examining' (the utilitarian theory), and Mr. Pickard-Cambridge takes me to task for this. He argues that the situation immediately suggested by my words ('a single . . . breaking of a promise') is not the situation we have to think of. My words, he says,

'suggest a single breach of promise occurring as an exception to the general practice, and in face of a general opinion that such breaches are wrong. What we have to ask is what would happen if this general opinion were scrapped, and if a breach of promise could appear in public with no halter round its neck, admired as a shrewd device, or at least approved as quite unobjectionable and lawful. Imitators would pour in as thickly as applicants for the dole.... In six months or less credit would be as dead as national solvency with a universal dole'.[2]

---

[1] *The Right and the Good*, 39.   [2] *Mind*, xli (1932), 154.

His reasoning here appears to me to be at fault. We must distinguish two questions. One is the question whether condemnation of promise-breaking by public opinion is justifiable on utilitarian grounds? I am willing to admit that it is. Undoubtedly general condonation of promise-breaking would lead to general breaking of promises, and undoubtedly this would lead to results which a utilitarian would deplore. But the question I was asking was a different question, viz. whether it is by its results that a particular act of promise-breaking is made to be wrong, or by its intrinsic nature *as* a breach of promise? If I were tempted to break a particular promise, I, if I were a utilitarian, should not be entitled to ask 'what would happen if promise-breaking were generally condoned', except in so far as I thought this particular breach of promise likely to lead to the general condonation of promise-breaking; for particular acts must by a utilitarian be judged only in the light of their probable consequences. Now I do not think that generally speaking a particular breach of promise is likely to have much influence in promoting the general condonation of promise-breaking. Is it not rather the case that it will be condoned only in so far as public opinion is already weak or perverted on the matter of promise-breaking? And is it not the case that a flagrant breach of promise often tends to *strengthen* the general opinion against promise-breaking, so that so far as this effect goes a utilitarian should welcome and approve it? I should say, for instance, that the breach of Belgian neutrality by Germany in 1914 strengthened rather than weakened in all impartial observers the sense that treaties ought to be observed. 'Recent history in Ireland or Chicago', says Mr. Pickard-Cambridge, 'sufficiently illustrates the situation which arises if murder be unsuppressed.'[1] But that is an argument not against the doing of a particular murder, but against the general condonation of murder by the state.

So far Mr. Pickard-Cambridge seems to have fallen into an *ignoratio elenchi*. He has confused the question, What are the

[1] Ibid. 155.

probable effects if I break this promise?, with the question, What are the probable effects if I do this and my act is generally condoned?; and since the bad effects in the latter case will be very great, and enough to condemn the act on utilitarian grounds, he assumes that in the former case also they will be so.

I pass to a part of his case which is more difficult to meet. He has shown great ingenuity in putting cases which do present some difficulty to one who believes in a *prima facie* duty to keep promises. (1) He puts first[1] the case of two sick musicians, A and B, of whom A has promised B that before 5 p.m. to-day he will put a new E-string on B's violin. If at 4.45 B is evidently dying, is A still bound by his promise? I agree, as I suppose every one would, that he is not. But my comment would be that Mr. Pickard-Cambridge in using this case as an argument against my view is pressing on the letter of the promise and not on its spirit. I ask for some common sense in the interpretation of the promise. A's verbal promise is: 'I will put a new E-string on your fiddle.' But the underlying assumption is that B will be well enough to play on the fiddle. In spirit the promise was: 'If you are alive and well enough to play on the fiddle, I will put it, in respect of its E-string, in condition for you to play on it.' The admission of such a qualifying clause would be dangerous if the qualification were one made secretly by the promiser to himself at the time of the promise, or extemporized by him afterwards in his own interests; but in this case it is one which, if it had occurred to A to make it openly at the time, would have been accepted by B, and which implicitly determines the nature of the understanding between the two men. Suppose the assumption were different: suppose that A had broken the string of B's violin, and his promise to B were implicitly a promise to make good this slight financial loss, he *would* be still bound to prevent this loss to B's heirs.

(2) Secondly,[2] he takes the case in which it is A's illness that takes a turn for the worse. If A is in pain and can hardly bear to move, then, says Mr. Pickard-Cambridge, he is under no

---

[1] *Mind*, xli (1932), 158.   [2] Ibid.

obligation to fulfil his promise. Again, I would ask that the promise be interpreted sensibly. The expectation of both men is that when the time comes to fulfil the promise the circumstances will not be very different from what they are. It is on this assumption that the promise is made, and that it is received. If, when the time comes to fulfil it, A is as ill as Mr. Pickard-Cambridge supposes, he could fairly say to B, 'Here is a change of circumstances which neither of us contemplated. The assumption on which the promise was made being falsified, do you consider my promise still binding?' Suppose, on the other hand, A's promise had been: 'However ill and weak I am, I will do this for you if I can', then we *should* consider him still *prima facie* bound to fulfil the promise if he can; whereas here also Mr. Pickard-Cambridge would apparently say that, although A's being very ill and weak was a possible contingency explicitly named in the promise, yet since, when the time comes, he *is* ill and weak, so that the pain caused to him by the fulfilment of the promise would outweigh the good it will do to B, there is no obligation to fulfil the promise. Now this is a case in which, since the promise is probably known only to the two persons concerned, the sapping of general mutual confidence by general condonation is not a consequence that need be considered. The only consequences that a utilitarian need consider are the pain caused to A by his fulfilling the promise, and the pain caused to B[1] by its not being fulfilled; and Mr. Pickard-Cambridge's view evidently is that, where other consequences are negligible, and A's pain would be greater than B's, A has no obligation to fulfil the promise. On this view, then, whenever A makes a promise to B, he is to be understood as saying, 'I will do so and so if and only if my doing so and so will cause me less pain or inconvenience than my not doing so will cause to you.' Mr. Pickard-Cambridge claims constantly that his view agrees better than the opposing view with the ordinary consciousness, but I think that this is *not* how the ordinary consciousness understands promises. I think we should want to know, when

---

[1] I use this phase, for brevity, as including his loss of pleasure.

some one makes us a promise, whether it is an ordinary promise or a Pickard-Cambridge promise that he is making.

(3)[1] I have promised (a) to play at a concert, (b) to send my score, (c) to send my partner's score. I fall ill, and it is clear that I shall not be able to play. Promise (a) therefore 'must be broken, because its fulfilment is impossible'. But, according to Mr. Pickard-Cambridge, I (on my theory) ought to maintain that it is still my duty to fulfil promises (b) and (c), which I still *can* fulfil. Again I ask for common sense in the interpretation of the promise. My verbal promises were as stated, and if I am to be held to the letter of my promises I am guilty of breach of promise if I break any one of them. But it is clear that the promise to play was subject to the tacit condition 'if I am able to play', and that the other two promises are subject to the same condition, and cease to be binding when the assumed condition is not fulfilled.

(4)[2] I promise (a) to call at X's house at 2 p.m. to-morrow and (b) to go for a walk with him. He falls ill, so that promise (b) cannot be fulfilled. Mr. Pickard-Cambridge says that on my theory I ought to maintain that promise (a) is still binding. But it is surely perfectly clear that the assumed condition of both promises is that both X and I are well enough to go for a walk, and that, this condition being unfulfilled, the *prima facie* obligation to fulfil either disappears. If, on the other hand, the promise to call at his house were independent of the assumed condition that he is well enough to go for a walk, it would still hold good. Once more Mr. Pickard-Cambridge is insisting on the letter of the promise and forgetting the spirit.

(5)[3] The vicar of my parish asks me to send my piano to the parish hall next Thursday afternoon. I promise categorically. I afterwards learn that he is arranging for a concert, and later that the concert is off. Mr. Pickard-Cambridge says I ought (on my theory) to think myself still bound to send the piano. But it seems to me clear that though categorical in words, my promise was made and accepted on the tacit understanding that

---

[1] *Mind*, xli (1932), 163–4.   [2] Ibid. 164–5.   [3] Ibid. 165.

my piano would serve some purpose of the vicar's, and that when this condition is known to be unfulfilled the *prima facie* obligation disappears.

(6)[1] A rich miser visits me *in forma pauperis*, and extracts a promise to pay him £100 in six months. 'If I discover the fraud in time, will anyone hold that my promise binds me?' The case seems to me a difficult one. I would deal with it tentatively as follows. If he had promised to do me a service, and I had promised to pay £100 on his doing so, it will be agreed that my promise would cease to be binding if its condition were not fulfilled by him. Now, in the actual case supposed, my promise to pay arose out of conversation with the miser, which was conducted under the implied contract to tell each other the truth. In breaking this contract, he has destroyed the basis on which my promise was made. It is as if I had said, 'If you are telling me the truth, I will pay you £100', and since he is not telling me the truth, the condition on which the promise was made is unfulfilled, and I shall not in spirit be breaking my promise in refusing to pay.

Suppose, however, that I do pay, is it not clear that he is under a very strong *prima facie* obligation to return the money —an obligation which good men would regard as in most cases overriding the question whether he or I or another man would make the best use of the money? Whatever we may think, in this difficult case, of the *prima facie* obligation to keep promises, does it not form a very clear case of another *prima facie* duty, that of restitution for injury done?

(7)[2] A poor man extracts from me a like promise, and comes into a fortune before the six months have elapsed. 'Am I bound to pay? Very few would think me bound to do so.' The case does not seem to me so easy. I think that a man with a very delicate sense of honour would consider that he ought to pay for his own carelessness in making the promise unconditionally. But alternatively it might be urged that the promise was in spirit a promise to pay £100 to a poor man, and ceased to be

---

[1] Ibid. 165–6.   [2] Ibid. 166.

H

binding when the poor man has become rich. In either case the *prima facie* obligation to keep promises does not seem to be placed in question. And surely, whatever we may think that the promiser ought to do, we should agree that if he does pay, the other ought to return the money. The case throws into high relief the *prima facie* duty of making a return for benefits received. So obvious is this that we should not think it necessary for the recipient of the £100 to consider anxiously whether he, or his benefactor, or some other person would make the best use of the money. He should send it straight back to his benefactor.

It would be tedious to go through all the cases put forward by Mr. Pickard-Cambridge; I have, I believe, said enough to indicate the lines on which they should be dealt with by one who believes in a *prima facie* obligation to fulfil promises, distinct from the obligation to seek the general good. But it may well be thought that I have been rather vague, in appealing to the spirit of a promise against its letter. 'A promise', it may be contended, 'is a statement that one will do something, and is not fulfilled unless this thing is done.' My reference to the spirit of the promise is simply a reference to the obvious fact that most promises, like most statements of any kind in ordinary life, are made without any attempt, and without any necessity, to state in full all their implied conditions and qualifications, since conversation would be very tedious if all of these were insisted upon. Between two men of good faith there will usually be agreement as to the unexpressed conditions to which a promise is subject; the spirit of the promise is perfectly well understood. To argue that one who takes the non-utilitarian view of promises is bound to interpret them according to the letter and not to the spirit is really to misinterpret the nature of ordinary speech.

Of course the presence of unexpressed conditions to which a promise is subject has its dangers; and in particular the presence of the very vague unexpressed condition 'if circumstances have not become very different'. Those who wish to break a treaty, for instance, are usually able to say with truth that conditions have become very different since the treaty was made. There are various ways in which this difficulty can be dealt with. One, of course, is to make every effort to state the conditions explicitly instead of leaving them to be tacitly understood. But however much care be taken, it is impossible to foresee all the changes of circumstances which might make the maintenance of a treaty unreasonable. No treaty, therefore, should be made binding for ever; every treaty should either be for a definite period, or should contain provisions for its own possible revision under suitable arrangements. The difficulty is not so serious in the case of most promises between individuals. As a rule, these are promises to do something within a comparatively short time, in which there is less danger of a change of conditions which will make the fulfilment of the promise unreasonably onerous. But it is plain that even in such private promises it would often be well to express the conditions more exactly than we usually do.

Another argument to which Mr. Pickard-Cambridge attaches weight is to this effect: If the making of a promise in itself constituted a *prima facie* obligation to fulfil the promise, the obligation, springing as it does from a single source, ought to be always equally great; whereas every one in fact regards a promise to attend an At Home, for instance, as much less binding than one to attend a dinner-party.[1] An attempt might be made to answer this objection by saying: 'This would be a fair argument to use if I thought the making of a promise was the *only* source of a *prima facie* obligation. But I do not; I think there is also a *prima facie* obligation to bring into being as great a balance of good over evil as one can. I am therefore bound to consider the consequences of my act, and in the one case the obligation to fulfil the promise is reinforced by the obligation to save my host the very considerable inconvenience of an empty place at his dinner-table, while in the other, where the inconvenience to him will be much less, the reinforcement is

[1] *Mind*, xli (1932), 159.

much less, and a less strong countervailing obligation will make me think it right to break my promise and do something else instead—e.g. spend the afternoon in the company of a sick friend.'

This, however, would not be in my opinion the correct answer. For it divides my responsibility to my host into a responsibility to fulfil a promise + a responsibility to produce good, the first responsibility being of uniform obligatoriness and the second being more obligatory according as the good to be produced is greater; and that is not how we really think about the matter. What we really think is that we have a single responsibility to our friend, to confer on him the promised benefit (our presence at the party being assumed to be a benefit to him).

There appears to be no reason why one who does not take the utilitarian view of promises should consider the bindingness of all promises to be equal. In our natural thought about it, I believe we think of it as being, as it were, a product of two factors. *One* of these is the value of the promised service in the eyes of the promisee; we clearly think ourselves more bound not to fail another person in an important matter, than not to fail him in an unimportant one; and if any one doubts this and thinks I am being dangerously lax in allowing degrees of bindingness here, let him suppose himself (*a*) to have promised to visit a sick friend whom he knows to be longing for his company, or alternatively (*b*) to have promised to go to the theatre with a party which he thinks will not miss him much if he does not go. In the absence of any other responsibility competing with either of these, each of them will be binding; but the second responsibility will be much more readily overridden by any competing responsibility, such as that of turning aside to help the victims of an accident.

The *other* factor tending to increase the obligation to fulfil a promise depends on the way in which and the time at which the promise has been made. Any one would feel that a promise made casually in a moment of half-attention is less binding than one made explicitly and repeatedly, and perhaps reinforced by oath. The recency of the promise seems also to add something to its bindingness; we say, 'Why, it was only yesterday that you promised to do it.' Such considerations make the promise more binding, because they intensify the promiser's awareness of its existence and the promisee's expectation of its fulfilment. We may, then, if we like to put the matter so, think of the responsibility for conferring a promised benefit as being n times as binding as the responsibility for conferring an exactly similar unpromised benefit, where n is always greater than 1, and, when the promise is very explicit, is much greater than 1. It will follow that it is always our duty to fulfil a promise, except when the uncovenanted benefit to be conferred is more than n times greater than the covenanted benefit. We are not able to assign a very definite value to n in any case, but I believe there is pretty general agreement that n is usually great enough to secure that when the alternative advantage to be conferred is not very different in amount, the promised advantage ought to be conferred.

From the duty of promise-keeping Mr. Pickard-Cambridge turns to consider briefly the duty of returning good for good, and that of punishment, and to argue that these also can be explained on utilitarian grounds. (1) 'To return a service, especially where it requires a sacrifice, is to show most unmistakably that the service has been appreciated, and to keep alive the benefactor's good-will. Not to return it is to choke the life of friendship in its infancy, by discouraging the effective good-will of the benefactor; or, if his good-will still continues to live and to express itself, the relation is inevitably, if unintentionally, diverted downhill from friendship into patronage.'[1] Is this the way in which any one not intent on defending a theory really thinks about the return of benefits? Is it really the wish to keep alive our benefactor's good-will, or to save him from becoming patronizing, that makes us think we ought to return benefits? Is not our actual thought more truly expressed in the simple phrase 'one good turn deserves another'?

[1] *Mind*, xli (1932), 168.

And is not this the expression of the sense of a *prima facie* obligation to return good for good, quite distinct from the duty of caring for the character of our benefactor?

(2) With regard to punishment also, Mr. Pickard-Cambridge seems to give up any notion of desert. 'The sufficient reason why *prima facie* it is a duty to punish only the guilty, is that they are the people who most need to be brought to reconsider their ways, and there is nothing so provocative of reflection as the inability to sit down in comfort.'[1] It follows that if we thought that in any particular situation equally good consequences would be produced by punishing a guilty person and by inflicting pain on an innocent one, we should think the one act no more right than the other. But this is not what we really think. We think of infliction of pain on the innocent only as something to be taken to in the last resort, when some overwhelming reason of public policy demands it. And the very reformative effect of punishment of which he speaks will take place only if the punished person thinks of his punishment not as an administrative device for furthering the general benefit, but as something that he has deserved by his misdoing.

In his third article[2] Mr. Pickard-Cambridge returns to the topic of promise-keeping. His argument is an elaborate one, but the only novel feature in it, I think, is a distinction which I had not brought out, and which is well worth bringing out. He distinguishes between what he calls the objective good brought about by the fulfilment of a promise, arising out of the nature of the service done to the promisee, and the subjective good, consisting in his gratification at getting what he expected to get; and similarly between the objective loss involved in the breaking of a promise, arising from the nature of what the promiser fails to give to the promisee, and the subjective evil consisting in his disappointment. And he argues that this enables him to justify on utilitarian grounds many acts of promise-keeping which it would be hard to justify on utilitarian grounds if we forgot the subjective good involved. He

---

[1] *Mind*, xli (1932), 169.   [2] Ibid. 311–40.

argues that if I should by keeping the promise confer 1,000 units of objective good on the promisee, and by doing an alternative act 1,002 units of objective good on some one else, I am on the strictest utilitarian grounds justified in keeping the promise if I think that more than one unit of *subjective* good will be conferred on the promisee in the one case, and more than one unit of *subjective* evil inflicted on him in the other.

He is surely not justified in laying the stress he does on the subjective good of a fulfilled promise to the promisee; for in general there is more subjective good involved in getting an unpromised and unexpected benefit than in getting a promised and expected one. But he is justified in attaching a good deal of importance to the subjective evil of *not* getting a promised and expected benefit; and this might, as he suggests, turn the scale, on utilitarian principles, in favour of keeping a promise which on other grounds a utilitarian would not think himself bound to keep. But I cannot accept the suggestion that, apart from the effect of my action in strengthening or weakening general mutual confidence, the obligation to keep a promise is entirely due to the sum of good objective and subjective to be conferred on the promisee. And I invite any one who accepts Mr. Pickard-Cambridge's view to consider the following cases.

(1) Where the objective goods to be conferred by keeping and by breaking the promise are equal, and the effects on general mutual confidence are negligible, he would make the reason for its being right to fulfil the promise, when it *is* right, lie in the gratification to be caused to the promisee. But now suppose that some one has through no fault of mine misunderstood me as promising to do a certain act—suppose, for instance, that he is a foreigner who has claimed to understand English perfectly but has in fact quite misunderstood some word or idiom I used, and therefore taken me to be promising to do act *A* when I was promising something different, or not promising anything at all; his gratification if I did or disappointment if I did not do what he was relying on me to do would be just as great as if I had promised to do it, but my thought about my duty would

be entirely different. I should very likely as a matter of benevolence save him the disappointment, if I could do so without
sacrificing some more stringent duty, but I should have none
of the *distinctive* thought which I have when I *have* made a
promise, that I am, simply for that reason, *prima facie* bound
to fulfil it. Mr. Pickard-Cambridge's view leads to a conclusion completely contrary to what we actually think in such
a case.

(2) Suppose that *A*, a dying man, has entrusted his property,
or some part of it, to *B* on the strength of *B*'s promise to hand
it over to *C*, who knows nothing of *A*'s wishes or of *B*'s
promise. Suppose that *B* does not believe in immortality, or
believes that at any rate the dead know nothing of the fortunes
of the living. Then there is for him no question of either subjective or objective good to be enjoyed by *A*, and since *C* knows
nothing of the affair there is no question of subjective good or
evil for him through the gratification or disappointment of his
hopes. If the transaction has been private, *B*'s act will have no
effect on general mutual confidence, unless he divulges the
transaction, which, if he breaks the promise, he is not likely to
do. There is no question, for one who disbelieves in immortality, of strengthening or weakening *A*'s friendship for him;
for *A* is dead. Then according to Mr. Pickard-Cambridge *B*
would be justified in simply considering what was the best use
that could be made of the property. If he thought a fourth
person *D* could make the best use of it, or that he himself
could, he ought to bestow it on *D* or keep it for himself.
There is, of course, the question of the effect on his own
character. If he breaks the promise, he will probably weaken
his own feeling for the sanctity of promises, and make it more
likely that he will break other promises which even on utilitarian grounds he ought to keep. But, for Mr. Pickard-Cambridge, the duty of keeping promises is always subject to the
more general duty of producing as much good as possible, so
that the promiser will be doing a worse thing, and doing more
harm to his character, if by keeping the promise he loses the

opportunity of doing the maximum good, than if he breaks the promise.

Is it not clear that this utilitarian way of considering such a case is not the way in which honest men actually would consider it? We should, in fact, regard the breaking of this promise as an outrageous breach of trust, and if we fear the effect on our character, it is because we consider the act itself detestable.

Some one might ask why I take such an artificial case, in which many of the goods and evils that usually result from the keeping or breaking of promises are eliminated. My answer would be that I have no need of such cases to convince me, or (I believe) most thinking people, that there is a *prima facie* duty to fulfil promises, distinct from the *prima facie* duty to produce what is good. This seems to me to stand out as a salient fact in the moral situation, even when the moral situation bristles with good utilitarian reasons for fulfilling promises, or for breaking them. But when we have to deal with theorists who do not admit this, perhaps the method of isolating the issue by eliminating other considerations affords the best hope of convincing them.

The view that the obligation to fulfil promises is distinct from that of producing the greatest good has also been criticized from another point of view, viz. that of the school of Brentano. Mr. G. Katkov, in his *Untersuchungen zur Werttheorie und Theodizee*,[1] has attempted to bring what we think about the sacredness of promises under the principle of the maximization of good, in the following way. He points out (1) that the receiver of a promise, on the strength of his belief that the promise will be fulfilled, undertakes certain sacrifices and risks which he would not otherwise have undertaken, so that the maker of the promise runs in turn the risk of inflicting great injury on the receiver if he breaks the promise.

This explanation plainly does not meet the case. The special characteristic of the situation created by a promise is that even

[1] pp. 136–41.

when we do *not* think the promisee likely to lose more by the breaking of the promise than some one else will gain, we think ourselves *prima facie* obliged to keep the promise.

Mr. Katkov falls back (2) on a second line of defence, which is much more interesting. He holds that we are not justified in breaking a promise in order to confer even the greatest good on another than the promisee, if there is the slightest probability that through our action the promisee will suffer an injury which makes his total 'balance of value' predominantly bad. This is very different from Mr. Pickard-Cambridge's light-hearted treatment of the interests of the promisee as standing on exactly the same level as any one else's; it is, in fact, the admission of a *prima facie* obligation independent of the obligation to maximize value. It is true that Mr. Katkov rests this *prima facie* obligation on a different principle from that of fidelity to promise; he makes our special obligation in this case to be an instance of the general law that we are not justified in inflicting harm on one person in order to confer a greater good on another. To say this is at once to give up the crude utilitarian principle that an evil conferred on any one can always (in the determination of our duty) be set off against an equal good conferred on some one else; and I have already[1] remarked that at this point Utilitarianism does not correspond to what we really think. But Mr. Katkov's admission fails to deal completely with the peculiarity of the situation created by a promise. This will be seen if we compare two situations. In one, *A* has made no promise to any one, and a certain act would confer a great good on *B* and a smaller injury on *C*. In the other, he has made a promise to *C* and none to *B*, and a breach of promise would confer a great good on *B* and a smaller injury on *C*. Any right-thinking person will, I believe, consider that the fact that this act would be a breach of promise is (whether decisive or not) a *further* argument against doing the act, *over and above* any objection which arises from its being an injuring of one person in order to benefit another.

[1] p. 75.

(3) Finally, Mr. Katkov denies the possibility of any *prima
facie* obligation which can conflict with the duty of producing
the best state of affairs, on the general ground that 'better' simply
means that which it is right to prefer. This is simply a cutting
of the knot. The position is this. Those who think as I do,
think (and claim that the moral consciousness when not
sophisticated by a particular theory agrees with us) that there
is a *prima facie* duty to fulfil promises even when no greater
good can be foreseen as likely to come into being by the
promise's being kept than by its being broken; and we think
that this shows that the rule 'produce the greatest good' is
not the only rule of conduct. The followers of Brentano
agree with us in thinking that when we have made a promise we are under a special obligation to the promisee, but
differ from us in thinking that it can be brought under the
general rule 'choose the greatest good'. But instead of trying to point out wherein the specific good to be produced by
keeping promises consists, they content themselves with
saying 'it must be the greatest good, because it is what we
ought to produce'. The utilitarian says 'you ought to do so-
and-so because by doing so you will produce the greatest
possible good': the follower of Brentano says 'do what you
ought to do, and you may be sure that in doing so you will be
choosing the greatest good, since "better" means nothing but
that to prefer which is right'.[1]

Mr. Katkov sees[2] that if this is all that 'better' means, his principle 'you ought to choose the best of what is attainable' is in
danger of being a mere tautology—'it is right to prefer what
it is right to prefer'. He can hardly be held to have escaped
from this conclusion by the remark[3] that 'in choice not a simple
preference, but the preference of an existence to a non-existence, or the opposite, is included, and so the utilitarian highest
practical principle comes pretty much to this, that whenever
one is faced by the choice between the existence of several
goods, he *should* always *prefer* the *existence* of the more

[1] Op. cit. 140.   [2] Ibid. 141.   [3] Ibid. 141.

excellent'. If 'better' only means 'such that one ought to prefer it', nothing can save the principle 'one ought to prefer the existence of the better' from being a tautology. And unless we can see a goodness in the state of affairs produced by a fulfilment of promise—a goodness not resting on or consisting in the fact that we ought to fulfil the promise—we cannot say that the duty of fulfilling the promise rests on the general duty of producing what is good.[1]

Although I think it is quite clear that a promise creates a *prima facie* obligation, or a responsibility, quite different from that which alone the utilitarian system recognizes, we must guard against stating the obligation in a way which would lead to consequences which our reflective moral consciousness would reject. What then is it, exactly, that a promise creates an obligation to do? We must first note that, if the promise is phrased in the way in which promises usually are phrased, we are *not* under an obligation to do that which we have promised. For promises usually take the form of saying 'I will do so-and-so', where 'doing so-and-so' is the effecting of some change in the state of affairs, paying a debt, returning a borrowed book, travelling to some place to meet some person, &c.; but if we are right in the contention put forward in another context,[2] we are under no obligation to effect changes, but only to set ourselves to do so. If, therefore, we want to limit ourselves to making promises which it will be our duty to fulfil, we should cast our promises in the form 'I will set myself, or do my best, to do so-and-so'. But it would be pedantic to insist upon this alteration, for in fact our promises are understood so by both parties. No one thinks that he has failed to do his duty if he has done his best, without success, to fulfil his promise; and no one thinks another has failed in his duty, though we may think he has failed to discharge a *legal* obligation, if he has done his best to bring about the change that was promised.

---

[1] I return to this subject later, when the meaning of 'good' comes to be discussed, p. 289.   [2] pp. 153–4, 160–1.

But even the obligation to *set oneself* to do that which was promised does not necessarily remain binding until the self-exertion in question has been performed. For in the first place, if it has become clearly impossible to effect the change in question, there remains no duty to set oneself to effect it. If I have promised to return a certain book to a friend, and if the book is meantime destroyed, it ceases to be my duty to set myself to return it; for my duty, when the time comes at which I had promised to return the book, is determined not solely by my promise but also by the later developments of the situation; and here the situation has developed in such a way as to abolish the duty—though it has created another instead.

Suppose that the fulfilment of the promise has become not impossible, but much more difficult than it appeared likely to be when the promise was made. Mr. Pickard-Cambridge evidently thinks that in that case too the duty is usually abolished. But I do not think that our reflective moral sense would support him there. Ease of performance is no necessary or even usual characteristic of that which is our duty. No doubt, if the effort to fulfil some difficult promise were likely to be such as to incapacitate us for many other useful services, we might consider ourselves absolved from the duty; but then the *prima facie* obligation would not have been abolished, but would merely be over-ridden, as any *prima facie* obligation may be over-ridden by another that is more stringent. No doubt, too, we should regard the fulfilment of a promise which had become much more difficult to fulfil since it was given, as better evidence of moral goodness than the performance of one which had remained relatively easy, and the failure to perform it as less evidence of moral badness than the failure to perform one that had remained relatively easy. But to say there is less moral badness in failing to do *A* than in failing to do *B* is quite different from saying that *A* is less our duty than *B*, still more from saying that it is not our duty to do *A* at all.

Apart from impossibility of fulfilment, there is one other condition that abolishes the *prima facie* obligation. The duty

of fulfilment of promise is not a duty of maintaining consistency between one's words and one's deeds. The sense of it is
distinct from any sense that one may have that, to be self-consistent, one ought to do something that one has said one will
do, just because one has said one will do it; and much stronger
than any such sense. It is essentially the sense of a duty not to
fail, not to 'let down', some one who has, on the ground of
one's promise, trusted one to do something that he wishes one
to do. If he convinces us that he has ceased to want it, we
feel ourselves no longer under even any *prima facie* obligation
to fulfil the promise, because we have no longer the thought
that otherwise we shall be failing our promisee. Here again,
the present duty depends not merely on the situation as it was
when we made the promise, but on its subsequent development; and the subsequent development has been such as to
make that cease to be a duty which at first was one. Indeed, if
we feel convinced, even on other grounds than his saying so,
that the promisee no longer wishes the promise to be fulfilled,
the *prima facie* obligation has disappeared. At first sight, this
seems to lend itself to the utilitarian explanation that it is
the thought of the promisee's future gratification that makes the
fulfilment of the promise a duty, so long as it is a duty. But
that this is not the true explanation is shown by the fact that we
all (I believe) think ourselves to be obliged on quite a different
ground to fulfil a promise to another person, from that on
which we think ourselves obliged to afford him an unpromised
gratification. It is further shown by the fact that we think ourselves bound by a promise to a man who has died since the
promise was made. Here, unless we think not only that he
survives in another mode of being, but that he is, in that mode
of being, aware of what happens on earth, and has the same
desires that he had on earth, there is no thought of his future
gratification; yet we feel the promise to be binding, whether
or not we hold these views about a future life. In his case, too,
we think the *prima facie* obligation is terminated if we are convinced that he, if he were alive and aware of the circumstances,

would no longer wish us to do what we have promised. But that is a consideration which no *utilitarian* can consistently permit himself. He must concern himself only with consequences that he thinks likely to happen, not with what might happen if things were not as they are, if the promisee were alive instead of dead.

It might be suggested that though we do not seriously think the dead man will be gratified by our fulfilment of our promise, we are yet obscurely under the influence of a superstitious tendency to think of him as likely to be gratified. This, no doubt, is sometimes so; but that it is not a complete account of our attitude is shown by the fact that we should think just in the same way in the case of a promise to a man who by reason of distance, or of some other cause distinct from death, is not likely to know whether the promise has been fulfilled, and to be gratified or disappointed accordingly.

Again, if we have promised to do several related actions, some of which we believe to be desired by the promisee only if the others also are done, then if the latter become impossible, we naturally are under no obligation to do the former. On the other hand, if we have promised to do a number of related actions, the fact that some have become impossible and some are no longer desired by the promisee, while some perhaps are neither possible nor desired by him, does not abolish the duty to do the others which are both possible and desired by him.

There is another change of circumstances, regarding which we must ask ourselves whether it abrogates the *prima facie* duty of fulfilling a promise. Suppose that it is still possible to fulfil it, and that the promisee still wishes for its fulfilment, but that we have become convinced that its fulfilment will do him harm, or less good than something else that we might do instead. Here we think of the promise as still binding upon us; we think of ourselves as still under the *prima facie* obligation. But this, like all *prima facie* obligations, is open to the competition of others, and it is only to be expected that when the advantage to be given to the promisee by some alternative act is very great, the sense of obligation to do that act should outweigh the sense of obligation to fulfil the promise. And in principle the same is true when it is not the promisee but some one else on whom the great advantage will be conferred by the alternative act.

The various considerations I have pointed out as having the effect of abolishing or over-riding the original duty of fulfilling a promise seem to me to account completely for the whole variety of cases cited by Mr. Pickard-Cambridge in which promises are not felt to be binding, without in the least involving the conclusion which he draws, that when they are binding they are binding only on the ground that their probable consequences are better than those which could be achieved by any alternative action.

While we are concerned with the duty of fulfilment of promise, it is worth while to consider the relation of this duty to that of telling the truth. These are apt to be thought of as distinct and complementary duties, the one a duty to say what is true, the other a duty to make true what one has said. But the relation between the two is more complex than this; the two are connected in the following way. You can break a promise without telling a lie (for it is only when the promise is made with the *intention* of breaking it, that a lie is told); but you cannot tell a lie without breaking a promise. This arises from the nature of language. If words had a natural affinity with the things they usually stand for, you could deceive without breaking a promise, by simply using words in an unnatural meaning. But, apart from a few onomatopoeic words, there is not, between words and the things they stand for, any natural affinity which makes the one the natural symbol for the other. There is no more affinity between the noise 'John is dead' and the fact which we usually express by saying that 'John is dead', than between the noise 'John is alive' and the fact which we usually express by saying that 'John is dead'. If some one asks me whether John is alive or dead, and I think that he is alive, it can be a duty for me to say 'John is alive' only in virtue of a pre-established expectation that when I make this noise I shall be thinking him to be in the state which we usually express by saying that he is alive. It is not to be supposed that there is a separate convention as to the meaning with which each word is to be used. But it *must* be supposed that there is a general convention that we shall not without notice use words in a meaning other than that in which they are generally used. If it were not for this, I should be at liberty to make the noise 'John is dead' when I think he is alive. But, there being this convention or understood promise, I am guilty of a breach of promise if I say he is dead when I think he is alive. Thus the telling of a lie is always a breach of promise.

The space I have given to discussing the duty of fulfilling promises might lay me open to the suspicion that I attach an undue importance to this duty. I do not think that that is the case. I have discussed it at length, partly because it is a very clear case of a duty which cannot be reduced to that of producing a maximum of good, and partly because the discussion has been forced on me by a particular critic. I do not suppose that I take, in fact, a more rigorous view of this duty than a utilitarian is likely to do; for on the one hand I am very conscious that there are other responsibilities which often outweigh that of fulfilling promises, and on the other hand a utilitarian is apt, in order to bring the rigour of his view about promises up to that of the ordinary moral consciousness, to make more of the utilitarian reasons for keeping promises than the facts warrant.[1] My object is not to suggest that the duty is more binding than a utilitarian thinks it is, but to suggest that it is binding on quite a different ground. The other principles of duty which, I have suggested,[2] fall outside the utilitarian scheme could be defended by arguments similar to those by which I have defended the independence of the principle of promise-keeping; but it would be tedious to develop such a defence. If I have convinced any one that there is one principle that falls outside the utilitarian scheme, he will probably be ready to admit that there are others also; and if I have not convinced him in this case, I should not be likely to do so in others.

[1] Cf. pp. 92–4.   [2] Cf. pp. 69–77.

VI

THE GENERAL NATURE OF WHAT IS RIGHT
SOME THEORIES

I TURN now to the question, What is the general nature of that which is obligatory on us?; and I will first state three alternatives which naturally present themselves: are we bound to do certain things, i.e. to effect certain changes in the state of affairs; or are we bound to be influenced by certain motives; or are we bound to do certain things under the influence of certain motives? The question may also be put in the form, Is what I ought to do what I ought to do because in doing it I shall be initiating a certain change in the state of affairs, or because in doing it I shall be acting from a certain motive, or because in doing it I shall be initiating a certain change under the influence of a certain motive? I am not sure that the second view is ever held, as a complete account of the nature of that which is obligatory. We sometimes use expressions which seem to harmonize with it, as when we say that a judge ought not to be influenced by partiality for either of the parties who appear before him. But when we say this we do not think that this is the whole content of his duty, even in this particular context; we also think that he should not under the influence of partiality do a certain act, i.e. give an unjust decision. It would seem highly paradoxical to make the nature of our motive in doing this or that act the *sole* ground of one act's being our duty and another's not being so. For it would imply that in trying to discover our duty we need not attend to the facts of the outer situation, but have only to consider the respective merits of different motives from which we might act; whereas it is obvious that our view of the outer facts of the situation is what mainly affects our judgement of what we ought to do. Those therefore who lay stress on motive in this connexion usually hold the third view, that we ought to do certain acts under the influence of certain motives; which really means that what is obligatory is always a complex thing, including the doing of a certain act and the being influenced by a certain motive. Now there are certain facts that seem to support this view. Suppose that a certain man pays a debt, but does it not from a sense of justice but solely in order to avoid a legal action against him; or suppose that he does it in order to tempt his creditor to reckless speculation with the money repaid; it seems natural to say that such a man has not done what he ought; that in the first case he has not done what he was obliged to do, and that in the second he has done what he was definitely obliged not to do. Yet we shall see that this way of thinking leads to very awkward consequences; and I think we shall see that there is another way of putting the matter which, without involving these awkward consequences, does justice to the dissatisfaction which we rightly feel when some one behaves in either of the ways indicated.

(1) The first objection I would urge against the view that what I ought to do is to act from a certain motive is this. To say that I ought to act from a certain motive means one of two things. It may mean that I ought first to have the motive, and in consequence to act under its influence. Now having a motive means, I think it will be agreed, thinking that a certain act would have a certain character, and desiring to do an act of that character. This is disguised by the brachylogical way in which we tend to refer to motives. We speak of love, or of pity, as a motive. But when we ask ourselves what we mean by acting from love, we must admit that we mean acting from the thought that a certain act would promote the well-being of a certain person, and from the desire to do such an act as would promote it; and a corresponding account can be given of pity, or of any other motive that can be named. To say that we ought to act from love is to say that we ought to think that a certain act would promote some one's welfare, that we ought to desire his welfare, and that we ought to do the act on that account. But it is surely clear that neither opinion nor desire is

under our immediate control. It cannot be my duty to think that a certain act would have a certain character, because I cannot by an act of choice produce this opinion in myself, any more than I can by choice produce any other opinion. And again, it cannot be my duty to desire to do such an act, because I cannot by choice produce this desire forthwith in myself, any more than I can by choice produce any other desire. I can no doubt take steps which may in the long run lead to my having a certain opinion; e.g. by attending to certain features of the act and ignoring others. And again I can by a suitable direction of my attention make it likely that a certain desire will arise in me. I can cultivate motives; but I cannot manufacture them at a moment's notice; and since my duty is my duty here and now, it can be no part of my duty to have a certain motive, since I cannot at choice have it here and now. Thus of the three things which the theory in question says I ought to do, only one is left as that which it can be my duty to do, namely, to do a certain act.

But to say that we ought to act from a certain motive may have another meaning. Some one might say 'though you cannot produce a motive at a moment's notice, and though it cannot be your duty to act from it if you have not got it, it is your duty to act from it if you *have* got it'. Suppose, for instance, that I have a wish to further A's well-being, and think that act M would do so, and wish to injure B, and think that act N would do so, ought I not to act from the one motive and not from the other? Undoubtedly I ought to do the act to which love points, and not that to which malevolence points. But it is not my duty to be under the influence of love; for that I already am, whereas my duty is that which is in the immediate future. My duty is simply to do the corresponding act; and what makes it my duty is not that in doing it I shall be acting from the wish to promote A's welfare, but the fact that I think it *will* promote A's welfare.

(2) The second argument I would put forward for holding that our duty is to do acts, and not to do them from certain motives, is this: it is commonly held that the highest of all

motives is the sense of duty. It is clear that whenever the sense of duty conflicts with any other motive, it is a morally better action to do that which we think to be our duty than to do any alternative act, whatever be the motive that points to it. And if sense of duty is the morally best motive when it points to a different action from that to which some other motive points, it is also the best single motive when it points to the *same* act to which some other motive points. It is better, for instance, to confer a benefit upon A from the reflective thought that that is the action which duty requires, than to do so from a mere instinctive love of A without considering the rights or the interests of other people. It would therefore be highly paradoxical to say that we ought to act from some other motive, but never from a sense of duty. Now it can be shown that it is never our duty to act from sense of duty. To say 'you ought to act from sense of duty' does not at first sight appear nonsensical. But it is seen to be so, as soon as we translate the vague phrase 'from sense of duty' into a more definite form. If the sense of duty is to be my motive for doing a certain act, it must be the sense that it is my duty to do the act. If, therefore, I say 'it is my duty to do act A from the sense of duty', this means 'it is my duty to do act A from the sense that it is my duty to do act A'. And this involves a self-contradiction. The whole sentence says that 'it is my duty to-do-act-A-from-the-sense-that-it-is-my-duty-to-do-act-A'; that all this and nothing less than this is my duty. But the last part of the expression involves that what I really think or ought to think, is that it is my duty to do-act-A simply. And if we try to amend the latter part of the expression to bring it into accordance with the theory, we get the result; 'it is my duty to do act A from the sense that it is my duty to do act A from the sense that it is my duty to do act A', where again the final part of the expression is in conflict with the theory. It is clear that a further similar amendment, and a further, and in the end an infinite series of amendments would be necessary in the attempt to bring the last part of the expression into accordance with the theory, and that even then we should not have succeeded in doing so. Any such expression would finish with the words 'from the sense that it is my duty to do act A', where it is implied that what I really think is that to do a certain act, and not to do it from the sense of duty, is what is my duty.

Again, suppose that I say to you 'it is your duty to do act A from the sense of duty'; that means 'it is your duty to do act A from the sense that it is your duty to do act A'. Then I think that it is your duty to act from a certain motive, but I am suggesting that *you* should act under the supposition that it is your duty to do a certain thing, irrespective of motive, i.e. under a supposition which I must think false, since it contradicts my own.

It is important to realize what is, and what is not, proved by this argument. It seems to be proved that it cannot be true that it is always, or even at any moment, our only duty to act from a sense of duty. For it is impossible to act merely from the sense that there are duties, or that I have duties, or even that I have certain particular duties, such as a duty to maximize the amount of good in the world. Even the more particular thought last mentioned, if it is to lead to any particular act, must be supplemented by the minor premiss that some particular act would in fact be the act which (of all the acts open to me) would most increase the amount of good in the world, and by the conclusion that I ought to do that particular act. Action from the sense of duty thus involves the thought that there is a duty to do a particular act, not because if done it will be done from a sense of duty, but because it will have a particular character such as that of maximizing the good in the world. And it can hardly be claimed that it is our duty to act from a mistaken thought; so that the very claim that we ought to act from a sense of duty involves the thought that there are duties other than that of acting from a sense of duty, acts the obligatoriness of which does not rest on the nature of the motive from which they will be done.

Can it then be contended that *besides* duties of this type

there is *also* the duty of acting from the sense of duty? This is the suggestion made in a criticism of my argument by Professor L. A. Reid.[1]

'If I say "It is my duty to do act *X* from a sense of duty", I do not mean of course that it is my duty (as well as to do act *X*) to have the "sense" of duty which is an innate capacity, for no one can, by willing, produce that. This must be assumed, as we have said, if we are to talk ethics at all. I mean by the above sentence that it is my duty to *summon* into action, with the freedom which I possess (and which is also assumed to exist) my capacity for apprehending and conating duty. I must do the act *X* which is my duty, and I must do it from a sense of duty which is the fulfilment of an innate capacity of mine.

'Further, there is no regress here, since the sense that *X* is a duty, and the sense that I ought to do *X* from a sense of duty (or that I ought to use in this instance the sense of duty which I possess) are not on the same footing. The one (*a*) has as its object an action, *X*, the other (*b*) has as its object a cognitional-conational state of mind, and whilst (*a*) without (*b*) is a concrete specific duty, (*b*) without (*a*) is a general capacity without special content. (*b*) needs some (*a*) to give it special content, so that some (*a*) is all the time and in every case the terminal object of a "sense of duty". As, in Ross's statement, the "duty to do *X*" and the "sense of duty" are not "duties" on the same level, there is no formal vicious regress involved.'

I must leave readers to judge whether this meets my argument. It seems to me not do so; for (apart from the fact that he does not address himself very closely to the precise form of the infinite regress argument), one of the things of which Professor Reid *assumes* the existence—'the sense that I ought to do *X* from a sense of duty'—is the very thing of which I was arguing for the non-existence. The theory he is maintaining is the theory that in any situation calling for moral choice we have two duties, to do a particular act and to be under the influence of the sense of duty when we do it; or he might prefer to say that we have a single complex duty including these two elements. Now we may ask, in what circum-

[1] *Creative Morality*, 64–5.

stances are we supposed to be faced with this choice? Is it suggested that we are already under the predominant influence of the sense of duty, or that we are not? Take the latter case first. It might be suggested that if one admires some one very greatly, and if that person urges one to act from a sense of duty, one might under the influence of admiration for him choose to act from a sense of duty. But surely this is a psychological impossibility. We might *wish* to substitute the sense of duty for admiration of a person, as our predominant motive, but we cannot effectively *choose* to do so, here and now. The most that we could possibly effectively choose would be to perform certain activities, either of action or of thought, which would gradually lead to the substitution of the one motive for the other; and then it would be the performing of these activities, and not the being under the influence of the sense of duty, that we ought to choose.

The only alternative is that we are already under the predominant influence of the sense of duty when we decide to do act X from the sense of duty. Then what we should be supposed to choose is to continue under that influence up to and including the time at which we do the act. But it is surely clear that this is not what happens. It is surely clear that when we decide to do our immediate duty, it is what we are to do that is the object of our choice, and not the motive from which we are to do it; and that for the simple reason that we do not question that the sense of duty, which is now the predominant motive, will continue to be so till the act is done.

To count the being under the influence of a certain motive, which is the precondition of the choice, as part of the object of choice, is to commit an error which is, in a very distant way, analogous to the error of treating the principles *upon* which we reason, as additional premisses *from* which we reason. What we choose is to do the act to which the already existing predominant motive points, and it is easy to fall into the error of supposing that what we choose is to act from that motive. What is **our** duty is to do the act to which the sense of duty points, and it is easy to fall into the error of supposing that what is our duty is to act from the sense of duty.

My insistence that it is always our duty to do certain acts, and not to act from certain motives, may seem to lay me open to the charge of making the moral life a very discontinuous thing, consisting of doing 'one damned thing after another', and having no real unity in itself. The good life, it might be argued against me, consists in becoming and in being a certain kind of person, not in doing certain kinds of thing. I should like to embrace what is true in this contention, and if possible to reconcile it with the general view I have put forward. I may begin by saying that it is one of our main duties to build up a good character in ourselves. The duties of special obligation by no means exhaust the range of duty. Besides them there is the duty of producing as much as possible of what is good; and in what is good goodness of character takes, I believe, the highest place; and for his own character a man has a special responsibility, since it is more under his control than that of any one else. I do not doubt that it is well for us, from time to time, to sit back, as it were, and review the way our character is developing, and take what steps seem necessary to develop it on better lines, by throwing ourselves, for example, into better surroundings. But improvement of character comes mainly not by anxious observation of our character but by faithful discharge of the other duties that arise for us hour by hour. This might no doubt lead to a one-sided development of character, since our existing surroundings might not call for the discharge of certain branches of duty. But, for a person leading his life in natural surroundings, these surroundings usually in fact yield occasions various enough to provide for an all-round development of character, and to provide for it better than a more self-directed attention does. I think Professor N. Hartmann is right in insisting that the development of character is best achieved when it arrives 'on the back of' the discharge of other duties; I think that if we study the lives of the best people we know we shall find this to be the case. The sense of duty and the various virtues are developed rather by acting in accordance with them, in so far as we have them already, than by searching anxiously to develop them further.

The only conclusion that can be drawn from our discussion is that our duty is to do certain things, not to do them from the sense of duty. If then it be still held that it is our duty to act from some motive, this can only mean that it is our duty to act from some other motive than the sense of duty, though the sense of duty is admittedly the highest motive; but such a paradoxical view is hardly likely to commend itself.

But, it might be replied, it is surely a very poor notion of the content of duty that you are putting forward, if you contend that a man who goes through life paying his debts from purely selfish motives, telling the truth simply to maintain a reputation for truthfulness, and so on, would nevertheless have done the whole duty of man. But to this there is the clear answer that a man who behaved in the way suggested, however many other duties he had done, would have failed to do one of his most important duties, that of cultivating the sense of duty. And it should be added that the duty of cultivating the sense of duty *is* the duty of cultivating the sense of duty, and *not* the duty of cultivating, from the sense of duty, the sense of duty.

An opponent might, however, return to the charge. He might say 'you are admitting that the man who acts from indifferent or bad motives must have neglected one important branch of duty, that of cultivating good motives. But you are nevertheless judging his particular acts of payment of debts and the like from indifferent or bad motives to be morally on the same level as acts of payment of debt from the sense of duty or some other unselfish motive; and that is what cannot be tolerated.' To this again the answer is quite clear. The man who pays his debts is doing this particular duty, from whatever motive he does it. But his action is morally worthless if he does so from certain motives, and morally worthy if he does it from others; for while an act's being my duty is quite independent of motive, the moral worth of my doing it depends mainly[1] on the worth of the motive. I discriminate just as rigidly as any one could between the conscientious and the selfish act; but I describe this as a difference of moral worth and not as a difference in respect of the one act's being a doing of duty and the other act's not being so. Both persons alike are doing these particular duties, but the one is doing them as duties, the other is doing them as it were by accident; and between these two things there is the greatest possible difference of moral goodness.

I would add two further considerations in support of the view I am urging. (3) When I set myself to ask in some particular situation what my duty is, it is because I intend, when I have come to know or think some particular act to be my duty, to do it for that reason. Now when we ask what it is that makes an act my duty, we are asking what is the *distinctive* feature of that act that makes it and not some other to be my duty. Now, *whichever* of two or more acts I decide to be my duty, I shall do it (if I carry out my intention) from the sense of duty. The motive will be the same whichever I do; the motive therefore can be no part of that which makes the one act my duty while the others are not, since the same motive will be the motive of whichever act I do.

That is the argument from the necessities of the case. And now for the corresponding *a posteriori* argument. (4) What is it to which we in fact find ourselves attending when we are trying to discover our duty in some situation? Is it not clear that what we attend to is the nature of the possible acts, considered apart from the motive from which we should do them —their tendency to affect the welfare of other people in this way or in that, their quality as fulfilments of promise or breaches of promise, and the like? This is certainly what I find myself attending to, and I venture to think that others will find the same.

[1] Cf. pp. 306-8.

But, it may be said, is not scrutiny of one's own motives a well-known part of the technique of moral deliberation? I think it is, but not as tending to show what is one's duty. Suppose that some attractive proposal is made to me, which I am tempted to accept straight off. I shall do well to ask myself what is the motive which is influencing me, i.e. whether it is not simply the desire to have some pleasant experience; for there is a real danger that such a desire may lead me either never to consider the question what is my duty, or to sophisticate myself into thinking that to be my duty which would merely be very pleasant. But if I can refrain from acting immediately from the desire for pleasure, and turn to ask seriously what is my duty, consideration of my motives will throw no light on *this* question; *this* question must be decided in the light of quite other considerations such as I have suggested above. The fact that in my original consideration of a proposed act I was being influenced simply by its pleasantness has no tendency to show that it is *not* in fact my duty, any more than it has any tendency to show that it *is*.

I turn now to consider two particular defences of the view that motive is, or may be, at least an element in causing that which is my duty to be my duty. The first attempt I will consider is that of Mr. Joseph, in chapters 2–5 of his *Some Problems in Ethics*. Mr. Joseph's general position, if I understand it rightly, is this. He holds that the obligatoriness of any action must be dependent on the goodness of something; he holds that it would be irrational to think of any action as being obligatory unless we first think of some element in the action, or something with which the action is connected, as good. 'My obligation to do what is right is to the performance not of an act without value, but of one which, if not related causally to good, must be somehow so related or in some way good itself.'[1] Now, as regards many obligatory actions, he accepts Professor Moore's account, that their obligatoriness depends

---

[1] Op. cit. 58.

on their tendency to produce good results; that is implied in the sentence quoted.[1] But he thinks that this account does not cover *all* obligatory action, and he thinks this for very much the same reasons that I do; he thinks, for instance, that it does not account for the sense that we have of an obligation to fulfil promises even when, so far as we can see, no more good would be *caused* by keeping the promise than by breaking it. Where, then, is he to find the goodness that makes such acts right? He first attempts to find it in the motive from which the act is done. He defends this view by urging first that all the acts to which moral judgements apply are motived acts. So far, I have no disposition to quarrel with him. There are indeed cases which at first sight seem to cast doubt on this statement. Take, for instance, the case of some one who knows that there is an invalid in a house but nevertheless stamps noisily upstairs. His making of the noise may have no motive; it may be the unthinking following of a habit. But we should certainly condemn a man who behaves so. And it is easy to see that this is but one of a large class of what may be called thoughtless acts, which are unmotived and which nevertheless we certainly condemn. Probably, however, we ought to be condemning the agent not for the thoughtless act, but for failure to do an act which if it had been done would have been done from a motive, viz. the act of controlling his habitual tendency to noisiness. The making of the noise is not merely not a motived act, but not even an intentional act, and no true subject of moral judgement. In fact, is it not clear that an intentional act must be a motived act? An intentional act is the conscious setting of oneself to bring some change into being, or to prevent some change from coming into being, and it seems clear that we never do this except when there is some feature, either in the act or in its consequences, which we wish to bring into being. The desire to do this will be the motive of the act.

I agree, then, that all the acts that are subjects of moral judge-

[1] Cf. *Some Problems in Ethics*, 28.

ment are motived acts. But I cannot agree with Mr. Joseph's analysis of a motived act. He analyses it into two things— (1) the motive and (2) a consequent physical movement.[1] He overlooks what seems to me a plainly existent third thing, viz. the setting oneself to produce the change in question. This is not a physical movement; it is a mental activity. And it is quite plainly to be distinguished from the motive. The motive is the wish to bring into being a state of things which we think will have a particular character, e.g. pleasantness. This is quite distinct from the setting oneself to bring into being a state of affairs which, we think, will have that character but will have others as well. And while it is true that no physical movement can be a subject of moral judgement, there is no antecedent reason why the *setting oneself to produce* a physical movement should not be the subject of the predicate right or wrong. I would add that the occurrence of a physical change is not even a necessary part of the whole thing which we call an action. No doubt in most cases what I set myself to do is to effect some change in the state of my body, and further consequential changes, as when I set myself to tell the truth or to pay a debt. But there is also such a thing as setting oneself to learn the truth or to improve one's own character, and here what one sets oneself to produce is a change in the state of one's own mind or of one's own character. Thus for the analysis of the motived action into motive and physical change, I would substitute the analysis of it into the setting oneself to effect some change, which may be either physical or mental, and the motive which leads us to do so, which in turn is analysable into the thought that the act will have a certain character and the desire to do an act of that character. Not merely, however, does Mr. Joseph ignore a vital element in a motived action, viz. the setting oneself to effect a certain change. He proceeds to speak as if a motived action were such a unity that no true ethical statement can be made about any element in it.

---

[1] Ibid. 38.

'No act exists except in the doing of it, and in the doing of it there is a motive; and you cannot separate the doing of it from the motive without substituting for action in the moral sense action in the physical, mere movements of bodies.'[1]

'A man who was fond of oysters might eat a plateful put before him for the sake of their flavour; a man who loathed them might do so to avoid hurting his host's feelings; a man who loathed or was indifferent to them might do so to prevent his neighbour, whom he knew to be fond of them and he disliked, from having two portions. I think these are three different acts, one morally good or else kindly, one morally bad or spiteful, one indifferent. They are not three instances of one act, viz. eating a plateful of oysters.'[2]

They are not of course three merely numerically different instances of something specifically the same. They are specifically different, since the motives are different. And in virtue of this difference three very different moral judgements are passed upon them, just as Mr. Joseph has said; one is morally good, one indifferent, one bad. But nevertheless they are specifically different instances of something that is generically the same, viz. of the act of setting oneself to eat a plateful of oysters; and while in virtue of their specific difference they differ in respect of moral goodness, there is no reason at all why in virtue of their generic resemblance they may not agree in possessing *another* moral attribute, viz. rightness (or wrongness).

Mr. Joseph speaks of the wrongness of 'separating' the act from the motive; and the word covers a dangerous ambiguity. Does he mean that it is wrong to suppose that the act could exist without a motive? I quite agree; I agree that all intentional acts are motived acts. But if he means that it is wrong to *consider* the act independently of the motive, to abstract from the motive and ask whether the act, which must be accompanied by *some* motive, has not some moral character of its own independent of whatever motive it is accompanied by, then I must reply that this is simply an instance of a type of objection which if it could properly be made here could equally be made to *all* abstract thinking. A body cannot have size without having shape, nor shape without having size; but it can have a certain size independently of its shape, or a certain shape independently of its size, and true statements may be made about either separately. A musical note cannot have pitch without having intensity, nor intensity without having pitch; but its pitch does not vary with its intensity, nor its intensity with its pitch, and pitch and intensity can profitably be studied separately. We shall not know the whole truth about the note till we have considered both, and we shall not know the whole truth about a motived act till we have considered both act and motive. But it is equally true that we shall never attain the whole truth about it till we have analysed it into its constituents and considered them first in isolation.

It may be remarked in passing that Mr. Joseph, who here attacks the consideration of acts apart from their motives, in a different context does this very thing himself, viz. where he points out that as regards acts which produce good results *their* rightness can be seen in certain cases to depend solely on the goodness of the results, without consideration of the motives.[1] In fact it is pretty clear that he thinks that the rightness of *most* right acts depends on their consequences (or intended, or probable, consequences)—that it is only two rather special types of right act that owe their rightness to their motives.[2]

So far I have only established that besides a motive and a physical change there is a third thing—the setting oneself to bring about a change, or in other words an intentional act— and that this is a *possible* subject of the predicate right or wrong; we have still to consider whether it is so in fact. (1) The first kind of case that we may consider is one propounded by Mr. Joseph.

'If I am prompted or inclined by affection to do some kindness that will cost me money, and simultaneously by desire of amusement to spend the money on myself, I may judge that I ought rather

---

[1] *Some Problems in Ethics*, 28.
[2] Ibid. 92–4. For the two types see my p. 129, n. 2.

to do the kindness; and the rightness because of which I judge that I ought to do it is its having the goodness that lies in its being an expression of affection, the alternative action, which is an expression of the desire for my own amusement, having thereby an inferior goodness or none at all.'[1]

That is a possible view. But clearly quite a different account might be given. It might be said that we simply see that any act tending to produce pleasure for another has therefore some degree of obligatoriness, quite apart from its motive, and that any act tending simply to produce pleasure for oneself has no degree of obligatoriness, whatever *its* motive. It is not very easy to choose between the two views. But I suggest a test case which will, I think, enable us to choose between them. Suppose that there are two acts possible for me. By one I shall produce a great deal of pleasure for a large number of people, but also a small amount of pain for some one *A* whom I dislike; and I may feel sure that if I do it I shall do it from a mixture of two motives, benevolence towards this set of people and malevolence towards *A*. By the other act I shall produce a much less amount of pleasure for the set of people concerned, but no pain to *A*, and I may feel sure that if I do it I shall do it simply from benevolence. On Mr. Joseph's theory the rightness of whichever act is right in such a case should depend partly on the goodness of its consequences, and partly on the goodness of its motive.[2] Therefore I should, before I can decide which I ought to do, have to ask myself anxiously whether the worth of my pure motive in the second case exceeds the worth of my mixed motive in the first case by a greater or less amount than that by which the net good to be *produced* in the first case exceeds the net good to be produced in the second. I suggest

---

[1] Op. cit. 47.

[2] His theory introduces goodness of motive as making right the act that is right, only in two types of case, viz. (1) where we think we ought to produce a pleasure for another rather than an equal pleasure for ourselves, (2) in such a case as promise-keeping, where we think we ought to fulfil a promise even when this does not seem likely to produce more good than an alternative act would. But if motive is the determinant of rightness here, it ought to be *a* determinant of rightness in other cases, such as the test case I suggest above.

that we do not in fact perform this comparison, but that, where some special obligation like that of keeping promises does not enter into the case, we judge directly that the act which will produce the greatest balance of good for others is the right act,[1] the motive not being considered at all.

I would add a further suggestion, which may or may not be true. If it is not true, it will not affect the truth of what I have been contending for; if it is true, it will tend to support it. Mr. Joseph thinks that we directly judge an act motived by the desire to *give* pleasure to be better than one motived by the desire to *get* pleasure, and for that reason judge that we ought to do the first rather than the second. I suggest that when we have reached moral maturity, we take one motive, the desire to do one's duty, as our standard of moral goodness, and judge other motives by the degree of their approximation to this. By the desire to do one's duty I understand the desire to act with the fullest possible regard to the various morally significant characteristics that the possible alternative acts would have. Now plainly a tendency to promote the happiness of others is one of these; and it seems to me equally clear that we do not think a tendency to promote one's own pleasure to be one of them. The reason why we judge kindness to be a better motive than the desire for pleasure is that it reveals, not indeed a reflective attention to all the morally significant aspects of an act, but at any rate an instinctive sensitiveness to one of them, viz. to its tendency to promote the happiness of others; while selfishness reveals only sensitiveness to a characteristic which we think has no moral significance, viz. the tendency to promote one's own happiness. I believe that it is on such a principle that we evaluate motives, good or bad; and it will be seen that it presupposes a prior judgement on acts as being right, wrong, or indifferent, in view of their characteristics apart from motive.

(2) What now are we to say of an act done from *sense of*

---

[1] Subject to the consideration that there is a more stringent obligation not to inflict injury on others, than there is to confer benefit on them; cf. p. 75.

duty? Are we to say that *its* obligatoriness depends on its being done from that motive? It might seem obvious that it cannot be so, because the sense of duty is already the sense that a certain action is obligatory; i.e. we are already satisfied of the rightness of the act by a consideration of its nature apart from its motive, and do not need to be satisfied of its rightness as we were (according to Mr. Joseph) in the former case,[1] viz. by considering the superiority of the motive from which if done it would be done. Mr. Joseph admits this:[2] 'Nor can the act owe its rightness to being a manifestation of that sense of duty to which it owes its morality.' Yet he seems to be hankering after an explanation of our sense of the rightness of such acts as promise-keeping, by the motive from which if done they will be done. For he goes on immediately to say: 'But I believe it is possible to distinguish between the sense of duty in general, and that of a duty to realize a goodness connected with the particular principle of the action which is recognized as my duty now.' The suggestion seems to be: 'The reason why I ought to keep a promise is that if I keep it I shall be acting out of respect for a certain principle, and that this is a better motive than that from which the alternative act would proceed.' 'I have to distinguish', says Mr. Joseph,[3] 'between the consciousness of duty in general, and that of my duty to act in a particular way here and now. It is this latter that may be the motive making the rightness of the action which, when moved by the former to ask myself what I ought to do, I recognize as the ground why one act rather than another is my duty now: this latter which, in such a case, takes the place of a particular good motive like affection.' This, I confess, seems to me an impossible position. What makes the act right is, we are told, a certain motive; and this motive is the thought that the objective act (or act considered apart from motive) is my duty here and now. This is surely impossible. I am represented *both* as thinking that I ought to do a certain act because of its own nature (e.g. because it is the keeping of a promise)

---

[1] That mentioned on p. 128, *supra.*   [2] *Some Problems in Ethics,* 48.   [3] Ibid. 50.

and as thinking that I ought to do it because if I do it I shall be doing it from this good motive. But I *cannot* think both things together, and if I think the first I do not need to think the second in order to be convinced that the act is my duty.

I am quite willing to admit Mr. Joseph's distinction between the consciousness of duty in general, and that of my duty to act in a particular way here and now. I might, for instance, think that I ought here and now to keep a certain promise, without realizing that in *all* normal circumstances there is something that is my duty. I might be alive to the duty of promise-keeping and blind to the duty of promoting the general good, or vice versa. It is not necessary to suppose that the sense of duty develops *pari passu* with regard to all the branches of duty. There are many people in whom fidelity to promises is strong but care for the general welfare weak, and others in whom the opposite state of affairs is found. But when Mr. Joseph tries to distinguish between the 'urgency' of the thought of a promise made and the sense of an obligation to fulfil it, and to make the obligation to fulfil it depend on the fact that if fulfilled it will be fulfilled as a result of the urgency of the thought,[1] he is (I believe) making a distinction without a difference. For if the urgent thought of the promise is to be such a motive as could give the action from it moral value, it must be the thought of the promise as binding, i.e. as being something I *ought* to fulfil; we are back at the immediate intuition of the rightness of fulfilling promises, and the reference to the excellence of the motive as making the act right is both unnecessary and inconsistent with what has gone before, since in what has gone before it has been admitted that the act is thought of as right apart from its motive. That Mr. Joseph is really making a distinction where there is no difference is seen incidentally from the fact that while he says[2] that the 'thought of a particular action' (e.g. of keeping a promise) of which he is speaking need not be the thought of an *obligation*, he describes it[3] as the thought of my *duty* to act in a particular way here and now.

---

[1] *Some Problems in Ethics*, 50–1.   [2] Ibid. 57.   [3] Ibid. 50.

Mr. Joseph, however, does not remain content with the
view put forward in these early chapters, that when the goodness connected with an action, on which its rightness depends,
is not to be found in its consequences, it is to be found in its
motive. In his eighth chapter he recurs to the question what
makes right acts right. He finds that besides the cases covered
by the utilitarian view, there are two other types of case: (1)
'the practice of what Hume called the indirect virtues, such as
justice, veracity, fidelity to promises',[1] and (2) 'an example of
the second kind occurs when a man judges that he ought to do
one rather than another of two actions, the resultant goods to
be expected from which appear equal, but would consist, if he
acted one way, in his enjoyment of certain advantages; if he
acted the other way, in another man's doing so'.[2] These, it will
be recognized, are just the types of act whose rightness in the
early of his book he describes as flowing from the motive
from which they are done. As regards both these types of
action, he rejects[3] the utilitarian theory that such actions are
made right by the fact that they produce or are likely to produce good results. But he also rejects his former explanation—
the view that they are made right by proceeding from good
motives. Or at least he admits that there are cases in which
there is no motive for the doing of either of two actions except
the sense of duty, and he admits that then 'in the judgement
which I have to make before action, when I ask which course
is right, which do I owe to do, it is assumed that the same
motive will have determined me in the adoption of either course;
and the determining difference must be a goodness in one
course that is not in the other'.[4] He goes on to offer a different
account of what it is in which this goodness lies, and this will
demand later consideration.[5] The important thing is that he
admits that where we act from a sense of duty alone, the action's
being a duty cannot spring from its being done from a sense of
duty.

[1] Ibid. 92.   [2] Ibid. 94.   [3] Ibid. 94.
[4] Ibid. 97.   [5] See pp. 140-5.

I turn now to a second attempt to vindicate the view that the rightness of right acts springs from the goodness of motives; that put forward by Professor Field in his article on Kant's First Moral Principle.[1] His view arises in this way. In considering the problem of conflict of duties, which arises when, for instance, we ask ourselves whether we ought to tell a particular lie or break a particular promise when we think that a balance of good consequences will arise from our doing so, I had said that our answer will sometimes be 'yes' and sometimes be 'no', so that we cannot maintain with Kant that it is *always* wrong to tell a lie or break a promise. I had added that there are certain moral principles that remain always true, e.g. that there is always a *prima facie* obligation to tell the truth or keep a promise, so that telling the truth or keeping a promise always tends as such to be right, even though in particular cases this tendency may be overborne by some other tendency which the act may have in virtue of some other rubric under which it falls, such as failing to produce a great advantage for some one else. This seems to me to be a straightforward account of what we really think about the matter. We think that whichever of the alternative acts we do in such a case is in one respect suitable to the situation and in another not, and in consequence we have a certain—not bad conscience, but compunction, if we either tell the truth and damn the consequences or secure the good consequences by telling a lie. Professor Field thinks this is a true account of how we feel about such a case, when we do not reflect deeply, but that it does not go to the root of the matter. The root difficulty arises, he thinks, from the fact that there are no kinds of *act* which as such either always are wrong (as Kant says) or even always tend to be wrong (as I have suggested). And he suggests that if we turn to motives, there and there only shall we find things that *always* have a certain moral character; hatred of a person and cruelty being always bad, and benevolence being presumably always good. Judgements such as that cruelty is bad are, he thinks, the primary moral judgements.

[1] *Mind*, xli (1932), pp. 17–36.

Now, he points out, there is a special connexion between certain motives and certain types of acts. The truth may be told from a variety of motives, but truth-telling has a special connexion with one motive, viz. the desire to tell the truth. Pain may be inflicted from a variety of motives, but the infliction of pain has a special connexion with cruelty, or the desire to inflict pain for its own sake. And because we judge a certain motive to be good or bad, we judge the kind of act which is thus specially connected with it to be *prima facie* right or wrong. Our judgement of acts is thus based on our judgement of motives.

Professor Field, it will be seen, goes a great deal farther than Mr. Joseph. Mr. Joseph thinks that the rightness of most right acts is due to the goodness of that which they bring about, or are meant to bring about, and it is only with regard to two classes of acts[1] that, finding no special good in what they bring about, he tries to find the ground of their rightness in the motive from which they proceed. Professor Field holds that the only primary moral facts are the facts that certain motives are good and certain others bad, and on these facts and these alone he bases the rightness of certain acts and the wrongness of others. Against this general view I would refer to the arguments I have already put forward,[2] which I believe to show that it is never on the goodness or badness of motives that the rightness or wrongness of acts is based. In particular, the sense of duty is always the sense of a duty to do an act of a certain kind, and to say that it is the sense of a duty to act from a sense of duty involves a self-contradiction.[3] This, the highest motive, already involves the recognition of a rightness and wrongness which is independent of motive.

Professor Field cites, as an example of the mode of reasoning which he thinks we use, a story that is told of Plato, that he said to a delinquent slave, 'I should have punished you, if I had not been angry.' But if Plato actually reasoned on Professor Field's lines, he can only be judged to have dealt very perfunc-

[1] Cf. p. 129, n. 2, *supra*. [2] pp. 114–24. [3] Cf. pp. 116–21.

torily with a case of conscience. His problem was, Should I inflict pain on this slave? If he really decided not to do so on the sole ground that he was angry, he would have been judging the suggested act in the light only of one of the characteristics it would have, viz. that it would be a satisfaction of his anger, and ignoring all its other characteristics, such as that it would be the punishment of a person who deserved punishment, that it was likely to have certain effects, some good, some bad, on the slave, that it was likely to deter other slaves from behaving similarly, and so on; whereas clearly he *ought* to have considered all these other circumstances. What I suppose Plato to have done was something very different—to have realized that he was so much under the influence of anger that he was not in a position to judge rightly of these other characteristics of the act, and therefore to have thought it safer not to do *without further reflection* an act which in his sober judgement he was just as likely to think wrong as right.

But, apart from the general objections to a view which makes the rightness of acts depend on the goodness of motives, we must consider whether Professor Field's account explains what we think in cases of 'conflict of duties', which is the problem that both the theory of *prima facie* obligations and his own theory are put forward to account for. Let us take a case in which an act, if done, will be done not from the motive from which it 'normally' proceeds, e.g. when a doctor considers whether he should deceive a patient, when the deception may be expected to be for the patient's good. Professor Field agrees that in such a case the doctor, if he is a good man, will, even if he decides to tell the lie, have some compunction in doing so. He thinks that the doctor infers from the badness of the love of telling lies that an act belonging to a type which would normally be connected with this motive, viz. the telling of the lie in question, has a tendency to be wrong, and this, he thinks, is what lies at the basis of our sense of *prima facie* obligations. The suggestion seems to me erroneous. Suppose that we grant, merely for the sake of argument, that the badness of a motive tends to make wrong an act proceeding from that motive. How can it tend to make wrong, or even be thought to tend to make wrong, an act which if done will *not* be done from that motive, but from a desire for the good of the patient? If the badness of a motive makes acts which proceed from it to be wrong, then we may say in a statistical sense that acts of deceit tend to be wrong because love of deceit is wrong; for acts of deceit normally proceed from love of deceit;[1] but an individual act of deceit which does not proceed from this motive can have *no* tendency to be wrong because most acts of deceit proceed from the love of deceit, and the love of deceit is bad. If, then, Professor Field's view were right, the doctor should have no compunction at all about telling the lie, and no objection to telling it. He should regard as sheer confusion of thought the notion that this lie can have any tendency to be wrong because *other* lies in virtue of proceeding from a *different* motive tend to be wrong. But the plain fact is that he thinks that his act's being a lie is a factor adverse to its being his duty, even if he decides that this is overborne by other factors tending to make it his duty.

Suppose the opposite process to take place, and all is plain sailing. Because we judge that the infliction of pain has a tendency to be wrong, we think that being attracted to the infliction of pain as such, i.e. in virtue of a characteristic in which it is known to tend to be wrong, is morally bad. The motive is judged bad because of the *prima facie* wrongness of that which it is an attraction towards.

I conclude that Professor Field's theory does not explain our actual judgements in cases of apparent conflict of duties. And I suggest that the view that we judge acts right or wrong in virtue of the motives from which they would normally proceed, and not motives good or bad in virtue of the *prima facie* rightness or wrongness of the actions which they are attractions or inclinations towards, is a putting of the cart before the horse.

Something should be said of Professor Field's reply to

---

[1] I admit this merely for the sake of argument; in fact most acts of deceit proceed from the desire of advantage to oneself.

another of the arguments I put forward for the view that our
duty is to do certain kinds of act and not to act from certain
motives, viz. that we *cannot* choose to act from a particular
motive. In reply to this he says[1] that 'in any sense in which we
can choose what action we shall do, we can choose what motive
we shall act from'. Now, choosing to do a certain act does not
necessarily involve choosing to act from a certain motive. For
there are acts which might proceed from any one of two or
more motives, and in such a case choosing to do the act is not
choosing to do it from any one of the motives, though it must
be from one of the motives that we make the choice. Let us
take, however, the case in which there is only one motive from
which the act could be done; say, sense of duty, or desire for
pleasure. Then it might seem that in choosing the act we are
choosing the motive, since the act can only be done from one
motive. But this is not really so. You might as well say that if
I choose to walk down the High Street of Oxford I am choosing to be still alive, and choosing that the High Street shall
exist, when the time comes at which I mean to take the walk;
for certainly I cannot walk down the street unless I am alive
and it exists. We do not choose that these things shall be; we
choose on the assumption that they will be, or perhaps we
should say 'without thinking of the possibility that they may
not be'. Similarly, though in the case supposed we could not
do the act except from the motive in question, what happens,
strictly speaking, is not that we choose to act from that
motive, but that from that motive we choose to do the act in
question, on the assumption that the motive will still exist in
our mind, or will have come to exist again, when the time for
doing the act arrives. When the choice or decision precedes the
act by only a short interval, the assumption is usually justified;
but when the interval is long, we are only too familiar with the
fact that the motive often fails to be present, or to be present
with sufficient strength, when it is needed.

It has been rather a surprise to me that so many writers have

[1] *Mind,* xli (1932), 33.

fallen foul of the view I expressed in *The Right and the Good* that obligatoriness attaches to acts independently of their motives, and moral goodness to them in consequence of their motives. I had thought that I was simply stating in a very explicit way what had always been implicit in the main lines of ethical theory. Possibly the doctrine is less likely to be rejected as a paradox if I indicate what a respectable ancestry it has. It is implicit in the doctrine of Aristotle, in which the whole content of the just, for example—of that which it is incumbent on us to do, in this particular department of duty—is described, without any reference to the motive of the agent, as arising from the nature of the situation in which he is acting (i.e. from the rights of the various persons affected by his action), and doing that which is just, doing this particular part of our duty, is described as consisting simply in the effecting of the proper distribution, compensation, or exchange—all this being distinguished from the doing of what is just 'as just men do it',[1] i.e. from the motive of love of justice. It is clearly implied that the one is what is obligatory, while the other is that which has moral goodness.

Again, the doctrine is stated very explicitly by Kant, when near the beginning of the *Grundlegung*[2] he distinguishes between doing what is your duty and acting from duty (i.e. from a sense of duty). He clearly implies that you can do the former even when your motive is a purely selfish one; and I believe that he consistently describes action from a sense of duty not as the only action that is right, but as the only action that has moral worth, thus making the motive (or, as he prefers to call it, the principle or maxim of action) the ground of moral goodness, but the nature of the action apart from its motive the ground of its rightness.

It is hardly necessary to point out that in this respect, if in no other, Utilitarianism joins hands with Kant. For utilitarians, the rightness of an act is determined by its consequences or else by its expected or probable consequences, and in no wise by its

---

[1] *Eth. Nic.* 1105 b 8.   [2] Akad, Ausgabe, iv. 397–9 (Abbott's translation, 15–18).

motive; witness Mill's well-known phrase 'the motive has nothing to do with the morality of the action, though much with the worth of the agent'.[1] And in this respect Mill's example is followed by the revised version of Utilitarianism associated with the name of Professor Moore.

This is perhaps the most convenient place to discuss the final part of Mr. Joseph's theory.[2] It has no direct connexion with the general view we have been considering, that the motive from which an act will be done, if it is done, forms, always or sometimes, all or part of the reason why we ought to do it. But in his mind it arises, as that view arose, from a consideration of actions whose obligatoriness cannot be accounted for, as that of many actions can, by their tending to produce good *results*. He has already insisted[3] that the word '*right*' is ambiguous; that besides standing for the fact that an act ought to be done, it stands for a common characteristic in virtue of which the acts that ought to be done ought to be done, and *this* rightness is, he maintains, 'a sort of goodness'.[4] Whether '*right*' can thus stand for the supposed common characteristic in virtue of which all acts that ought to be done ought to be done, is only a question about the use of language; the important question is whether Mr. Joseph can detect such a common characteristic, which is itself a form of goodness. He makes this impossible for himself, if I have grasped his view aright, by accepting the instrumental or utilitarian account of the source of the obligatoriness of many—I think, most—of the acts we ought to do. Most acts that are right are so, according to him, because they are productive of good. But productivity of good is, I would maintain, *not* a form of goodness in any strict sense of the word '*good*', and is most certainly not the same thing which he describes as the basis of the obligatoriness of two other kinds of act, to which he thinks the utilitarian account inapplicable.[5]

---

[1] *Utilitarianism*, copyright editions, 26. Cf. the note on the same page.
[2] Referred to above, p. 133.   [3] *Some Problems in Ethics*, ch. vi.
[4] Ibid. 92.   [5] Viz. those mentioned above, p. 129, n. 2.

As regards both these kinds of action, he rejects[1] the utilitarian theory that such actions are made right by the fact that they produce, or are likely to produce, good results. And he rejects[2] the view that they are made right by their proceeding from good motives. His view, then, is that such actions are obligatory because they have a rightness, which is a form of goodness, independent both of results and of motives. And his positive suggestion as to the source of the rightness of such an act is that it is the goodness 'of the system which it forms with its context'.[3]

This view seems to me open to serious criticism on two grounds. (1) If I contemplate one of the acts in question, an act, say, in which a promise is kept, or an act in which A brings into being a certain pleasure for B, when he might have brought into being an equal or greater pleasure for himself, and ask myself whether it is good, apart both from results and from motives, I can find no goodness in it. The fact is that when some one keeps a promise we can see no intrinsic worth in that; we must first know from what motive the promise was kept. It may have been kept in order later to procure some satisfaction from the promisee; then the keeping of the promise from that motive is indifferent. It may have been kept to spite some third person; the keeping of it from that motive is positively bad.

If I am right in holding that such acts are *not* as such good (but only the doing of them from a sense of duty or from some other good motive), then Mr. Joseph's view as to the source of the goodness he ascribes to them must be wrong. But since some readers may not have been convinced by what I have said on the first head, it is worth while (2) to examine his view as to the source of the goodness of such acts. This view is differently expressed by him in different places. One of his ways of putting it is to say that the goodness belongs not so much to the act but to 'the system which it forms with its context'.[4] Another is that it belongs to 'the rule of action of which it' (the action) 'is

---

[1] *Some Problems in Ethics*, 94.　　　　[2] Ibid. 97.
[3] Ibid. 97.　　　　　　　　　　　　　[4] Ibid. 97.

a manifestation.'[1] But finally[2] we are told that 'we must look to the whole form of life in some community, to which all the actions manifesting this rule would belong, and ask whether it, or some other form of life is better, which would be lived by the community instead, if this rule were not helping to determine it. If we judge that it is better, then the particular action is right, for the sake of the better system to which it belongs'.

The view has perhaps been suggested by Kant's attempt to test the rightness of an act by asking whether the principle involved in it could without self-contradiction be made a universal law of conduct for all rational beings.[3] But Mr. Joseph does not contend that the rule of life, of which keeping promises is one manifestation, is the *only* self-consistent rule; he sees that Kant failed to make this out.[4] What he claims is that 'the form of life requiring the particular action in the working out of its plan' is *better* than any other.[5] The suggestion, then, is that we have an imaginative vision of a certain kind of life in a community which we see would be better than any other, and that, reading off its implications, we see that among them are, for instance, that we should keep promises, that we should produce happiness for others rather than for ourselves, and the like. To this I have three objections. (1) One is that already made, that we can see *no* intrinsic goodness attaching to the life of a community merely because promises are kept in it. Before judging that the life of a promise-keeping community was good, we should insist on knowing whether the promises were being kept from good or from indifferent or from bad motives. (2) Mr. Joseph seems to me to be putting the cart before the horse. We do not start with a general notion of the ideal life of a community, and read off, as consequences that can be deduced from this, that promises should be kept, and the like. Rather, because we see that promises ought to be kept, that people should make restitution for the ills they have done, and render good for the good they have received, as well as promot-

---

[1] *Some Problems in Ethics*, 98.   [2] Ibid. 98.   [3] Cf. ibid. 98.
[4] Ibid. 99.   [5] Ibid. 99.

ing the general welfare, we build up from these intuitive insights the conception of an ideal community in which people would do these things, and do them because they know them to be right. If Mr. Joseph holds that we read the particular types of duty off as consequences from a single ideal, he may fairly be asked to state the general ideal in much more definite language than he ever does, and exhibit the deduction of the several branches of duty from it.

(3) No element in a system can owe its goodness merely to the goodness of the system; for neither presence in a good system, nor even presence as a necessary element in a good system, can guarantee the goodness of everything that is thus present. Thus, whatever be the merits of Mr. Joseph's view that certain actions owe their *rightness* to inclusion in a good system, they cannot be *good* by virtue of this, and therefore their rightness is not, as he maintains it is, a sort of goodness.

In fact his view, so far from finding a single source of the obligatoriness of all acts that are obligatory, describes some as being obligatory because their consequences are good,[1] some as being so because their motives are good,[2] and some as being so because the system to which they belong is good.[3] In no case is rightness shown to be itself 'a sort of goodness'.

Some light is thrown on his view by a comparison which he later[4] makes between ethics and mathematics. In mathematics

'a man may come to know, independently one of another, many facts between which he later discovers necessary connexion. Indeed in this field it is hard to doubt that all facts are mutually involved, though we cannot show this. Some have urged that, if this is so, the apprehension of the facts in their isolation is not properly to be called knowledge of them; we do not really know anything unless we know it in all its linkages. Perhaps there is a parallel here between Ethics and Mathematics. We think we know of certain actions separately that we ought to do or forbear them. But if the obliga-

[1] Cf. pp. 124–5, *supra*.   [2] Cf. pp. 125–32, *supra*.
[3] Cf. pp. 140–1, *supra*.   [4] *Some Problems of Ethics*, 108.

tion is grounded in some goodness or badness which the action would have, and which is not independent of its being so linked with other actions as to make good or bad the form of life to which it and they would belong, it might be said that we could not really know our obligation till we viewed the action in these linkages. Yet in both fields some isolated judgments seem true, though the facts cannot be so independent of each other as the judgments are isolated.'

Mr. Joseph seems to me to adopt, though rather half-heartedly, a coherence view of truth both as regards mathematics and as regards ethics. That view, if accepted whole-heartedly, involves that no proposition can be known to be true until it can be seen to imply and be implied by all the other true propositions within the given field (ethics, say, or mathematics). And since, admittedly, we do not know all the linkages of implication between our axioms, it follows, on this view, that we do not know the axioms, and in fact strictly know nothing. But Mr. Joseph is in two respects half-hearted. (a) He admits that we *do* know the axioms. 'A man may come to *know*,[1] independently one of another, many facts between which he later discovers necessary connexion.' Then we do know the axioms, and even if we should later be able to discover logical connexions between them, that cannot rob them of their self-evidence. (b) He treats mathematics and ethics as independent fields of knowledge, but if he were consistent in his allegiance to the coherence theory he should say that nothing can be known in ethics till it can be seen to imply and be implied by what is true in mathematics, and vice versa. We could not know that promises should be kept unless we could see it to be implied by what we know about the nature of numbers; and we could not know that 2 and 2 make 4 unless we could see it to be implied by what we know about duty.

As against this theory, what I suggest is that both in mathematics and in ethics we have certain crystal-clear intuitions from which we build up all that we can know about the nature of numbers and the nature of duty. And, to return to our proper

[1] Italics mine.

subject, we do not read off our knowledge of particular branches of duty from a single ideal of the good life, but build up our ideal of the good life from intuitions into particular branches of duty. In the course of our thinking we come to know more, but we should never come to know more if we did not *know* what we start with.

VII

THE GENERAL NATURE OF WHAT IS RIGHT
POSITIVE CONSIDERATION OF THE QUESTION

I TURN now to consider more precisely the general nature of what it is that moral laws bid us to do. Let me start by supposing that we accept the general account of rightness that has been offered, viz. that 'right' means 'suitable, in a unique and indefinable way which we may express by the phrase "morally suitable", to the situation in which an agent finds himself'. This situation contains two elements, what we may call the objective and the subjective element. The objective element consists of the facts about the various persons and things involved in the situation, in virtue of which a certain act would in fact be the best possible fulfilment of the various *prima facie* obligations resting on the agent. Suppose, for instance, that the situation is one in which none of the special obligations such as that of keeping a promise or of making reparation for an injury rests upon the agent, but only the responsibility for bringing as much good as possible into being. Then the act which would in fact produce the maximum good will be that which best fits the objective element of the situation, and will be in this respect the right act.

The subjective element consists of the agent's thoughts about the situation. These are as much parts of the total situation as are the objective facts. And the act which is morally suitable to them, i.e. the act which the agent, in view of his opinion about the situation, thinks will be the maximum fulfilment of obligation, will be in that respect right; while in order to be *completely* right an act will have to be suitable both to the objective and to the subjective element, which it can be only if the agent's opinions correspond to the realities of the situation.

It is clear that when we call an act right we sometimes mean that it suits the objective features of the situation, and sometimes that it suits the subjective features. And when people express different opinions about the rightness or wrongness of an act, the difference is often due to the fact that one of them is thinking of objective and the other of subjective rightness. The recognition of the difference between the two is therefore in itself important as tending to reconcile what might otherwise seem irreconcilable differences of opinion. But the question remains, which of the characteristics—objective or subjective rightness—is ethically the more important, which of the two acts is that which we ought to do. There are various considerations that tell in favour of the objective view. When we are in a difficult moral situation, what we *want* to know is not what act we think likely to produce certain results, but what act *will* produce certain results. And we are often driven to admit that we do not know what we ought to do, while if what we ought to do depended on what we think, we could always ascertain by reflection what we think, and therefore what we ought to do.

Again, moral laws are often expressed in a form which implies the objective view. It will be enough to take two instances. The moral law about promise-keeping is usually expressed in the form 'keep your promises', and a promise is usually expressed as a promise to effect a certain change in the situation, e.g. to restore a book to a friend. If we accept the moral principle as it is usually expressed, it follows that the act we ought to do is that which will in fact lead to our friend's reception of the book, and that if we so deal with the book that it reaches him we shall have done our duty, while if we so deal with it that it does not reach him we shall not have done our duty, even if in the first case we have dealt carelessly with it and in the second case carefully. This no doubt seems paradoxical, but I formerly thought that the paradox could be removed by saying that while the first act is the right act, the latter is the morally better act, since it is done with greater conscientiousness.

Again, the moral principle relating to the production of good is usually couched in the form 'do that which will produce most good', and this, like the usual formulation of the duty of promise-keeping, implies the objective view. It implies that not the act which the agent thinks will produce the most good, but that which will in fact produce the most good, is the act that ought to be done. And, as before, we might hold that we had removed the apparent paradox involved in calling a care-less act which in fact produced most good the right act, by admitting that it is morally inferior to a more careful and con-scientious act which in fact produced less good.

Nevertheless, I have come to hold the opposite opinion, that it is the subjectively right act that is obligatory. I owe my con-version to Professor Prichard's Lecture on 'Duty and Igno-rance of Fact'. His reasoning is so conclusive that I cannot do better than reproduce the main features of his argument. He starts by pointing out that the moral rules which are the generalization of our thought as to the characteristics which make particular acts which are our duties to be duties, habitually take the form of saying we ought to *do so-and-so*, to speak the truth, to carry out the rules of one's government, &c. He points out that the *doing something* which is implied in such formulations always means causing a change of state of some existing thing; that e.g. telling the truth means causing some one else to have a true opinion about the state of one's own belief about something. Further, when we reflect on the changes which we think we ought to bring about, we find that they are always changes which we can only bring about in-directly, by bringing about something else directly—e.g. we can cause another man to know our thoughts only by causing certain sounds, or making certain marks on paper, or the like. Thus the general form of a moral rule is 'a man ought, or ought not, to bring about a thing of a certain kind indirectly'. But when we bring about something indirectly, the result is not wholly due to us. The only changes we can be said quite strictly to bring about are those which we bring about directly. Thus if a moral rule is stated in terms of 'doing something' and of 'bringing about something' in the strict sense, it will take the form, 'A man ought to do such an act or acts as will cause a thing of the kind A to assume a state of the kind x'.

But this expression is elliptical in two respects. In saying that a man ought to support his indigent parents, we do not mean that he should support them whether he has or has not such parents, or that he should support them whether he can or not. Thus the full form of a moral rule will be: 'When the situation in which a man is contains a thing of the kind A capable of having a state of the kind x effected in it, and when also it is such that some state or combination of states which the man can bring about directly will cause a state of the kind x in A, the man ought to bring about that state or combination of states'.

The formulation of any moral rule in this way, which we have seen to be the proper expression of our normal formulation of moral laws, implies the objective view of the basis of moral obligation. And this view, Professor Prichard points out, we find in two ways attractive. (1) We tend naturally to think that obligation does not depend on our thought about the situation, but on the nature of the situation itself; and when we try to resolve our doubt about what our duty is, we often try to do so by resolving our doubt about the facts. And (2) this view implies that if some action is a duty, it would actually bring about some state referred to in a moral rule, such as the recovery of a sick man, and would not merely be an act which we think likely to do so; and we value this implication because we should like to think that if we have done a duty, we have actually achieved some such change.

Yet this view has awkward consequences. (1) In order to know that some moral rule is applicable to me here and now, I must know (*a*) that the situation contains a thing of the kind A capable of having a state of the kind x effected in it, and (*b*) that it is such that some act that I can do would cause this A to assume a state of the kind x. Now (*a*) is not always fulfilled. I may not know whether my parents are in difficulties, or whether a man I meet is ill. And (*b*) is *never* fulfilled; I never *know* nor can come to *know* that some state which I can bring about will produce an effect of the kind *x*, though I may have reason to *think* it. Thus if duty be such as the objective theory conceives it to be, I can never know that I have any particular duty, or even that any one has ever had or will ever have a duty.

It is worth while to note in passing just what is proved and what is not proved by this argument. In constructing or in following a geometrical proof, we never know that we have before us a triangle, for instance; but we treat the figure before us as if it were a triangle, and we come to *know* that if it were, it would have certain properties. Similarly, we never know that an act we could do would produce a certain effect, but we may think that it would, and may *know* that if it would, it would be our duty to do it; and we might proceed from this to generalized moral rules, which would be hypothetical in character; e.g. 'if you can ever produce a true opinion in the mind of some one else as to what you think, you ought to do so.' Thus the objective view is not fatal to the possibility of knowing moral rules. But it is fatal to the possibility of recognizing particular duties incumbent on us here and now, since we can never know, for instance, that we *can* produce a true opinion as to our thought in any one else's mind.

Further consequences of the objective view are (2) that we can never do a duty because it is a duty, since this must mean 'because we know it to be a duty', (3) that some past act of mine may have been morally obligatory though I believed it was one I ought not to do, and (4) that I may do some act which is obligatory, though I do not even suspect that it will have the effect which renders it a duty.

These difficulties all arise from supposing that an act is made my duty by the objective facts of the situation. The only alternative is to suppose that it is made a duty by the subjective facts of the situation, viz. by my state of knowledge or opinion about the facts of the case. The most obvious way of describing the state of mind which makes an act my duty is to say that it is my thinking certain things likely; e.g. that a man near me has fainted and that my shouting would revive him. This view has the advantage of making it possible to discover our duties; for we can always or almost always know what it is that we think likely. This view also has the advantage of making it possible to do a duty knowing it to be a duty. It is, however, open to this objection, that since the question whether a certain act is a duty depends not merely on our thinking that there is *some* probability of its having a certain effect, but on our thinking it at least *in a certain degree* likely that it will, 'there will be border-line cases in which I shall be unable to discover whether the degree to which I think the act likely to confer a certain benefit is sufficient to render it a duty'.[1] Thus even on this view I may have a duty without being able to discover that I have it—although there are other duties which we *can* discover ourselves to have.

The only way to choose between the objective and the subjective view is to ask ourselves which corresponds better with what we actually think to be duties. Professor Prichard points out two ways in which our thought *seems* to imply the objective view. (1) We often think without question both that the situation contains something in a certain state, and that some action we could do would produce a change in it of a certain kind, and then we think without question that we ought to do the action. Here we seem to be implying that what makes us bound to do the act is not our opinion, but the fact, that the situation is of a certain kind and that the act would have a certain effect in that situation. (2) We often seek to change the mind of some one else about a duty by trying to convince him that he is wrong about the facts. 'Thus, where *A* thinks he ought to vote for *X* rather than *Y*, *B* may try to convince *A* that he ought to vote for *Y* by arguing that *X* and *Y* will, if elected, act otherwise than as *A* expects.'[2] Here we seem to imply that what *A* ought to do depends not on how he thinks *X* and *Y* would behave, but on how they would in fact behave.

On the other hand, much of our ordinary thought is in con-

---

[1] Op. cit. 13.   [2] Ibid. 17.

152 THE GENERAL NATURE OF WHAT IS RIGHT

flict with the objective view. (A) One instance will suffice to show this. Suppose one is driving a car from a side-road into a main road; the question arises, ought one to slow down before entering the main road.

'If the objective view be right, (1) there will be a duty to slow down only if in fact there is traffic; (2) we shall be entitled only to think it likely ... that we are bound to slow down; and (3) if afterwards we find no traffic, we ought to conclude that our opinion that we were bound to slow down was mistaken. ... Indeed the objective view is in direct conflict with all the numerous cases in which we think without question that we ought to do something which we are thinking of as of the nature of an *insurance* in the interest of some one else.'[1]

(B) 'The extent to which our ordinary thought involves the subjective view is usually obscured for us by our tendency to think that the terms "likely" and "probable" refer to facts in nature. For we are apt, for instance, to express our thought that some one has probably fainted, and that shouting would probably revive him, by the statements: "He has probably fainted" and "Shouting would probably revive him". We are then apt to think that these statements state the existence of certain facts in nature called probabilities.'[2]

But there cannot be probabilities in nature. Whatever the precise nature of the fact expressed by the statement '*X* has probably fainted' may be, the fact must consist in our mind's being in a certain state. Once this is realized it becomes clear that most of our ordinary thought involves the subjective view.

(C) Even when we try to change some one else's mind about a duty, we do not really imply the objective view. 'This is shown by our thinking that when our attempt to change his opinion about the facts is over, then, whether we have or have not succeeded, the question whether he is bound to do the action will turn on the nature of *his opinion* about the facts.'[3] We are not really trying to convince him that his duty is not what he thinks it is, but, thinking that his doing of his duty would result in very bad consequences, we try to put him into

[1] Ibid. 17–18.   [2] Ibid. 18.   [3] Ibid. 19.

a different state of opinion on the facts, a state of opinion in which an act which we think will have *good* consequences will have *become* his duty, because his opinion about the facts has changed.

Thus on the whole the subjective view is more in agreement with our ordinary thought than the objective. Yet it is exposed to various difficulties, of which the chief are (1) that on this view knowledge of the existence of border-line cases precludes us from thinking that we can always discern our duties, and (2) (a more fundamental difficulty) that this view represents the duty of doing some action as depending not on the fact that the action would have a certain character, but on our thinking it likely that it would. To maintain this seems impossible, and we seem therefore to be in an impasse.

Professor Prichard now turns to consider a difficulty which is common to both views, and which if well founded will lead us to modify both. We have hitherto assumed that an obligation is an obligation to do some *action*, i.e. to produce some change in something. But we must ask whether this is true. An obligation must be an obligation to be *active*, and not to be *affected*, in a particular way. To say that an obligation is always an obligation to do some action implies that there is a particular kind of activity, distinct from other activities such as thinking or imagining, whose nature is to be the bringing about of something. But there is no type of mental activity of which the general nature is to be the producing of a change in some physical object, such as the moving of a hand or a foot. On the contrary, if we ask *how* we move a hand or a foot, the natural answer is that we do so by setting ourselves to do so. There is a type of mental activity of which the generic nature is to be the setting oneself to effect a change in a physical object, and of which setting oneself to move a hand or a foot is an instance. The change in the physical object, when it follows, is merely the result—the intended result, of course—of the mental activity.

Again, if we ask what we mean when we say 'I can make a

loud noise', we find that what we mean is not that there is a special kind of activity of which we are capable consisting in bringing about a loud noise, but rather that a special kind of activity of which we are capable, consisting of setting ourselves to make a loud noise, would have a loud noise as an effect.

Two conclusions follow: (1) that the true answer to any question of the form 'can I do so-and-so?' must be 'I don't know'. This is obvious in certain cases. Obviously I cannot *know* whether I can succeed in threading a needle. But even where we usually assume that we can effect certain changes, such as the movement of a hand or a foot, we can never *know* that we can, since we may have become paralysed since we last tried. And (2) whatever we are setting ourselves to do, we never *know* that we are doing what we are setting ourselves to do. The mental activity may be of exactly the same kind whether we do or do not by performing it bring about the bodily change intended.

'As regards an obligation, the moral is obvious. It is simply that, contrary to the implication of ordinary language and of moral rules in particular, an obligation must be an obligation, not to *do* something, but to perform an activity of a totally different kind, that of setting or exerting ourselves to do something, i.e. to bring something about.'[1]

The question now arises whether the substitution of 'setting ourselves to bring about some result' for 'bringing about some result' makes it easier to decide between the objective and the subjective view. Professor Prichard points out that in one respect it does. 'For once it has become common ground that the kind of activity which an obligation is an obligation to perform is one which may bring about nothing at all, viz. setting ourselves to bring about something, we are less inclined to think that, for there to be an obligation to perform some particular activity, it must have a certain indirect effect. To this extent the modification diminishes the force of the objective view without in any way impairing that of its rival'.[2]

[1] Ibid. 24.　　　　　　　[2] Ibid. 25.

But the main difficulty of the subjective view remains, that it represents 'the obligation to do some action as depending not on the fact that the action would have a certain character, if we were to do it, but on our thinking it likely that it would'.[1]

This difficulty Professor Prichard removes in the following way:

'We are apt', he says, 'to think of an obligation to do some action as if it were, like its goodness or badness, a sort of quality or character of the action. . . . And this tendency is fostered by our habit of using the terms "right" and "wrong" as equivalents for "ought" and "ought not". For when we express our thought that we ought, or ought not, to do some action by saying that the act would be right, or wrong, our language inevitably implies that the obligation or disobligation is a certain character which the act would have if we were to do it. . . . And when we think this, we inevitably go on to think that the obligation or disobligation must depend on some character which the act would have. But, as we recognize when we reflect, there are no such characteristics of an action as ought-to-be-doneness and ought-not-to-be-doneness. This is obvious; for, since the existence of an obligation to do some action cannot possibly depend on actual performance of the action, the obligation cannot itself be a property which the action would have, if it were done. What does exist is the fact that you, or that I, ought, or ought not, to do a certain action, or rather to set ourselves to do a certain action. And when we make an assertion containing the term "ought" or "ought not", that to which we are attributing a certain character is not a certain activity but a certain man. If our being bound to set ourselves to do some action were a character which the activity would have, its existence would, no doubt, have to depend on the fact that the activity would have a certain character, and it could not depend on our thinking that it would. Yet since, in fact, it is a character of ourselves, there is nothing to prevent its existence depending on our having certain thoughts about the situation and, therefore, about the nature of the activity in respect of the effects. Indeed, for this reason, its existence must depend upon some fact about ourselves. And while the truth could not be expressed by saying: "*My setting myself to do so-and-so* would *be*

[1] Ibid. 25.

right, because *I think* that it would have a certain effect"—a statement which would be as vicious in principle as the statement: "*Doing so-and-so* would *be* right because I *think* it would be right" —there is nothing to prevent its being expressible in the form: "*I* ought to set myself to do so-and-so, because *I* think that it would have a certain effect."[1]

This last part of Professor Prichard's theory, while both true and important, is not necessary for the saving of the subjective view. For even if we think that there is a character of rightness that attaches to an activity, it will, on the subjective view as now restated, be a character which belongs to the activity not because of the activity's being thought to have a certain character but because of its actually being of a certain character, the character of being the setting oneself to bring about a certain effect. This character it actually has, and there is in principle no reason why it should not be the ground of a further character of rightness. Thus, even apart from Professor Prichard's last contention, the subjective view is safe from the objections which seemed fatal to it.

There is another mode of argument by which we may, I think, satisfy ourselves of the truth of the subjective view. It might be agreed, I believe, that the act which a man in any situation ought to do is that which it would be *reasonable* for him to do if he wanted to do his duty in that situation. And I think we can on reflection discover two possible but wrong answers to the question what it would be reasonable for him to do. (1) There may be some change, by setting himself to bring which about he would in fact produce the result the production of which would be objectively right, e.g. would succeed in returning to a friend a book he had promised to return; a change, however, which no human foresight could foresee to be about to have this effect—e.g. a book despatched in the most careless way may by the vigilance of the Post Office or of some individual unexpectedly reach its destination. And it might

[1] Ibid. 26–7.

happen that owing to unforeseen circumstances the careful despatch of the book might fail to lead to its reaching its destination. Yet if no human foresight can foresee these facts, no one would say that it was reasonable for a man who wanted to do his duty by his friend to despatch the book carelessly, since the successful result of this neither is nor could be foreseen by the sender. (2) There may be circumstances which the agent does not foresee, but which a wiser or better-informed person might foresee, which would in fact cause a certain activity of the agent's to produce a certain result, the production of which would be objectively right. Yet it would not be reasonable for the agent, if he wished to do his duty, to perform such an activity, since *ex hypothesi* he neither knows nor thinks the activity would have this result. The fact that other people might know or think this has no tendency to make it reasonable for *him* to act thus. What *he* ought to set himself to do, then, is neither that which will in fact produce the result in question, nor that which in the judgement of better-informed people is likely to produce it, but that which *he* thinks likely to produce it.

Yet we do not think that an agent should necessarily forthwith perform that activity of self-exertion which in his present state of opinion about the facts seems to him likely to produce the objectively right result. We often raise the problem what we ought to do, some time before the time at which whatever action is to be taken must be taken. In such a case the agent should have before his mind, as the ideal, that self-exertion which would in fact produce the right result. This, however, he cannot know; and so he must fall back on a secondary ideal, viz. that self-exertion which on the fullest consideration that he can give to the matter within the time at his disposal would seem most likely to produce the result. And he should set himself to *act* only when either the time-limit is on the verge of arriving, or he has reached the point of thinking that no further consideration would enable him to judge better of the circumstances and of the probable effects of alternative exertions. What he does after such consideration may reasonably be expected to be nearer to the objectively right act than what he would do after a first hasty consideration.

At first sight it might seem that in substituting 'setting himself to bring about a certain result' as that which the agent ought to do rather than 'bringing about a certain result', we have, contrary to our earlier conclusion, introduced motive into the structure of that which we ought to do. For 'to set oneself to bring about a certain result' seems to be perilously near to being actuated to action by the desire to bring about that result; i.e. by a certain motive. Yet the two things are quite different. Suppose we imagine, for instance, that in some situation none of the special responsibilities such as that of keeping a promise is in question, and the only responsibility that arises is that of setting ourselves to produce as much good as possible. What we ought to do, then, strictly speaking, is just to set ourselves to produce this. And that is different from doing so from any special motive, such as sense of duty or benevolence. For we may set ourselves to produce the result from any one of a *variety* of motives. We may think, for instance, that in setting ourselves to produce the greatest good we are also likely to acquire a good reputation for ourselves, or to get in a high degree the pleasure of having a good conscience; and either of these may be our motive. But a self-exertion which may proceed from any one of several motives cannot be identified with self-exertion from any one motive; and if it is the self-exertion that is our duty, it is not the self-exertion from any particular motive that is our duty. Or again, suppose that the main responsibility in some situation is that of fulfilling a promise, e.g. of paying a debt. We may set ourselves to do this either from the motive of sense of duty, or from the wish to avoid a legal action against us, or from the wish to injure our creditor by putting him in possession of more money than is good for him. A self-exertion which may arise from any one of these motives is not identical with a self-exertion from the sense of duty, and it is the former and not the latter that is our duty.

We are now in a position to see that two views which we have rejected owe their plausibility to an ambiguity in the notion of right action. A right action means in general one that is morally suitable to the situation. But an action may be described as morally suitable to the situation either because it is suitable to the objective elements in the situation, i.e. because it is that which would in fact produce the result which we think we ought to aim at; or because it is suitable to the subjective elements in the situation, i.e. to our thoughts about the situation and about the probable results of alternative actions. Both actions are undeniably, in different respects, right; and because the former is right in a respect in which the latter is not, it is easy to fall into the supposition that it is it that is obligatory. But it is also true that the latter is right in a respect in which the former is not, and we have seen good reasons for holding that it is it that is in fact obligatory.

Again, an action done from a certain motive is undeniably right, or morally suitable to a situation, in a sense in which a mere action, irrespective of its motive, is not. Where, for instance, the only responsibility is that of producing a maximum of good, it is more completely fitting that we should set ourselves to produce a maximum of good, from the sense of duty to do so, than that we should barely set ourselves to produce a maximum of good, it may be from some unworthy motive. And where the fulfilling of a promise is the main responsibility, it is more completely fitting that we should set ourselves to fulfil it from the sense of duty, than that we should barely set ourselves to fulfil it. And since the action from a certain motive is more fully fitting, morally, than the bare action, more completely right, it is easy to fall into the supposition that it is our duty. But we have seen good reasons for holding that this view, although it is one into which we easily fall, is not the true view. Both the view that it is our duty to produce certain results, and the view that it is our duty to act from certain motives, are natural enough perversions of what seems to be the true view, that it is our duty to set ourselves to produce certain results. It is sometimes said that it is neither results nor motives but intentions that make actions right or wrong, and this is almost true. There is a certain danger in laying the stress on intention, since intentions may remain idle; but it would be true to say that the nature of what is intended *in an act* is what makes the act right or wrong.

The most important point, I think, which emerges from Professor Prichard's discussion is that the only thing to which a man can be morally obliged is what I will call a self-exertion, a setting oneself to effect this or that change or set of changes. He cannot be obliged to perform an 'act', in the ordinary sense. For the noun 'act', as we ordinarily use it, stands for a complex thing; viz. the causing of a certain change by setting oneself to cause it; and this includes as an element in it the occurrence of the change. It would be absurd to say 'I killed him, and in consequence he died'; to say 'I killed him' includes the statement that he died. It would not, indeed, be absurd to say 'I hit him, and in consequence he died', but it *would* be absurd to say 'I hit him, and in consequence he suffered a blow'. Now the occurrence of the bodily change involved in the use of such words or phrases as 'kill', 'hit', 'tell the truth' cannot even be part of what is right or of what is wrong. This follows directly from the fact that if a man had, without knowing it, become paralysed since the last time he had tried to effect the given type of change, his self-exertion, though it would not produce the effect, would obviously be of exactly the same character as it would have been if he had remained unparalysed and it had therefore produced the effect. The exertion is all that is his and therefore all that he can be morally obliged to; whether the result follows is due to certain causal laws which he can perhaps know but certainly cannot control, and to a circumstance, viz. his being or not being paralysed, which he cannot control, and cannot know until he performs the exertion.

Now, assuming that the only thing that can be obligatory or disobligatory is a self-exertion, it can be seen that the only thing to which there can be a *prima facie* obligation, or to which some one else can have a claim, is also a self-exertion. For only those things are *prima facie* obligatory which, if there are no more pressing *prima facie* obligations, are actually obligatory. No one, for instance, can, have a claim to have his life saved by me; the most that any one can have is a claim to my self-exertion to that end.

At the same time, it is very natural that in our ordinary thought we should think that it is actions and not self-exertions that are right or wrong. For (1) the most direct results of the self-exertion, those within the agent's own body, have followed so constantly, within his experience, upon the self-exertion, that he not unnaturally thinks of the self-exertion + its most direct results as if they formed one single event; and (2) where the self-exertion produces its desired result, there is a further connexion between it and its result, over and above that which there usually is between a cause and its result, viz. that the one is just the attempt to produce the other.

Now we may distinguish several different self-exertions which might have some claim to be considered right, or what the agent ought to do:

(A) The self-exertion which is morally most suitable to the objective circumstances, in the sense of 'the circumstances other than the agent's own state of knowledge or opinion'; e.g., in a case where only beneficence is in question, the self-exertion which would in fact benefit humanity most.

(B) The self-exertion which is morally most suitable to the agent's state of mind about the circumstances, in which there may be included ignorance and false opinion as well as knowledge and true opinion; i.e. the self-exertion which would be morally most suitable if the circumstances were such as he supposes them to be.

(C) The self-exertion which he *thinks* to be morally most suitable in the circumstances as he takes them to be.

(B) may differ from (A), in consequence of a divergence from the truth in the agent's opinion about the circumstances.

(C) may differ from (B), in virtue of a divergence from truth in the agent's opinion as to what is morally suitable to the supposed circumstances. The one difference is due to a divergence from truth on a non-moral question, the other to a divergence from truth on a moral question.

All these acts are in different senses right or morally suitable —the first suitable to the objective circumstances, the second to the agent's opinion on the non-moral question, the third to his opinion on the moral question. Which of them is the action that the agent ought to do? Professor Prichard's argument seems to me to have shown that it is not the first. No one would say that the driver of a car had done right in driving fast round a corner if he thought there might quite probably be a car meeting him but in fact there were none. But the question may be asked, should we not go a stage farther and say that it is rather the third than the second that is the right act, since that alone is suitable to the agent's complete state of opinion, including his opinion on the moral as well as on the non-moral question. The suggestion is at first sight open to the objection that we should be saying that act (C) is the right act for the agent to do, simply because he thinks it is the right act. It is clear on epistemological grounds that nothing can have a character simply by being thought to have it; but we are not suggesting that act (C) has a certain character by being thought to have that character. The agent *thinks* it is the act suitable to, or harmonious with, his opinion on the question 'what are the circumstances?'; and in consequence it *is* the act suitable to his opinion on the question 'what is the act suitable to the circumstances?'. Thus the act has one suitability by being thought to have another. If our suggestion thus escapes the epistemological objection, there seems to be no objection to saying that it is the suitability that act (C) has, and not that which act (B) has, that makes an act one's duty. For, just as it was felt to be paradoxical to say 'you ought to do the act which will produce certain consequences, because it will produce these consequences, and though you think it will not', so it is paradoxical to say 'you ought to do the act which is most suitable to your opinion about the circumstances, because it is the most suitable to your opinion, and though you think it is not'.

It is only by thus distinguishing different rightnesses or suitabilities and by making duty depend on the last of the three, that we can do justice to a thought which is inseparable from the thought of duty. This is the thought that anything that we ought to do must be something that we not only can do, but can do with the knowledge or at least the opinion that it is our duty. Suppose that we blame a man for not doing his duty, and he replies 'but I did not know or even think it to be my duty, and therefore could not do it with the knowledge or even the opinion that it was my duty'; it would be a poor response to say 'no, but you might have done it from some quite different motive'; for clearly a man who had acted from a different motive would have been more blameworthy than the man who did what he honestly thought was his duty. Now, when a man's opinion about the circumstances is mistaken, he cannot do act A with the knowledge or even the opinion that it is right in sense A. And when his moral insight is at fault, he cannot do act B with the knowledge or even the opinion that it is right in sense B. But even if both his opinion about the facts and his moral insight are at fault, he can always do act C with the knowledge that it is right in sense C, i.e. that it is the act which is most suitable to his opinion on the question what act is most suitable to the circumstances as he takes them to be.

There is another consideration which tends to show that it is what is right in this sense that we think an agent is obliged to do. The notion of obligation carries with it very strongly the notion that the non-discharge of an obligation is blameworthy. Now suppose that of two men one does that which he mistakenly believes to be his objective duty, and the other does that which is his objective duty, believing it not to be so, we should regard the former as at least less blameworthy than the latter; and in fact we should not regard the former as directly blameable for the act, but only, if at all, for previous acts by which he has blunted his sense of what is objectively right.

It may at first sight seem dangerous to admit this double dose of subjectivity into the answer to the question 'what is my duty?', by making it depend on my *opinion* as to what is morally suitable to what is in my *opinion* the state of the facts; and that is, I think, the strongest apparent objection to which this account is exposed. But 'subjective' is notoriously one of the vaguest of philosophical terms, and we must ask ourselves whether the account given above is a subjective account in any objectionable sense. The kind of subjective account which it seems to me important to avoid is one which says that acts are made to have some moral characteristic by being thought to have it, or (which comes to the same thing) that the opinion that an act has a certain characteristic is no more true and no more false than the opinion that it has not. Now, we are not giving such an account of 'right' in any of the three senses we have distinguished. In any particular situation in which a particular man is placed, there is one act which, if he had complete knowledge about the circumstances and a completely correct moral insight, he would see to be right in the first sense. There is no suspicion, even, of subjectivity in what is right in this sense. Secondly, suppose him to be mistaken about the circumstances; there is an act which is right in the second sense, in the sense of being appropriate to his opinion about the circumstances. That act is not made right in this second sense by being thought to be so; it bears the same sort of relation to the supposed situation as the first act does to the actual situation; the same kind of harmony exists in the one case as in the other; the harmony is not created by being thought to exist, it exists independently of the agent's thought about it. Thirdly, the agent may be mistaken in his moral judgement of his duty in the supposed situation; but so long as he thinks as he does, the act in which he acts on his conviction has the same sort of harmony with his conviction as an act in which a man acts on a correct conviction has with that conviction, a harmony which is not created by his opinion but is there for all to apprehend.

Error in this region arises, it would seem, only if we confuse, as we often do, one kind of rightness with another. Although, if one acts with imperfect moral insight or in accordance with insight that is morally correct but based on an incorrect view of the facts, one does what is right in one sense, and in what is from one point of view the most important sense, since it is that to which praise is appropriate (for a man is more to be blamed for acting against his convictions than for doing contrary to his convictions an act that is right in the first sense), no one should be content to have done so. He should be rather ashamed of having done an act which owes its rightness to its harmony with incorrect moral insight or incorrect opinion about the facts, and should realize that it would have been better if he could have amended his moral insight or his opinion of the circumstances, or both, so that in doing what was right in the third sense he would have also been doing what was right in the second or even in the first. If to act in accordance with one's conviction is always, in one sense, to do one's duty, it remains true that one's conscience may be very much mistaken and in need of improvement.

We may now, in the light of this discussion, consider the question of the relation of the morally good act to the right act. Is a morally good act necessarily right? Is a right act necessarily morally good? Or are the two characteristics quite independent?

If by a right act we mean an objectively right act, i.e. the act which out of all those open to a particular agent in particular circumstances will in fact produce the maximum fulfilment of the claims that exist against him, we must maintain the complete non-dependence of moral goodness and rightness upon one another. For an action's being morally good depends mainly[1] on the motive from which it is done, and the goodness of the motive neither guarantees nor is guaranteed by the nature

[1] Cf. pp. 306–8, 325–6.

of the results that the act actually produces. Take, for instance, the case in which the motive is the sense of duty, i.e. the desire to do one's duty +the thought that a certain act is one's duty. This thought in turn rests on the thought that the act will produce certain results; and the thought that it will do so furnishes no guarantee that it actually will do so. And conversely, of course, the fact that it will do so furnishes no guarantee that it was done from the thought that it would do so and the thought that therefore it was our duty to do it. Thus a morally good act may be objectively wrong, and an objectively right act may be morally bad, or indifferent.

It is important to maintain this, as a corrective of the view that, so long as we act conscientiously, all is well. Conscience, when not accompanied by clear insight into the situation, and by foresight of the effects which acts are likely to have, has often led to acts which objectively considered were deplorably wrong, which failed lamentably to fulfil the *prima facie* obligations of the agent. On the other hand, we are not bound to think that there is *no* connexion between moral goodness and objective rightness, that a morally good act is no more likely to be objectively right than a morally bad or indifferent act, or an objectively right act no more likely to be morally good than an objectively wrong act. For the motive of a morally good act is either the sense of duty or the desire to bring some particular good thing into being, as being good, and an act so motived is far more likely to conform to objective duty than one of which the motive is either self-interest or malevolence.

Again, the act which is right in the first of the two subjective senses, the act which would be right if the situation were as the agent supposes it to be, is not necessarily morally good, nor vice versa. For on the one hand, such an act may be done with a bad motive, and will not then be morally good; and on the other hand, an act done with a good motive, and therefore morally good, may through failure of moral insight not be the act which would actually be right in the circumstances as the agent supposes them to be.

The relation between rightness in the third sense, conformity to the agent's thought on the question as to what is right in the circumstances, and moral goodness, cannot be stated so simply. The motive of a morally good act may be either the sense of duty or the wish to bring some good thing into being, as being good. In the first case the morally good act is necessarily right in the third sense; it is the act which harmonizes with the agent's thought about his duty. In the second case, it is not so. The act may be done without the agent's thinking about his duty, and then the act cannot be said to harmonize with the agent's thought about his duty, since he has no such thought. Or again he may think that act *A* is his duty, but do act *B* from some other good motive (e.g. that of kindness to an individual), and in such a case his act has some moral goodness, but does not harmonize with his thought about his duty, and is not right in the third sense.[1]

And conversely, rightness in this sense never guarantees moral goodness. For an act may be the act which the agent thinks to be his duty, and yet be done from an indifferent or bad motive, and therefore be morally indifferent or bad.

---

[1] Later, however, I will mention (pp. 306–9) a consideration which enables us to state a closer connexion between moral goodness and rightness than that pointed out in this paragraph.

VIII

THE KNOWLEDGE OF WHAT IS RIGHT

I TURN next to the epistemological questions connected with duty. Can we be said to *know* our duty? And if we can, how do we acquire this knowledge? I will start with a simple case. I am walking along the street, and I see a blind man at a loss to get across the street through the stream of traffic. I probably do not ask myself what I ought to do, but more or less instinctively take him by the arm and pilot him across. But if afterwards I stop to ask whether I have done what I ought, I shall almost certainly say 'Yes'; and if for any reason I ask myself, before doing the act, whether I ought to do it, I shall give the same answer. Now it is clear that it is in virtue of my thinking the act to have some other character that I think I ought to do it. Rightness is always a resultant attribute, an attribute that an act has because it has another attribute. It is not an attribute that its subject is just directly perceived in experience to have, as I perceive a particular extended patch to be yellow, or a particular noise to be loud. No doubt there are causes which cause this patch to be yellow, or that noise to be loud; but I can perceive the one to be yellow, or the other to be loud, without knowing anything of the causes that account for this. I see the attributes in question to attach to the subjects merely as these subjects, not as subjects of such and such a character. On the other hand, it is only by knowing or thinking my act to have a particular character, out of the many that it in fact has, that I know or think it to be right. It is, among other things, the directing of a physical body in a certain direction, but I never dream that it is right in consequence of that. I think that it is right because it is the relieving of a human being from distress. Now it seems at first sight to follow from this that our perception of the particular duty follows from the perception of a general duty to relieve human beings in distress.

And, generalizing, we might feel inclined to say that our perception of particular duties is always an act of inference, in which the major premiss is some general moral principle. And no doubt my grasp of the principle that I should relieve human beings in distress precedes my grasp of the fact that I should relieve this blind man, since up to this moment I may not have known of the existence of this man, and certainly did not know of his desire to cross this particular street; while I certainly had at least a latent awareness of the general principle, an awareness which the occurrence of *any* instance falling under the principle might call into activity—just as I have a latent knowledge of the laws of arithmetic or of English grammar before I proceed to make up my accounts or to write a letter.

Yet it will not do to make our perception of particular duties essentially inference from general principles. For it may, I suppose, be taken for granted that man was a practical being before he became a theoretical one, and that in particular he answered somehow the question how he ought to behave in particular circumstances, before he engaged in general speculation on the principles of duty. No doubt there was an earlier stage still, when men in fact did right acts without ever asking whether they were right, when, for instance, they helped one another in distress without thinking of any duty to do so. We see disinterested help being given by men to one another every day, without any thought of duty. Aristotle puts the point simply:

'Parent seems by nature to feel friendship for offspring and offspring for parent, not only among men but among birds and among most animals; it is felt mutually by members of the same race, and especially by men. . . . We may see even in our travels how near and dear every man is to every other.'[1]

Butler puts the matter more eloquently:

'There is such a natural principle of attraction in man towards man, that having trod the same tract of land, having breathed in the same

---

[1] *Eth. Nic.* 1155 a 16–22.

climate, barely having been born in the same artificial district or division, becomes the occasion of contracting acquaintances and familiarities many years after: for any thing may serve the purpose. Thus relations merely nominal are sought and invented, not by governors, but by the lowest of the people; which are found sufficient to hold mankind together in little fraternities and copartnerships: weak ties indeed, and what may afford fund enough for ridicule, if they are absurdly considered as the real principles of that union: but they are in truth merely the occasions, as any thing may be of any thing, upon which our nature carries us on according to its own previous bent and bias; which occasions therefore would be nothing at all, were there not this prior disposition and bias of nature.'[1]

Aristotle's reference is perhaps the more interesting, in two respects. In the first place, it takes the practice of disinterested aid further back in time, by asserting its existence not merely among men, but among animals. He opens up the vista of the development of disinterested action, as it exists in man, from the instinctive co-operation of the members of an animal community. And secondly, he points to what is much the most striking and universal example of disinterested action, the operation of parental love, from which perhaps all disinterested action may be supposed to have developed.

In such action, in its earliest form, there was no thought of duty. We must suppose that when a certain degree of mental maturity had been reached, and a certain amount of attention had been, for whatever reason, focused on acts which had hitherto been done without any thought of their rightness, they came to be recognized, first rather vaguely as *suitable* to the situation, and then, with more urgency, as *called for* by the situation. *Thus* first, as belonging to particular acts in virtue of a particular character they possessed, was rightness recognized. Their rightness was not deduced from any general principle; rather the general principle was later recognized by intuitive induction as being implied in the judgements already passed on particular acts.

[1] Sermon I (Gladstone's ed.), 38–9.

The question may, however, be asked: 'Once the general principles have been reached, are particular acts recognized as right by deduction from general principles, or by direct reflection on the acts as particular acts having a certain character?' Do we, without seeing directly that the particular act is right, read off its rightness from the general principle, or do we directly see its rightness? Either would be a possible account of what happens. But when I reflect on my own attitude towards particular acts, I seem to find that it is not by deduction but by direct insight that I see them to be right, or wrong. I never seem to be in the position of not seeing directly the rightness of a particular act of kindness, for instance, and of having to read this off from a general principle—'all acts of kindness are right, and therefore this must be, though I cannot see its rightness directly'.

It appears to me that we apprehend individual facts by deduction from general principles in two kinds of situation, and in no more. (1) We may have no real insight that the attribute A implies the presence of the attribute B. But we may have accepted on what we believe to be good grounds the *belief* that A always implies B, and we then may say to ourselves, 'This is an instance of A, and therefore it must be an instance of B; I cannot see it for myself to be so, but I think it must be, because of a general principle which I have for good reason accepted'. Or (2) the general principle may be one that is not self-evident, but known as the consequence of a proof; and we may remember the principle while we have forgotten the proof. There again, we shall not see with self-evidence that the particular A is also a B, but we shall read this conclusion off from the remembered general principle 'all A is B'.

Both these situations actually occur in morals. (1) In most people's lives there is a stage at which they accept some moral principle on authority before they have really come to recognize its truth for themselves; and in such a case the rightness or wrongness of the particular act is not apprehended on its own merits but read off from the general principle. The suggestion is indeed sometimes made that we never pass beyond this stage of acceptance of moral principles on authority to a fresh original recognition of them. But the difficulty at once arises, that the reference to authority either lands us in an infinite regress, or leads back to *some one* who recognized the principle for himself. *A* may believe it because *B* said it was true, and *B* because *C* said it was true, but sooner or later we come to some one who believed it on its merits. Further, I think we can by careful introspection distinguish the acceptance of a moral principle on authority from its acceptance on its own merits, as we can distinguish the stage at which we accepted mathematical principles on our teacher's authority from that at which we came to recognize their truth for ourselves. It is probably the case that many people all through their lives remain in the condition of accepting most of their moral principles on authority, but we can hardly fail to recognize in the best and most enlightened of men an absolutely original and direct insight into moral principles, and in many others the power of seeing for themselves the truth of moral principles when these are pointed out to them. There is really no more reason to doubt this than to doubt that there are people who can grasp mathematical principles and proofs for themselves.

(2) The other situation in which we read off the rightness of particular acts from some general principle also arises. The general principle may have been accepted not on authority but on its merits, but it may have involved for its recognition a fairly elaborate consideration of the probable consequences of a certain type of act; this would be true of such a principle as the principle that indiscriminate charity is wrong. In such a case the rightness or wrongness of an individual act falling under such a description is by no means self-evident. It would involve for its recognition a tracing out of the probable consequences, which we in fact do not perform; but we remember the general principle, while we have forgotten, or do not take the time to recollect, the arguments for it; and so we read off the rightness or wrongness of the particular act from it.

Our insight into the basic principles of morality is not of this order. When we consider a particular act as a lie, or as the breaking of a promise, or as a gratuitous infliction of pain, we do not need to, and do not, fall back on a remembered general principle; we see the individual act to be by its very nature wrong.

So far I have considered the type of case in which the thought of a conflict of duties does not occur to us, but we regard an act straight off as right or wrong in view of some obvious character that it has. It must be admitted that in a great part of our lives we think and act so. When we are asked a question, we do not as a rule doubt whether it is our duty to give a true answer. When we have made a promise, we do not as a rule doubt whether we ought to keep it. When we see an opportunity of relieving pain or distress without, so far as we can see, producing any bad ulterior results, we do not doubt whether we ought to do so. Yet in fact all these acts of ours will produce further consequences, and the probability is that any of them will produce some bad consequences. It may be asked whether we are justified in habitually ignoring this possibility. We cannot take Kant's line, that of holding that the act is so right in virtue of being a telling of the truth or a keeping of a promise that no further consequences it has can possibly make it wrong. For apart from the paradoxical consequences that this simple faith leads to, it is clear that the problem of conflict of duties breaks out even among the duties of perfect obligation, which Kant treats as absolute, and even within a single one of these duties. I may, for instance, be unable to keep one promise without breaking another.

Sometimes our simplification of the moral problem by viewing an act only under one category is plainly unjustified. A very little reflection would reveal probable consequences which make the act which we take to be right plainly wrong. Where the simplification *is* justified, it is justified by such considerations as these: An action which presents itself *prima facie* as right in virtue of some character it possesses—say, that of being the keeping of a promise or the relieving of another's pain—starts with reasons in its favour which go beyond what is expressed in describing it as the keeping of a promise or the relieving of another's pain. When we keep a promise we do more than keep faith with another person; we usually do something to strengthen the whole system of mutual confidence on which society is built up. When we break a promise, we do something to weaken this. So, too, when we tell the truth or tell a lie—which are in fact particular instances of keeping or breaking faith with another person.[1] Again, if the immediate and most striking effect of an action is to relieve the pain or improve the character of another person, the argument for doing the act is not exhausted by that; for we know that happiness tends to radiate outwards from any one who is made happy, and goodness to radiate outwards from any one who is helped towards goodness, while pain and badness also tend to spread and radiate from one person to another. Thus an act which presents itself most obviously as conforming to one of the basic principles of morals starts with strong arguments in its favour; and we usually and justifiably suppose that unless some probable bad consequence reveals itself on a fairly brief inspection, the bad consequences are not sufficiently probable, or if sufficiently probable are not sufficiently weighty, to upset the strong *prima facie* argument in its favour.

Not only is it often justifiable to accept the fact that an act falls under one of the basic principles of morality, as sufficient reason for regarding it as right (or wrong) without further consideration. It is often justifiable to accept in the same way the fact that it falls under one of the *media axiomata* of morality. For mankind has for more generations than we can tell been exploring the consequences of certain types of acts and drawing conclusions accordingly about the rightness or wrongness of types of acts, and the *media axiomata* are the crystallized product of the experience and reflection of many generations. Suppose there is a *medium axioma* that actions of type *A* are

[1] Cf. pp. 112–13.

wrong. Then any one who lightly does an act of this type, because he thinks some particular good result is likely to come of it and does not foresee equivalent bad results as likely to come of it, is in effect setting up his own very narrow experience against the experience of countless generations. He is in principle committing the same error as a child does who sets up his own very limited experience and immature judgement against the experience and judgement of older people. In the last resort we must use our own judgement as to what is right and what is wrong; but one of the factors of the situation which should very seriously affect our judgement is the fact that the *orbis terrarum*, although for reasons which may not be entirely clear to us, judges thus or thus about the type of act we propose to do.

It often happens, however, that no course of action presents itself as obviously called for by any basic moral principle or even by any *medium axioma*, or that incompatible actions present themselves as so called for. In such a case there is no escaping from the task of thinking out what it is that we ought to do. This task is one of greater or of less difficulty according to whether, when we come to reflect, some principle of special obligation, such as that of fulfilment of promise, is or is not seen to be involved. The latter is the less difficult case, and with it I will begin. Here the only principle of duty that we see to be applicable is that which bids us set ourselves to produce the greatest good. Our problem, then, is a twofold one: (*a*) to forecast the consequences of alternative actions, and (*b*) to estimate the comparative goodness of these consequences. In considering (*a*) a very strange fact at once presents itself. Generally speaking, no wish to produce a certain remote result leads to action which is effective in producing the result unless it is accompanied by knowledge of or opinion about some means which will effect the result. We do not need to know or have opinions about *all* the causal links that intervene between the means we set ourselves to produce and the final result we wish to produce. When I press the accelerator of my car, I produce the result that my car accelerates, though I may know nothing of the elaborate mechanism that produces this result. I may merely have discovered empirically that pressing the accelerator produces this result, or have learned from authority that it will. But at least, to make the car accelerate, it is not enough to wish or even to try to make it do so; I must set myself to press the accelerator. But at the very beginning of the causative process starting with an act of will quite a different state of affairs presents itself. If the teachings of physiology are correct, movements of members of the body, such as arms, or legs, or tongue, depend on movements of the controlling muscles; these depend on the stimulation of nerves passing from the brain to the muscle, and this in turn on some alteration in the brain. Thus, if the general order which I have stated held good in this case, we could effect a movement in a member only by setting ourselves to effect a certain change in the brain which we know or think will effect a certain change in the member we wish to move. But the fact is that, while any one who studies physiology may come to know this causal sequence, as ordinary moral agents we know nothing of it. If we have enough of a smattering of physiology to know in general that such a sequence exists, we certainly have not the remotest idea *what* sort of change in the brain will produce the wished for movement of the member. Thus we have something happening within the body that never happens outside the body, viz. that we can at will produce a certain result without having any knowledge or even opinion about any of the changes which are necessary preliminaries to this result. So far as our own awareness goes, we skip as it were the intermediate stages, and it seems to ourselves as if the mental effort to move the limb directly produced the movement.

I mention the problem, not because I have any light to throw on its solution, nor because I think it *ethically* important, but because it is interesting in itself and takes us deep into the whole problem of the relation of mind and body.

Whatever be the explanation, we start, then, not indeed with the *knowledge* that the mental effort to move a certain limb will in fact move it (for some lesion in brain or nerve or muscle may prevent this), but with what for practical purposes is generally as good as knowledge. And further, within certain limits of accuracy we may be said to 'know' the *kind* of movement that our effort will produce, that by trying to move an arm forward we shall in fact move it forward and not backward. As regards the further effects of an act of will, on bodies and on minds, we depend on analogical reasoning. We have a good deal, if not of knowledge, at least of highly probable opinion, as to the present condition of many of the bodies in our immediate vicinity and of the minds connected with them. The condition of the things in my environment and the final intra-corporeal effect of my act of will are the joint causes which will determine the first extra-corporeal effect; and using such probable opinion as we have of the condition of the things in our environment, and our experience of what effects similar intra-corporeal changes have had on bodies and minds similarly conditioned in the past (and we have amassed a good deal of such experience before we begin to think morally), we can form fairly probable opinions as to the first extra-corporeal effects of our act of will.

Our knowledge of its later effects is very much less, or rather our opinions about them are much less likely to be right. We can see that in this way. Let us first suppose, merely for the sake of argument, that there is no other agency at work except oneself causing changes in the world, or at least in one's environment. Then we may suppose that an action of ours will affect some of the things (minds and bodies) in our environment, while leaving others approximately unchanged. Let us denote things (substances) by capital letters and their successive states by attached numbers. Then by our action a set of things $A_1 B_1 C_1 D_1 E_1 F_1$ will be so changed as to become a set of things $A_2 B_2 C_2 D_1 E_1 F_1$. Then by the interaction of these things a further state of things will be produced, in which again some of the things will have been changed by their interaction, while others will be approximately unchanged. This state we may denote by $A_3\,B_3\,C_2\,D_2\,E_1\,F_1$. Now we can perhaps anticipate with reasonable accuracy that the immediate result of our action will be to change $A_1\,B_1\,C_1\,D_1\,E_1\,F_1$ into $A_2\,B_2\,C_2'\,D_1\,E_1\,F_1$; but we could foresee that its later result would be to produce the condition of affairs $A_3\,B_3\,C_2\,D_2\,E_1\,F_1$, only if in addition to anticipating the change from $A_1\,B_1\,C_1\,D_1\,E_1\,F_1$ to $A_2\,B_2\,C_2\,D_1\,E_1\,F_1$, we could foresee the further change from this latter state to $A_3\,B_3\,C_2\,D_2\,E_1\,F_1$. If our chance of being right about each change separately is one in two, for example, our chance of being right about the final result of both is much less. And it will diminish as we try to forecast effects further and further from us in time.

But the position is much worse than this in fact. We have simplified the problem immensely by supposing ourselves to be the only active agency at work. In fact, there are many other agencies, bodies and minds, at work altering our environment. We can foresee the first change with some approach to accuracy because the state of things $A_1\,B_1\,C_1\,D_1\,E_1\,F_1$ is already in existence and more or less open to our observation. But we cannot anticipate with certainty that at time 2 the state of affairs will be $A_2\,B_2\,C_2\,D_1\,E_1\,F_1$, as we could if we were the only agency at work and if we could rightly estimate the effect of our agency. By that time other agencies will or may have produced other changes in some or all of the substances in question. People, for instance, who are now alive and whom we may expect to be affected in some way by our action may by that time be dead or at a distance. Thus the difficulty of forecasting the future increases more rapidly than we have above suggested, as the future we try to forecast is a more and more distant future.

In the attempt to forecast the effects of our action, we are not limited entirely to reasoning by analogy from experience. To a very limited extent perhaps even bodily change may be anticipated *a priori*; it seems probable that a few simple laws of dynamics are known *a priori* to be true. But in forecasting effects on minds we can use *a priori* reasoning much more. We can anticipate, even apart from experience, that the announcement of a forthcoming pleasure will itself produce pleasure, and the announcement of a future pain, pain, that the news of some one's success will cause pain to his enemies, that that which is enjoyed while it is possessed will be to some extent missed when it is taken away. We have, I think, far more *a priori* insight into mental causation than into physical. But if many of our major premisses are won by insight and not by experience, the minor premisses which we must fit on to these if we are to draw conclusions about the future must be borrowed from experience. It is only by the help of experience that we can know that A is B's friend or that C is D's enemy, that E has enjoyed experience F in the past and will therefore be glad to be promised the future enjoyment of it, or that G has found experience H painful and will be sorry to hear that he is to have it again. All things considered, the difficulty of forecasting the future is so great that the slenderness of our insight into it is not to be wondered at. It is perhaps more surprising that wise men can often form such shrewd forecasts as they do.

When we turn (*b*) to estimating the *goodness* of the results of alternative actions, further difficulties confront us. These would be great enough even if pleasure were the only good; for not only is it extremely difficult to compare the intensity, and therefore the pleasure-value, of pleasures of very different quality, such as those of pushpin and poetry, to take Bentham's instances; it is extremely difficult to compare with accuracy the pleasure-value even of similar experiences. Yet it seems that in comparing somewhat similar pleasures we often have no difficulty in recognizing that one is more intense than another. And if we pass from a pair of similar pleasures to a pair of less similar pleasures, and so on, there does not seem to be in principle any point at which we should be justified in drawing the line and saying 'up to this point comparison is possible; here it becomes impossible'. Thus in principle it seems to me that all pleasures fall on one scale in respect of intensity and are comparable in respect of it, though when the pleasures are very different in character it is only a very considerable difference in intensity that one can detect.

If we recognize, as I think we should, other goods than pleasure—virtuous emotion and action, and the exercise of intelligence—the difficulty of comparison becomes much greater.

Two views seem to be here possible. It may be held that all these things, including pleasures, are good in the same sense of 'good'. Then the position will be that, just as it is easier to compare two similar pleasures in respect of intensity (and therefore of goodness) than two dissimilar ones, and yet dissimilar pleasures must be in principle comparable, so it is easier to compare two similar activities (e.g. two virtuous actions) in respect of goodness than to compare a virtuous action with an exercise of intelligence or with a pleasure, and yet in principle all three are comparable. If, on the other hand, as I think to be the case, good actions are good in a different sense of 'good' from that in which any pleasures as such are so, then good actions will not be comparable in respect of goodness with pleasures as such. Then, when we try to decide whether we ought to set ourselves to produce some good activity or some pleasure, the two things to be produced will not fall on one scale of goodness, but the two *prima facie* duties will still fall on one scale of obligatoriness and will be comparable thereon.

The choice between these two views must be deferred to the chapter in which the meanings of 'good' will be discussed.[1] Meantime, however, we may discuss the position with regard to any good things which *are* good in the same sense of 'good', as, for instance, two virtuous actions may be properly held to be.

It has been suggested[2] that there are not amounts, but only degrees, of goodness, and that in consequence all that we are entitled to assign to different goods is not cardinal numbers, implying that each good contains a certain number of units of goodness, but only ordinal numbers, implying that the two goods occupy different places on a scale of goodness, or are unequally far removed from the zero-point of indifference.

---

[1] Ch. 11.   [2] By Professor H. H. Price, in *Mind*, xl (1931), 353.

Now such a state of affairs would be all that is needed if we had, in choosing which of two actions we should do, to compare a single good which will be produced by one with a single good which will be produced by the other. But this is not usually the case. Far more often we have to recognize that one or both of the two actions will affect for good or evil more than one person; and in such a case we are bound to attempt some summation of the goods and evils to be effected by each action. Let us for simplicity's sake suppose that only *good* effects are anticipated, and that only three goods are involved, whose order on the scale of goods is *A*, *B*, *C* (*A* being the nearest to zero), and that we have to choose between two actions, one of which will produce one, and the other the other two, of these goods. Then if (as the theory in question supposes) we knew only the order, but had no notion of the amount of goodness in any of the three goods, we should know that it was preferable to produce $A+C$ rather than B, and $B+C$ rather than A, but we should have no notion whether it was better to produce $A+B$ rather than C. Similarly, if four goods were involved whose order on the scale of goods is *A*, *B*, *C*, *D* (*A* being the nearest to zero), and if at least one of the two actions will produce at least two of the goods, then we could (if goods had only ordinal and not cardinal numbers answering to them) in most of the cases[1] decide which action would produce more

---

[1] Viz. (ignoring cases in which the effects of the two actions include an identical good, which may be cancelled out) when the effects of the two actions are to be as follows:

First action	Second action
A	$B+C+D$
A	$B+C$
A	$B+D$
A	$C+D$
B	$A+C+D$
B	$A+C$
B	$A+D$
B	$C+D$
C	$A+B+D$
C	$A+D$
C	$B+D$
$A+B$	$C+D$
$A+C$	$B+D$

good, but we should be quite unable to deal with the cases in which the effects of the two actions were to be as follows:

First action	Second action
C	$A+B$
D	$A+B+C$
D	$A+B$
D	$A+C$
D	$B+C$
$A+D$	$B+C$

Now, in practice we are not conscious of this particular limitation. It certainly sometimes happens that when we think one action will produce one single good and the other a combination of lesser goods, we judge without hesitation, in some cases that the action which produces the single great good is rather to be done than the other, and in other cases that the other is rather to be done than it. I do not suggest that this is always so; it is perfectly clear that very often we should in such a case find it quite impossible to say whether the single good or the combination was to be preferred. But in principle, if we ever are justified in thinking that a certain combination of lesser goods is more worth (or that it is less worth) producing than a single greater good, we must know more about the goods than that they fall in a certain order on the scale of goods.

Nor will it be enough to know the size of the intervals that separate the goods. Suppose we know that $B = A+M$ and that $C = B+N$. Then we know that $A+B = 2A+M$, and that $C = A+M+N$; but we should not know whether A is greater or less than N. We should need to be able to compare the intervals which separate the goods from one another with that which separates the smallest of them from zero. And this seems to me indistinguishable from recognizing each of the goods as containing a certain number of times a certain unit of goodness, i.e. from assigning to them cardinal as well as ordinal numbers.

If, then, we are ever able to say with confidence, comparing one greater good with the sum of a number of smaller ones, that it is more (or that it is less) worth producing than they, it is implied that each of the goods contains a definite number of times some unit of good. There is, of course, no natural unit of good. But we can arbitrarily take some small good and say that the goods we are comparing are twice, five times, &c., as good as it. Or, without having any particular unit of good in mind, we can say 'whatever unit of good be taken, B would be worth twice as many of it as A, C five times as many as A', and so on.

Now in fact we can never speak with as great precision as that. The position is rather this: the most that we can say with confidence is that B is worth not less than m times and not more than n times as much as A, and so on. It is clear that if we have this type of knowledge, then we shall sometimes be able and sometimes be unable to say of good C (for instance) that it is worth more (or less) than $A+B$. Suppose, for instance, that, taking some good G as unit, we can say

$$'A = \text{not less than } 2G \text{ nor more than } 3G$$
$$B = \text{not less than } 3G \text{ nor more than } 4G$$
$$C = \text{not less than } 5G \text{ nor more than } 7G',$$

we shall not be able to say whether C is greater or less than $A+B$. But if we can say 'C = not less than $8G$,' we shall know that in any case it is worth more than $A+B$.

This is, I believe, the kind of position in which we actually find ourselves. We should be justified, I think, in supposing that any good contains a definite amount of goodness, but since we cannot estimate this exactly but only as falling within certain limits, our knowledge is often not enough to enable us to compare one greater with two or more lesser goods. And, of course, the same difficulty often makes it impossible to say whether, of two single goods A and B, A or B is greater or A and B are equal.

The question may at this point be raised, whether such assessment of the goodness of the results of an action (or of the goodness of anything, for that matter) as we can reach is or is not reached by inference. The answer seems to be that it is not. If it were to be reached by inference, it would have to be either from premisses in one of which the term 'good' already occurred, or from premisses in which it did not occur. Now the latter is logically impossible; you cannot import a term into your conclusion which did not occur in one or other premiss. The former is not logically impossible. It would be logically possible that all judgements about the goodness of any particular results were deduced from premisses, of which *one* stated the goodness of a class of things and the *other* brought the individual thing under the class. But while this is logically possible, it seems to me, for reasons similar to those given before, with reference to rightness,[1] not to be true in the case of our appreciation of goodness. If this view be correct, the apprehension of the degree of goodness of particular goods is logically immediate. But, of course, it does not follow that it is psychologically immediate. Goodness is a resultant attribute; it belongs to anything to which it does belong, because of the nature of the thing in some respect or other—because, for instance, it is a brave and not a cowardly act. And while even the vaguest apprehension of the goodness or badness of anything depends on some previous insight into the nature of the thing, an apprehension of the *degree* of its goodness will depend on close study of its nature, upon which the apprehension of the degree of its goodness supervenes, not as a logical conclusion but as a psychological result.

The psychological preliminaries to the judgement on the goodness of the results of an act will, of course, differ according to whether we are judging of an act already done, or of one not yet done. In the former case some of the results have probably already taken place and will be open to observation; but others lie in the future and require an effort of imagination for their envisagement. In the latter case *all* the results can only be apprehended by an effort of imagination. In both cases the

[1] pp. 169-73.

imagination will presuppose reasoning—reasoning to the probable consequences of an act, based upon analogies drawn from previous experience. Thus in no case are the psychological preliminaries at all simple, and the more accurate our judgement of goodness is to be, the more careful must be our observation of achieved results and our imagination of results not yet achieved. It is hardly necessary to dwell on the difficulties of the analogical reasoning of which I have spoken— of the danger, for instance, of supposing that because one act has affected in a certain way the people mainly affected by it, a similar act will affect similarly quite different people.

A special complication is introduced into the judgement of goodness by the well-known principle of organic values, i.e. of values of wholes which are not equal to the sums of the values of their parts. But here the broad principle which I have stated above holds good—that the judgement of the goodness of the whole is logically immediate, but psychologically mediated by a study of the goodness of the parts. Take, for instance, the whole state of things constituted by a vicious act and the pain of the subsequent punishment. Here both elements, taken apart, are bad, but the whole has not a badness equal to the sum of the badnesses of the parts.[1] We cannot, therefore, deduce its value from the values (using 'value' non-committally to cover badness as well as goodness) of its parts. Yet it is only if we envisage clearly the degree of badness of the vicious act and the degree of badness of the pain suffered that we can arrive at any definite view of the value of the whole which they compose.

It is not to be supposed that the existence of organic values vitiates any and every computation of the goodness of the total results of an act by summing the values of its individual results. Where the different effects of an act are effects on different persons, they do not, so far as I can see, coalesce into

---

[1] If the parts are, as I think, bad in two different senses of 'bad' (cf. pp. 271–9), there is, of course, no sum of their badnesses. But even if they are bad in the same sense, the whole has not a badness equal to the sum of the badnesses of the parts, since the fittingness of the punishment to the sin takes away from the badness of the whole.

organic wholes, and it appears therefore to be safe to arrive at the goodness of the total results of an act by summing the goodnesses of the individual results—though, of course, the effects on any one person may form an organic whole whose goodness cannot be assessed by the process of summation.

One further complication remains. It will be remembered that in our consideration of the epistemological questions connected with the judgement of duty, we have so far considered only the duty of producing the maximum good. But there are other duties than this, the duty of fulfilling promises, the duty of making reparation for wrongs we have done, the duty of making a return for good we have received. Where such a special *prima facie* duty exists, as well as the general *prima facie* duty of producing the maximum good, our final judgement about our duty depends not on a comparison of goods but on a comparison of *prima facie* duties. But the same general principle reappears, that the final judgement is not a logical conclusion, but yet is something that presupposes preliminary mental acts, in which we study the situation in detail, till the morally significant features of it become clear to us.

Epistemologically, the position about duties of special obligation seems to me to be this. We all recognize their existence, but in two very important respects our judgements about them differ. (1) To most plain men these present themselves as duties independent of the duty of promoting the general good. To some philosophers they present themselves as merely derivative principles, flowing from the duty of promoting the general good, and ceasing to have any binding force whenever action according to them seems unlikely to promote in fact the general good. But (2) apart from this difference of view about the ground of the obligation to behave in these ways, people probably differ a good deal with regard to the *degree* of obligation which they think to attach to these principles of action. We may consider (*a*) how in this respect people who hold the teleological view will differ from those who hold the intuitionistic view. In general, the former will

probably think that less obligatoriness attaches to the fulfilment
of promises, for example, for they will think it is always outweighed by the obligatoriness of any act which is likely to
increase more the general good; while holders of the intuitional
view will hold that some fulfilments of promise are more obligatory than some actions which are likely to increase more
the general good. This is the general position; but it would be
a mistake to expect that holders of the teleological theory will
always take a laxer view about fulfilment of promise than holders
of the intuitionist view. For teleologists, having to account
somehow for the stubborn general disposition to regard fulfilment of promises as binding, are apt to explain this by referring
to the tendency which breach of promise has to break down
mutual confidence, and, in doing so, they are apt to exaggerate
this tendency; so that a plain man recognizing an independent
duty of fulfilling promises may easily think that *much* more
good might be achieved by doing something else which involves breaking a promise, and that in this case the duty of
promoting the general good outweighs the other, while a teleo-
logist may have persuaded himself that the keeping of the
promise will in fact bring more good into existence than any
other act and that therefore the promise should be kept.

Apart from this difference between the attitude of teleologists and that of intuitionists towards promise-keeping,
there are (*b*) no doubt considerable differences between intuitionists as to the degree of obligatoriness of promise-keeping.
All that Intuitionism implies is the view that the duty of
promise-keeping is independent and *sui generis*; it implies no
particular view about the relative weight of this *prima facie*
obligation compared with others. Within Intuitionism, we can
have at one extreme the view of Kant that duties of perfect
obligation always outweigh those of imperfect obligation.
At the other end we might have people who think the duty of
promise-keeping to be *sui generis* but yet to be one which very
rarely outweighs the duty of promoting the general good.
Thus in a particular case of conflict of duties of these two kinds,

different intuitionists (or different plain men) will give quite different answers. But this casts no doubt on the truth of the intuitionist view. It simply points to the fact that in this region our knowledge is very limited, that while we *know* certain types of act to be *prima facie* obligatory, we have only opinion about the degree of their obligatoriness. An exactly similar situation would reveal itself among teleologists, as soon as they began to face the question of the comparative goodness of different goods. Suppose them to agree that virtuous action, intelligent thought, and pleasure are goods; yet there is certainly no agreement about the *comparative* worth of these things. That casts no doubt on their being goods, and goods with different degrees of objective goodness; it only shows that our knowledge in this field is very limited. And so it is with regard to our knowledge of the relative obligatoriness of different *prima facie* duties.

It would perhaps be appropriate here to take account of an objection recently made to the kind of view I have been trying to state.[1]

'If the most significant kind of morality is creative morality (and whether it is or is not can only be judged by the success of the application of the idea of creativeness to ethical concepts), then the ethics of intuitionism or deontology approaches from the wrong end. If we begin with the consideration of rational general rules we are bound to find out in time that the rules are inadequate to meet all cases and if we modify the theory and speak of "prima facie" duty *versus* "duty proper" or "actual duty", we have still in the end to acknowledge a remainder, the surd of the individuality of the individual. We have to quote Aristotle again and say, "The decision lies with perception". Indeed the *root* of the matter lies with perception, and at the best with a deeply imaginative perception linked to a consciousness of a larger good. This comes first, this is of prime importance, and what is left over, the considerable amount of life that is routine, may be dealt with approximately enough by rules and formulae. I for one, anyhow, believe that we get a fresher view of morality if we look at it from this angle.'

[1] L. A. Reid, *Creative Morality*, 109 f.

This objection, I think, rests on a misconception. If I have understood aright what Professor Reid means by creative morality, it is its aspect of spontaneity, of freedom from routine rules, that he wishes to emphasize. Now Intuitionism, in the form in which I hold it true, does not in any way condemn the moral life to routine. Such a charge might perhaps be brought against Kant's form of Intuitionism, in which it is held that the rightness or wrongness of an individual act can be inferred with certainty from its falling or not falling under a rule capable of being universalized. My criticism of this view is that it unduly simplifies the moral life. It ignores the fact that in many situations there is more than one claim upon our action, that these claims often conflict, and that while we can see with certainty that the claims exist, it becomes a matter of individual and fallible judgement to say which claim is in the circumstances the overriding one. In many such situations, equally good men would form different judgements as to what their duty is. They cannot all be right, but it is often impossible to say which is right; each person must judge according to his own individual sense of the comparative strength of various claims.

The criticism which Intuitionism as I hold it makes upon teleological ethics is that teleological ethics, in a different way from Kant's, over-simplifies the moral life; that it recognizes only one type of claim, the claim that we shall act so as to produce most good, while in fact there are claims arising from other grounds, arising from what we have already done (e.g. from our having made a promise, or inflicted an injury) and not merely from the kind of result our action will have, or may be expected to have. Intuitionism of *this* kind seems to me not to be hostile to creative morality in any sense in which creative morality is a good thing. I suppose that there could be no better instance of creative morality than the case of a man who, going beyond the routine of the duties commonly recognized by those round him, becomes convinced of some new duty and devotes his life to the discharge of it, as for example

Wilberforce did when he devoted his life to the abolition of the slave-trade and of slavery. Creative morality involves not the denial or belittlement of the claims whose existence has long been recognized, but the coming to recognize new ones. If Intuitionism meant that people are to accept as absolute all the claims that are commonly recognized, and never to accept new ones, it would indeed be adverse to creative morality. But it means neither of these things. The general principles which it regards as intuitively seen to be true are very few in number and very general in character. With regard to all *media axiomata*, which are attempts to apply these general principles to particular types of situation, it preserves an open mind. It recognizes that new circumstances sometimes abrogate old claims and sometimes create new ones, and that we must be constantly alive to recognize such changes and to act on them.

So far I have been speaking of the problem of discovering which of the actions open to one would be objectively right, would discharge in the fullest possible measure the various claims or *prima facie* duties that are involved in the situation. This is what we should *like* to know; and it is clear, in view of the various difficulties I have pointed out—the difficulty of comparing the goodness of various results, the difficulty of balancing the duty of producing the greatest good against special obligations—that we can never *know* our duty in this sense, but can only reach more or less probable opinion about it. At the same time the difficulties are not so great as to make the attempt useless. We can by the use of analogical reasoning from experience, and of *a priori* reasoning, forecast with some confidence the nearer consequences of our acts; and in certain cases (as we have seen[1]) there is some reason to suppose that of two acts that which has the better proximate consequences will also have the better remote consequences. And again in comparing goods, and in comparing *prima facie* duties, while we are often in doubt which is the greater good or the more

---

[1] pp. 173-5.

stringent obligation, in other cases, where the one good is *much* the greater or the one obligation *much* the more stringent, we seem to be able to grasp these facts with certainty. The fact that in many individual cases the people whose judgement we have learned most to respect in ethical matters will pronounce the same judgement on acts is some guarantee that objectivity has been attained.

We have, however, in an earlier chapter[1] come to see that besides the objective duty of which we have been speaking, there is a subjective duty; there is an act which we *think* likely to be the maximum fulfilment of objective duty. In our attempt to discover objective duty, whether it succeeds or fails, we can at least discover our subjective duty; for we can come to know what it is that we think. At the same time, there are cases in which we do not even think any one act to be likely to be the completest fulfilment of our *prima facie* duties—in which we are quite doubtful as between two or more acts. But even so we are not completely ignorant; for we at least think that the right act is one of a limited number of acts. In such a case it is our subjective duty, and we know that it is, to do one or other of the acts, of which we think one or other to be our objective duty.

[1] Ch. 7.

IX

THE PSYCHOLOGY OF MORAL ACTION

I PROPOSE next to attempt some discussion of the psychology of moral action, i.e. of any action to which either the epithet good or bad, or the epithet right or wrong, is applicable. For a reason which will appear later,[1] I postpone for the present actions done from a sense of duty. It will, I think, be admitted that, with the possible exception of action from a sense of duty, all moral action is motivated by the desire of an end. Every student is familiar with Aristotle's account of action as either being, or (as I think he would rather have said) being immediately preceded by, choice of certain means, which by deliberation have come to be thought of as the means most likely to achieve a pre-desired end;[2] and his account is pretty generally accepted. Nevertheless it needs reconsideration. To begin with, it is evident that not every desire of an end sets up a process of deliberation which in turn leads to the choice of means to that end. We have many idle desires which arise in us, and may remain as part of the colouring of our mental life, but never lead to deliberation, still less to action. There are careers, for instance, which one is attracted by, but nothing more; one realizes the attractions, in certain respects, of being Prime Minister or Lord Chancellor, or an England cricketer or a champion golfer, but of all those who are attracted, momentarily or even permanently, by such objects, few do anything about it, even to the extent of deliberating how they could be attained. It would seem that, to be effective as a determinant of deliberate action, an end must not merely be desired, but be chosen.

The difference between deliberate and impulsive action seems to be this, that impulsive action follows directly upon a desire, or upon the strongest of two or more conflicting desires,

[1] p. 205. [2] *Eth. Nic.* 1111 b 4–1113 a 14, 1139 a 33–b 13.

whereas in the case of deliberate action a choice intervenes between desire and action. This choice or decision is itself a conation, an activity not of intellect but of will; but it is often preceded by a decision in another sense, an intellectual activity of judging that something is the case. With regard to this intellectual activity two questions arise: (1) whether it is a necessary preliminary to choice, and (2) what it is that is judged to be the case. With regard to the first question, I can neither see *a priori* that such an intellectual decision is necessary, nor be sure by introspection that it always happens. It seems to me possible that there is a semi-impulsive form of action, which is preceded by a choice but not by an intellectual decision. With regard to the second question, two possibilities suggest themselves—(*a*) that we judge one desire to be the strongest, and (*b*) that we judge one end to be the most attractive. So far as I can make out by introspection, the latter is the judgement that we actually form. Our attention seems to be directed not to the comparative strength of our desires, but to the nature of their objects. It may be *because* the desire for A is stronger than the desire for B that we judge A to be more attractive than B, but what we actually judge seems to be that A is the more attractive.

It seems to me further that the attractiveness which we ascribe to ends may be ascribed to them on different grounds. One imagined state of affairs may be thought attractive because it will be a state of pleasure for ourselves; another because it will be a state of pleasure for some one else in whom we are interested; another because it will be a state that we think good in itself. There seems to be no foundation in fact for the view that what attracts us, and what is judged to be attractive, must be an imagined state of oneself, still less for the view that it must be a state of oneself *qua* pleasant.

If the one decision is an intellectual and the other a conative act, we must not for a moment suppose that there are two entities within us, an intelligence and a will, functioning side by side and independently. We should not choose or decide on the end if we had not made previous judgements about its nature. We should not decide that it is more worth pursuing than any alternative if we did not start with certain conative tendencies, a tendency in one man, for instance, to a life of effort and in another to a life of ease, in one man to selfish and in another to unselfish activity. Intelligence and will act and react on one another, or rather, since even to say this is to reify them too much, the whole man, in virtue of certain judgements which he has made and certain desiderative tendencies which he has, both judges that a certain end is the most worth pursuing, and decides to pursue it.

We have already seen that to desire is not to choose; we must further realize that to desire an end more than its alternatives is not to choose it. A man may in fact be desiring an end more than any alternative, but he cannot be said to choose it until he performs a perfectly specific new kind of mental act, which can by introspection be distinguished from any sort of desire.

This act may equally well be called an act of decision. Any decision is in fact, even if the word 'decision' does not bring out this aspect of it as distinctly as the word 'choice', a choice of one thing in preference to all others. The others may be clearly conceived, or they may be very vaguely conceived. In either case preferential choice—of a rather than b or c, or of a rather than anything else—is involved.

It is clear that the mere desire of an end does not necessarily set in train a process of deliberation that leads up to action. Yet it would be wrong to say that an end must be *chosen* before the process of deliberation on means can be begun. To set up such a process, a strong attraction towards an end, which yet does not lead immediately to the choice of the end against all alternatives, is enough. Any fairly strong attraction, provided there is not some counter-attraction which is both stronger and recognized to be incompatible with it, may set up two processes of thought—(1) a process of thinking out more in detail what the end in question involves as part of its essence or of its

necessary or probable consequences, and (2) a process of thinking out the steps necessary for its attainment. If one feels
attracted by the idea of being Prime Minister, one naturally
sets oneself to think on the one hand of the attractive and the
unattractive features of the position itself, the enormous power
and prestige balanced by the incessant toil and the crushing
responsibility, and on the other hand of the long, toilsome, and
often tedious course of action necessary for the attainment of
the position. And either of these trains of thought may lead to
the desired end *not* becoming a chosen end; we say 'that object
is attractive when considered abstractly but not when considered in detail', or again 'it is highly attractive in itself but
it + the steps necessary for the attaining of it form a whole
which is unattractive, or less attractive than some more modest
career'. Let us suppose, however, that the desired end survives
these objections, and becomes our chosen end. Then we continue no further the one train of thought, the thought about the
detailed nature and consequences of the end. We know that
by further reflection we could learn more about them, but
we think this unnecessary; we think we know enough about
them to know that this end is more worth pursuing than
any alternative—though of course features of the end that
come to our notice may later make us change our minds. For
the present we have made a definite choice of the end as
our end.

So far, it looks as if we should have to give up Aristotle's
doctrine, that choice is not of ends but only of means. It looks,
so far, as if we ought to recognize the existence of choice of
an end (to be followed usually by another choice, which is the
choice of certain means to it). But we must consider more
closely what it is that we choose. To the word 'choose' we
may append as object either a noun, or an infinitive preceded by
'to'; and we see more clearly what it is that we choose if we
concentrate on the latter form. That this is justified becomes
obvious if we reflect that we have admitted choice to be identical with decision; for with 'decide' we can only use the 'to'

form or what is in principle identical with it, the form 'to decide on' a certain course of action.

What then is it that we choose or decide to do? It is not to desire an end. That we must already be doing, for choice to take place. Not, again, to go on desiring an end which we desire already. Not, again, to *have* or *possess* a certain end, since that depends on circumstances beyond our control. What we choose or decide is to *seek* a certain end, i.e. to take whatever steps are expedient to the attaining of the end. To choose is to choose to take means to an end. And the distinction between this choice and the choice which follows is not that the one is a choice of end and the other a choice of means, but that the one is a choice to take *whatever* means are expedient to the attainment of an end, and the other is a choice to take *certain* means which we have come to think of as the means expedient to the end. It is only if we think of choice as a certain kind of desire that we shall feel tempted to relate the first choice to the end rather than to the means. But choice is by introspection seen to be a completely different activity from desire of any kind.

A certain amount of deliberation as to particular means has probably taken place before the choice 'to take the means to a certain end'. For a wise man, at any rate, will not choose so unless he has satisfied himself that the unpleasantness or the unworthiness of the means does not make the end an end not worth pursuing at the price. But it is enough at this stage to have assured oneself that there *are* means such that the end is worth aiming at by the use of them. The agent may have assured himself of so much, without having assured himself that he has thought of the *best* means to the end. Thus after the first choice, the next step is a further deliberation, in which the problem he is trying to solve is not, as before, what end he is to take the means to, but what means he is to take to the end he has already decided to pursue.

Aristotle, perhaps only for purposes of exposition, describes this process very simply. He speaks as if we worked, in thought, steadily back from the distant end to be achieved to the means to be taken here and now, step by step, never retracing our steps. What he suggests is this: that we see that the means on which the end A would immediately follow is B; that the means on which B would immediately follow is C; and so on till we see that means Y can be achieved by means Z, which is immediately in our power. Really the process is much more complex. There may be several means which would directly produce end A. If we proceeded in the purely linear fashion, we should decide upon one of these means, presumably in virtue of two considerations—which of them would most probably secure end A, and which of them, if it secured it at all, would secure it in the fullest measure. Means B_1 would be preferred to means B_2, B_3, &c., as the result of a joint consideration of these two points. If, for instance, the probability of B_1's securing A were $\frac{1}{2}$ and that of B_2's securing A were $\frac{1}{3}$, but B_2 if it secured A at all would secure it in a certain degree d, while B_1 if it secured A would secure it in a certain degree $\frac{d}{2}$, then the choiceworthiness of B_1 would be $\frac{d}{4}$ and that of B_2 $\frac{d}{3}$. If we thought this, we should probably forthwith decide on B_2 as the means to A to be adopted in preference to B_1, and our sole concern henceforth would be with the means to be adopted as means to B_2.

These two considerations do undoubtedly come into our choice of means. But other considerations come in to complicate the choice, and to prevent us from proceeding in the purely linear way, from distant end to distant means, to less distant means . . . to immediate means. In the first place, though B_2 is preferable to all its alternatives in respect of the two considerations named above, there may be features about B_2, e.g. its painfulness to us, or its painfulness to other people, which may make us decide that means B_1 or B_3 is rather to be chosen, even if it be a less effective means to A. Secondly, even if B_2 survived this consideration, a wise man would not choose B_2 unless he had satisfied himself that B_2 can really be reached by means which it is in his power to effect here and now. Thus he must perform the whole process of deliberation in a tentative way, right down to the means to be adopted here and now, before he can properly decide on any of the distant means. And finally, even if he has satisfied himself that he could bring B_2 into being, he will not decide on B_2 unless he has assured himself that there are means by which it could be brought into being, which are not in themselves so repugnant as to make it better to adopt means to B_1 or B_3. Thus, instead of proceeding in linear fashion from distant to near means, we have to run over the whole series (and indeed many times), judging of means at each stage (1) in view of the likelihood of their leading to A, (2) in view of the degree of A which they will lead to, if they lead to it at all, (3) in view of their own attractiveness, (4) in view of the probability of their realization, and (5) in view of the attractiveness of the means by which they can be realized. And what we choose in the end is a line of action which in view of all these considerations applied to each of its stages is judged to be the best.

On this choice there supervenes a mental activity of quite a different type—the activity of setting oneself to bring about the change which is the chosen immediate means to the attainment of the chosen end. The distinctness of the two activities is often obscured by the fact that the second follows immediately on the first. When little time elapses between the arising of the situation and the time at which action must be taken if it is to be taken effectively, exertion follows on choice so rapidly that the difference may escape a hasty introspection. And the difference is also obscured by the fact that we tend to speak of both kinds of activity under the colourless name 'acts of will'. Let us drop the colourless and indefinite phrase and ask ourselves whether we cannot by introspection distinguish the act of setting oneself to bring about a change, as entirely different from the choosing or deciding to bring it about. Not only does introspection show them to be quite different in character, but a considerable time may elapse between the one and the other; for a decision may be a decision to do something a minute, an hour, a day, a year, indeed any length of time later, or may be a decision to do it 'sometime', while a 'setting oneself' is a setting oneself to bring about a change forthwith.

The train of means which we choose as the best way of attaining the chosen end may be of either of two kinds. In the simpler kind, it is only in the bringing into being of the first link in the chain that our own activity is involved. We launch a single action, as it were, into the world, and trust to external circumstances to do the rest. Of this type of case psychology has, of course, nothing more to say. But more often further action on the part of the agent will be needed if his chosen means are in fact to lead to the chosen end. In the normal case, there will be a series of self-exertions which will reproduce in reverse order the series of choices which worked back from the end to the means to be adopted here and now. But in fact the normal series of actions contemplated by Aristotle often fails to take place. We have already seen that the process of deliberation does not proceed smoothly in one line from end to means, but that a choice of end is only provisional until there has been some consideration of means as well, and that the scale of end and means may be run up and down many times before either end or means is finally chosen. There is, however, another fact which makes our actual deliberation often depart still more widely from the Aristotelian model. Aristotle speaks as if desire for an end were the only possible starting-point of deliberation. But we are perfectly familiar with cases in which deliberation starts at the other end, by some action being suggested to us, and by our going on to consider what effects it is likely to produce. There are countless cases in which we are advised, requested, begged, or commanded to do some action, or it is hinted to us that we might, or we are asked whether we are going to do it. In all these cases the thought of the immediate action is in our minds before any thought of a distant end; the stimulus to deliberation comes from the opposite end to that contemplated by Aristotle. And apart from these very obvious cases of suggestion by another person, it constantly happens that something in our environment suggests to us the doing of some action here and now, and deliberation takes, not the Aristotelian form of asking what means will produce such-and-such an end, but that of asking what effects such-and-such an action will have.

Human beings might be divided into two types—what may perhaps be called the planning type and the suggestible type—according as the train of thought leading up to their choice of action habitually starts from the thought of an end and works back to means, or starts with the thought of an action suggested by the circumstances, and goes on to consider with more or less thoroughness its probable consequences. I do not suggest that these types are cut off from one another with a hatchet. Every one sometimes reasons in the one and sometimes in the other way; but some people *tend* to reason in the one and some in the other way. We have, on the one hand, the people with more or less settled purposes in life, who scrutinize possible lines of action, in all important matters at least, as lines of action tending to conduce to or to be unfavourable to the attainment of their purposes. We have, on the other hand, those who live more from day to day, acting more or less on the suggestion of the moment and as a rule not thinking out to the end the probable bearing of their actions on any ultimate purpose. The distinction is, of course, by no means the same as that between good men and bad men. The purposes of the first type may be mean and selfish, no less than in other cases they are high and unselfish; and the impulses of the second type may be generous or they may be low and narrow. It is rather the distinction between strength and weakness of character than between goodness and badness. It may safely be said that the men who make history, for good or for evil—great statesmen, for instance, and great soldiers—are men who by fixity of purpose correspond to the first type, and that the great mass of mankind corresponds to the second.

As a result of this to-and-fro movement of thought, partly working from desired ends to the means most likely to secure them, partly working from suggested actions to their probable effects, a decision is usually arrived at. Not always; for an indecisive mind, or any mind when faced with a situation of special difficulty, may prolong the time of deliberation till some more urgent problem supersedes the original problem. But suppose that a decision is taken. The circumstances may be such that the corresponding action, if it is to be done at all, must be done at once; and then the decision is immediately followed by the act decided on. Or they may be such that an interval should be allowed to elapse before the action is initiated. Or again, they may be such that, so far as we can see, it makes no difference whether the first practical step be taken at once or after some time. It is an interesting question whether, in the two latter cases, a renewed decision has to be taken before the act of 'setting oneself' can be done, or whether the momentum of the original decision is enough, as it were, to carry us on to the first practical step. This is a question to be decided by introspection, and I am not certain what the answer is. But so far as I can judge from observing the working of my own mind, I am inclined to think that the momentum of an original decision will only carry over a very short interval. Suppose, for instance, that I waken at seven, and decide to get up in half an hour. I find that at the end of the half hour I do not automatically set myself to get up, but have to renew my decision.

Whether a renewed decision is always necessary or not, it seems that it is usually desirable; for between the original decision and the time for action the circumstances may have so changed as to make the action decided on no longer the rational one to take, with a view to gaining one's end. Not that the original deliberation need all be performed over again; it may be enough to ask whether the circumstances have so changed. If we think they have not, the original decision should simply be renewed. If we think they have, the hard mental work of deliberation will not have, as a rule, to be done all over again; for usually the situation will not have been revolutionized but only changed in some details. *Some* probable consequences of any of the alternative actions will remain unchanged, and it will only be necessary to consider those that *are* changed.

Special interest attaches to the case in which it does not appear to matter when, within certain limits of time, the action decided on is to be taken. To reach the conclusion that it does not matter, we must satisfy ourselves of two things: (1) that, if the relevant circumstances do not change unexpectedly, an action done at any time within the limits is as likely as an action done at any other time within the same limits to produce a certain set of results, and (2) that the relevant circumstances are very unlikely to change unexpectedly, or that if they do change, they are not likely to change in such a way as to make any other action more effective. It is, of course, very hard to assure oneself on the latter point, and if we make this assumption, it must be in the main because we have to admit our almost total ignorance of whether the relevant circumstances are likely to change, and if so, how. When we are in such a state of ignorance, the assumption is a reasonable one to make. Why, then, does common sense prefer the man who 'does it now'? By not doing it now, we run the risk that the circumstances may change so that the action decided on will become impossible or less effective, and we shall be left only with a choice between actions less effective than it would have been; but it is equally possible that the circumstances may change so as to make possible some other action *more* effective than it. This possibility also is recognized by common sense in the maxim 'don't cross your bridges till you come to them'. If common sense on the whole prefers the man who carries out his resolutions speedily, that is to be justified on two grounds: (*a*) that if you put off action till near the end of the time available, unforeseen accidents may make it impossible for you within the time limit to carry out your policy of action, or to carry it out with the proper amount of care at each stage, and (*b*) that action which is resolved upon with some enthusiasm, when its linkage with the ends you desire is clearly recognized, is apt to become less attractive when that linkage has receded into the background of memory and the disagreeable features of the action have come into the foreground of attention; so that there is a danger that it may not be done at all if it is put off too long.

I have tried to give an account of the process leading up to and including a fully deliberate act, the kind of act which we are usually thinking of when we speak either of the rightness or of the moral goodness of acts. We have seen that in this process there is involved not only the activity of setting oneself to bring about some change, but the previous activity of resolving so to set oneself. Moral philosophy usually speaks as if it were the former alone that is the subject of moral judgements; but it is surely clear that resolutions also are manifestations of moral character, that they, no less than acts, can be morally good or bad. It seems to me also that they, no less than acts, can be right or wrong, obligatory or the reverse. But this is much less clear than it is that they can be morally good or bad. The view that they are right or wrong might be attacked on either or both of two grounds. (1) It might be said 'what matters is that we should set ourselves to *do* certain things. Now, we can set ourselves to do things without having previously resolved to do so, and if so we shall have done our whole duty. The previous resolution, even if it is a manifestation of good character, is superfluous and no part of our duty.' We have, then, to examine whether it is possible to 'set oneself' without previous resolution, and even without previous deliberation, without which I take resolution to be impossible. There is no doubt that this can happen. If some one asks us a question, for instance, we usually reply truly, without deliberating whether we shall, or resolving to do so. The momentum, as it were, of our character and habits carries us straight into the right act. Yet there remain two classes of cases in which previous deliberation and resolution seem to be included in our duty. The one is that class of case in which various *prima facie* obligations conflict, so that it is not at all clear what our duty is, and only careful deliberation will reveal this. He would be a foolish man who trusted to the inspiration of the moment to yield the right action in such cases as these. The other is the class of cases in which, while our duty is clear enough, we have a strong inclination to do something else. A man may, for instance, have a strong ingrained habit of telling the truth when his own interests are not involved; but this habit cannot be trusted to carry him straight to the telling of the truth when he stands to lose personally by doing so. In both these types of case the right action is in fact usually preceded by deliberation and resolution, and there can be no guarantee that it would be done if they were dispensed with.

(2) The other objection that can be made is this: 'Even if resolution is in such cases necessary as a condition of the right action, why resolve *now* to do my duty to-morrow, or next week, or next year? Why not leave the resolution till just before the time comes for the action?' The answer to this is that if we do not now put ourselves into the state of mind called intention (and resolving is just putting ourselves into this state), we shall be very likely to do meantime, on the suggestion of the moment, or in pursuit of other aims, things which will prevent us from doing, when the time comes, what it would be our duty to do if we could. Take, for instance, a debt which I ought to pay, but am under no obligation to pay till next year. If I do not now resolve to pay, and thus keep the duty of payment before my mind, I may easily be led into expenditure which will make it impossible to pay when the time comes. Or again, it is a man's duty to choose a career some time before the occasion arises for taking the first practical step in pursuit of it, because if he does not, he will very likely be led into actions which will make it impossible to pursue the career which but for them it would have been his duty to pursue.

The duty of resolving, then, seems to arise when either what is our duty is not perfectly clear, or there are desires which militate against the doing of it; and in either case it is a duty arising from the primary duty of *acting* in a certain way.

When I said, at the beginning of this chapter, that all moral action is motived by desire, I admitted one possible exception, viz. action from a sense of duty. Kant said that action from a sense of duty is not motived by desire at all—that its only preconditions are the knowledge that a certain act is one's duty, and the emotion of respect which that thought arouses in us. I do not think we can say *a priori* that this is impossible. It would seem *a priori* possible that an emotion may serve as the precondition of action, no less than a desire. But whether Kant was right or wrong in his view, it seems clear that his reasons for holding it were insufficient. He held it because he assumed that desire belongs altogether to a lower stratum of our nature than reason, a purely animal stratum to which no worth can attach. This complete degradation of desire is not justified. It is clear that, quite apart from a desire to do our duty, we have many desires which we could not have if we were not rational beings. Take, for instance, the desire to understand. It would be absurd to say that this belongs to the purely animal part of our nature. On the contrary, it springs directly from our possession of reason; and if it has developed continuously out of animal curiosity, I would rather say that animals, if they have curiosity, must have some spark of reason, than that curiosity must be irrational because animals can have it. And there are many other desires—the desire, for instance, to follow a certain career or occupy a certain position—which we should never feel unless reason had been at work, apprehending the nature of human relationships and the consequent desirability of such a career or such a position. We are, in fact, not limited in our choice to Hume's view of reason as the slave of the desires and Kant's view of it as their inveterate foe; many of our desires owe their very being to our possession of reason.

Kant's distrust of desire leads him to hold that all actions springing from desire are quite lacking in moral value—that an action done from kindness or love, unaccompanied by the sense of duty, is worth no more than the most selfish or the most cruel action. We can agree with him in thinking that the sense of duty is the highest motive, without following him in putting all other motives on the same dead level. Kant simplifies the moral life too much in making it a contest between one element which alone has worth and a multitude of others which have none; the truth rather is that it is a struggle between a multiplicity of desires having various degrees of worth.

If it be granted that we have desires that spring from our possession of reason, it is only natural that there should arise a desire, itself springing from our rational apprehension of principles of duty, not to be the slave of lower desires but to regulate our life by these principles. To say that conscientious action springs from such a desire, the desire to do one's duty, is in no way to degrade conscientious action, as Kant thought it would be. And in fact, when I ask myself why I do my duty (*when* I do it, and do it conscientiously), the truest answer I can find is that I do it because, then at least, I desire to do my duty more than I desire anything else.

The question now arises, whether conscientious action can, like other deliberate action, be described as the adoption of means to an end. An answer which naturally suggests itself is the following: 'From one point of view, conscientious action is not the adoption of means to an end; for in so far as one's object is to do one's duty, this is something that is already achieved in the immediate act of self-exertion. The doing of one's duty may, indeed, be described as an object of desire, but not as a desired *end*, in so far as speaking of an end implies that the end is something to be achieved by the use of means. Yet this is not the whole truth, as we may see by considering some particular conscientious act. Suppose that someone conscientiously sets himself to relieve another person's pain; his desire to do his duty will be satisfied by his exerting himself in the way that seems to him best for the purpose, but he will not be *completely* satisfied unless the means adopted actually secures the relief of the other's suffering. He has two

desires, the desire to do his duty, which is, of course, satisfied
by his doing his duty (i.e. by his exerting himself in what
seems the best way of helping the other man), and the desire
to achieve the relief of a suffering person, which will be satisfied only if the means adopted turn out effective.'

This is, however, not the true account of a *purely* conscientious act, i.e. of one in which the only effective motive is
the desire to do one's duty; it is an account of an act in which
there co-operates with this desire an independent desire,
springing from natural kindliness, to relieve the other man's
distress. In a purely conscientious act (and in using the word
'purely' I do not mean to suggest that such an act is superior to
one springing from the combination of the two motives, but
only to call attention to the singleness of the motive[1]), there is
no wish to promote the relief of another man's suffering, independent of the thought that it is one's duty to do so. Suppose
the agent has decided that the greatest claim on him in a given
situation is the claim of a sick man to his help. Then he has
but one primary desire, the desire to do an act of self-exertion
which will result in relief to the sick man, as being the doing of
his duty. And this desire will not be satisfied unless his action
has the effect in question. What he desires primarily is to do
his objective duty. But, knowing the difficulty of knowing
what act will be the doing of his objective duty, i.e. will produce the effect in question, he has also a secondary desire,
the desire to do his subjective duty, i.e. the act which he *thinks*
to be his objective duty. And he can derive some satisfaction
from the doing of this even if his primary desire fails to be
satisfied.

Thus conscientious action *is* the adopting of means to an
end—not, however, because the end is desired, but because the
self-exertion which will bring about the end is desired, as being
the doing of one's duty.

[1] Cf. p. 305.

X

INDETERMINACY AND INDETERMINISM

NO discussion of fundamental questions of ethics would be complete without some discussion of the problem of free will; and I must therefore say something about the subject, even if I do not feel that I have anything very new to contribute. One can at least attempt some survey of the present position of the problem. The problem has been once more brought to the front by the appearance among physicists of the doctrine known as that of indeterminacy, which might at first sight appear to offer an analogy in physics to what libertarians claim to exist in moral action. I have been helped by studying the symposium on the subject in an extra volume of the Aristotelian Society's Proceedings.[1] Professor Broad opens the discussion, and starts, after a few preliminaries, by considering the *a priori* argument for determinism, which he rightly treats as far the most important. His main contention is that determinism is not *self*-evident, but follows only from a certain view of the universe which itself when closely examined turns out not to be self-evident. He urges that if a determinist were asked why he feels sure of the truth of determinism, his answer would be, 'If everything else in the world up to a certain date had been exactly as it in fact was, and yet the subject *S* had then been in a different state from that in which it actually was, *S* would have had to have a different inner nature from that which it in fact had. But anything that had had a different inner nature from *S* would not have been *S* but a substance of a different kind and therefore a different substance.' Here the second premiss raises difficult questions; it might be suggested, for instance, that *S* might have had an inner nature different in some respects from that which it had, without necessarily losing its self-identity. And to set this possibility aside we

[1] *Indeterminism, Formalism, and Value*, 135-96.

should have to examine what we mean by the inner nature of a substance, much in the manner in which Professor Broad proceeds to do so. But it is surely clear that the determinist does not need this second premiss. His first premiss is 'if everything else had been the same and yet *S* had been in a different state from that in which it was, *S* would have had to have a different nature from that which it had'. Professor Broad makes the determinist go on to supply as his second premiss 'but *S could not have had* a different nature'. But it is obviously enough for him to say 'but *S had not* a different nature from that which it had', without raising the question whether it *could* or could not have had it. From the new premiss +the first it will equally well follow that, everything else being as it was, *S* could not have been in a different state from that in which it was. The determinist is in fact saying that the question whether *S* is at a certain moment to be in one state or in another must depend on *something*, and that if it does not depend on anything else in the universe (as *ex hypothesi* it does not, since everything else is supposed to be the same), it *must* depend on something in *S*. And this is surely as self-evident as anything could be.

I think, therefore, that Professor Broad's analysis of the inner nature of a substance is unnecessary for the discussion of determinism. At the same time, it will be only fair to follow his exposition in detail; and I do not question the value, in its own place, of his analysis. It may be summarized as follows:

'To ascribe a property to a subject is to assert that its states are connected with its previous states and relations by a causal formula. A property of the first order is a causal formula in which none of the variables are themselves properties, but all are simple attributes like, say, greenness. Instances of first-order properties are the magnetic property, the properties of a solid, the properties of a liquid, the properties of a gas. Now any given subject may change in respect of any such first-order property; e.g. it may pass from the liquid to the gaseous state. But if so, there will be a second-order property which is the property of changing in respect of a certain first-order property under certain conditions. Thus it is a second-order property of water to lose the property of liquidity and acquire that of gaseousness at a certain temperature under any given pressure. There may be a third-order property which is the property of losing one second-order property and acquiring another under certain conditions, and there may be properties of still higher order. But there must be some *ultimate* property of the nth order which determines changes in respect of properties of the $(n-1)$th order, which property in turn determines changes in respect of properties of the $(n-2)$th order, and so on, so that in the long run all changes the substance undergoes are determined by one of its ultimate properties. This ultimate property is, or these ultimate properties are, its inner nature, in accordance with which all its changes must take place.'

The determinist assumption is next formulated, as follows:

'(i) Every substance has a set of ultimate properties, each of which is of finite order.

'(ii) No substance can change in respect of any of its ultimate properties.

'(iii) Any substance whose ultimate properties had differed in any respect from those which S in fact has would necessarily have been a different substance from S.

'(iv) The value of any variable property of a substance at any moment is inferrible from one or more of its higher-order properties by substituting in the latter the determinate values of its states and relations immediately before that moment.

'(v) The state of a substance at any moment with respect to any characteristic which is not a property is inferrible from its first-order properties at that moment by inserting in one or more of them the determinate values of its states and relations immediately before that moment.'[1]

From this complex assumption Professor Broad rightly says that determinism follows at once. But he thinks that certain parts of the assumption are not certainly true. On the first three propositions he comments that they are involved in the notion of substance, but that it is doubtful whether there are

[1] Ibid. 144.

substances, and whether, if so, all events must be states of substances. Now to me, in spite of the very great difficulties involved in thinking out the nature of substance, it seems self-evident that there must be substances, and that all events must happen in or to substances. And I think that if empirical evidence were needed of the existence of substances, i.e. of beings which undergo change and yet retain their self-identity through it, we have the clearest evidence of it in the facts of self-consciousness, and particularly of memory, in which we certainly seem to have direct awareness that that which re-members is one and the same being that had the experience which it remembers. But the difficulties in thinking out the notion of substance are certainly sufficiently great to raise in many minds an honest doubt whether there are or ever could be substances, and whether the world is not to be interpreted solely in terms of qualities, relations, and events. I would therefore prefer not to rest the principle of determinism on the belief in substances. But I may remark in passing that if a case could be made out for libertarianism by criticizing the notion of substance, the gain for the theory of morals would be one that would not be worth having at the price it would cost, the price of forgoing any belief in a permanent self-identical self.

On the fifth proposition Professor Broad says that it does not seem to him self-evident that a substance must have so many first-order properties as to determine its states at any moment down to the last degree of determinateness. He thinks it possible that its first-order properties might suffice only to confine its states, with respect to various characteristics, within narrow limits, leaving free play within these limits. And he makes a similar remark about proposition (iv). Let us see what this suggestion implies. It means that, all the properties, states, and relations of a substance being what they are (and in saying 'all its relations being what they are', we imply 'all things else in the universe, in so far as they can influence the object, being what they are'), any one of several different states can yet indifferently come into being in the subject. And this is to say that whatever state does emerge, its taking the *precise* form that it does is accounted for by nothing whatever in the whole preceding state of the universe. To say this is to imply the existence of causation as regards the broad features of any state of affairs, and to deny it about the details; and for this I can see no justification whatever. It would be more rational to go the whole way with Hume and say that 'all events are entirely loose and separate', one state of the universe, or rather one set of simultaneous states of the various things that are, succeeding another without being in any way determined by it. Our conviction that things cannot be as Professor Broad suggests they are, seems to me not to depend on the assumption of the existence of substances, but to be equally clear if we try to think of mere events coming into existence, determined as to their general nature but undetermined as to their precise form. Professor Broad's analysis surely only leads us back to the original question, which is the question whether we are or are not certain that there must be *something* to account for each event's happening precisely as it does.

If our conviction of the law of causation rested on *a posteriori* evidence, such a half-hearted belief in causation might be justified. For it cannot be claimed that our powers of observation and measurement are such that we could ever on the ground of *experience* assert complete determinism. We can measure only down to the degree of accuracy of our measuring instruments, including our eyes. We do not know the *precise* determinate value of the variables either in the earlier or in the later of two states of the universe, or of two states of a single substance, and as far as observation goes two antecedent states might be exactly alike and the two subsequent states slightly different, or two antecedent states slightly different and the subsequent states exactly alike. All that experience can enable us to do is to correlate limitation within certain limits in the antecedent state with limitation within certain limits in the subsequent. Now I venture to think that were it not that some recent physical observations have suggested to some observers that precise determination in the antecedent state is consistent with slight variations in the subsequent state, no philosopher would have suggested indeterminism, at any rate as regards physical events, as a possibly true view. But it is surely clear that empirical evidence can never establish indeterminism, any more than it can establish determinism. The most that observation can justify a man of science in saying is, 'I find here a variation in respect of a certain characteristic, which I cannot correlate with any variation in the antecedent state of the universe which is at all likely to be relevant to it'. He can never be in a position to say '*there is* no corresponding variation in the antecedent state'; he can only say, 'I cannot observe any'. Now while empirical evidence could never prove the truth of determinism, it has gone a very long way to confirm its truth, which I believe we know independently of such evidence. The whole progress of science has depended on the assumption that the *precise* form of every event has a *precise* cause to account for it, and the history of science has provided a series of triumphant vindications of this assumption. Over and over again, where common sense sees no variation in the antecedent to account for a variation in the consequent, science by more careful measurement and stricter reasoning has discovered such a variation to exist. At present physics has reached a point at which in regard to certain phenomena it cannot detect such a variation. But to sit down before this defeat and say 'no variation existed; the event just happened so, without cause', is to be untrue to the whole history of science, to give up because of a temporary defeat a principle which has everywhere else carried it to victory.

I have just described the belief in the law of causation as having been often vindicated by experience; but such an expression needs careful qualification. Strictly speaking, neither the law of causation nor its denial can be confirmed by experience. This follows from the nature of the law. The law may be formulated in various ways, which in principle come to the same thing. One way, which will serve as well as another, is to say, 'for every variation between two events, there must be some variation between the antecedent circumstances, without which the variation between the events would not have existed'. This cannot be proved by experience, because no set of experiences could claim to have covered all past events, let alone those that are still in the future. Nor can it be disproved by experience, because all that can be said on the basis of experience is 'no variation has been observed', not 'no variation existed'. Not only the law of causation, but any law of the form 'for any A there is always a B', when the number of A's is infinite, is incapable of being proved by experience. But furthermore, the law of causation cannot even, strictly speaking, be confirmed or even partly confirmed by experience. For the law says not merely 'wherever there is a variation in the events, there is a variation in the previous conditions', but 'wherever there is a variation in the events, there *must be* a variation in the conditions *without which the variation in the events could not have existed*'; and experience, even where it verifies the existence of a variation in the previous conditions, can never assure us that without it the variation in the events could not have taken place. In other words, while experience can prove the existence of a constant conjunction within the limits of the experience, it can never discover the existence of a necessity; only reason or insight can do that.

If one says, then, that experience confirms or vindicates the law of causation, it can only be in a Pickwickian sense. Whenever experience verifies the existence of a variation in the conditions answering to a variation in the events, this confirms the belief in the law of causation only in the sense that it weakens the case of one who denies the law on the ground that experience presents us with numbers of cases in which the one variation exists without the other, by diminishing the number of instances on which he might otherwise rely.

What has given rise in the last few years to a doubt or denial, by some physicists, of the universality of the law of causation, is certain facts with regard to the behaviour of atoms. The original form of the so-called principle of indeterminacy was this: The atom was thought of as consisting of a nucleus, with electrons rotating round it in a certain restricted set of orbits. Radiation from the atom was supposed to take place when and only when an electron jumps from one to another of this set of orbits, and the principle of indeterminacy asserted that the jumping or not jumping of an electron from one orbit to another was undetermined. It is surely obvious that the only ground which could have led any one, in this situation, to think that the movement was undetermined was that there was no *known* difference between the constitution and circumstances of one electron and those of another, which could account for the one's behaving in one way and the other's behaving in another. And it is equally clear that the rational conclusion to draw was, not that there was *no* difference to account for this, but that there was a *not yet known* difference which accounted for it. But, since this way of stating the principle of indeterminacy seems now to have been abandoned in most quarters, we need not dwell on it. In the later form of the theory, the pictorial representation of the atom is given up. There is much diversity in the statement of the later form of the theory, and it may be of some assistance to the reader if I quote some typical statements. Mr. Birtwistle[1] states the matter as follows:

'At the instant when the position is determined the momentum of the electron is suddenly changed. This change of momentum is all the greater the shorter the wave-length of the light used, i.e. the more accurate the determination of position is. Thus at the moment when the position of the electron is known, its momentum can only be known to an order equal to the discontinuous change. Hence the more exactly a coordinate q is determined, the less exactly can its momentum p be found; and conversely.'

Mr. Dirac's[2] statement of the matter is this:

'We find that our wave packet represents a state for which a measurement of q is almost certain to lead to a result lying in a domain of

[1] G. Birtwistle, *The New Quantum Mechanics*, 276–7.
[2] P. A. M. Dirac, *The Principles of Quantum Mechanics*[2], 103.

width $\Delta q'$ and a measurement of p is almost certain to lead to a result lying in a domain of width $\Delta p'$. We may say that for this state q has a definite value with an error of order $\Delta q'$ and p has a definite value with an error of order $\Delta p'$. The product of these two errors is

$$\Delta q' \, \Delta p' = h.$$

Thus the more accurately one of the variables q, p has a definite value, the less accurately the other has a definite value.'

Mr. Frenkel's[1] statement is as follows:

'Since the position itself can be observed with only a limited accuracy of the order of magnitude λ and the corresponding uncertainty in the value of the momentum is of the order of magnitude h/λ, the product of the two inaccuracies—or rather of the *inaccuracy* of the observation of the coordinates of the particle and the resulting *uncertainty* in the evaluation of its momentum *for the instant of observation*—is approximately equal to h. . . . It is impossible to *measure simultaneously* with any degree of precision the position and the momentum of a material particle, because the measurement of the one implies, or produces, an uncertainty in the estimation of the other.'

If it is said that certain experiments with regard to atoms reveal that an electron has not at any moment both a determinate position and a determinate momentum (though, the more indeterminate the one is, the less indeterminate is the other), this saying seems to me susceptible of three different meanings. It may be taken to mean that science is not in a position to assign definite values to both the position and the momentum. This would indicate a regrettable gap in the state of our knowledge, and possibly in any future state of our knowledge, but can have no bearing on the metaphysical problem of indeterminism. Or it may be taken to mean that while an electron has a position and a momentum, these are not in fact definite; and this cannot be anything but nonsense. If, as is now thought, electrons are not, as they were earlier conceived to be, 'particles concentrated almost into points', but partake at the

---

[1] J. Frenkel, *Wave Mechanics, Elementary Theory*[2], 48–9.

same time of the nature of 'waves spreading throughout space',[1] then it may be improper to describe them as having position or momentum at a moment at all (they being entities too complicated to have a single position or momentum), but what is surely quite clear is that nothing in the world can have a position which is not a definite position or a momentum which is not a definite momentum. Or, thirdly, the phrase may be taken to mean that, while an electron has a definite position and a definite momentum, these are not completely determined by pre-existing conditions. It is only in this third form that the newer conception has any direct bearing on the problem of indeterminism; and in its third form it is in principle the same as the older 'principle of indeterminacy', in which electrons were thought of as small solid particles whose jumps from orbit to orbit are not determined; and precisely the same comment must be made on it as on the older theory.

Mr. Birtwistle and Mr. Frenkel state the matter with perfect propriety in the first of these three ways. They do not suggest that the electron has not a definite position and momentum, or that it has a position and a momentum which are not determined by previous conditions; they only say that we cannot find out precisely both its position and its momentum. Again, Mr. Dirac does not suggest that the position and the momentum are not determined by previous conditions; and when he says 'the more accurately one of the variables q, p has a definite value, the less accurately the other has a definite value', this must, I think, be interpreted in the light of the fuller preceding statement in which he says 'q has a definite value with an error of order q' and p has a definite value with an error of order p''; i.e. q and p have definite values, but values which we cannot discover exactly.

The most authoritative statement, however, of Heisenberg's principle of indeterminacy is that by Heisenberg himself. Towards the end of his famous article[2] he says:[3] 'An der scharfen Formulierung des Kausalgesetzes: "Wenn wir die Gegenwart

---

[1] H. Dingle, *Through Science to Philosophy*, 289.
[2] *Zeitschrift für Physik*, 43 (1927), 172–98. [3] Ibid. 197.

genau kennen, können wir die Zukunft berechnen", ist nicht der Nachsatz, sonder die Voraussetzung falsch. Wir *können* die Gegenwart in allen Bestimmungsstücken prinzipiell *nicht* kennenlernen.' Now clearly to deny that the if-clause of the statement 'if we know the present, we can calculate the future' is ever fulfilled is not to deny the statement itself, and therefore not to cast any doubt on the law of causality. Heisenberg, however, goes on to ask whether behind the perceived, merely 'statistical world' a real world conceals itself, in which the causal law is valid, and proceeds to say: 'Weil alle Experimente den Gesetzen der Quantenmechanik und damit der Gleichung $(1)^1$ unterworfen sind, so wird durch die Quantenmechanik die Ungültigkeit des Kausalgesetzes definitiv festgestellt.' The conclusion is clearly not warranted. If it is true, as we may well admit, that the state of a particle can never be known with complete precision in respect of all its properties, then we can never establish the law of causality inductively by showing that each later state is completely determined by an earlier state: but any one who regards the law of causality as self-evident and needing no proof, inductive or of any other kind, will not be shaken by being told that an inductive proof of it is impossible.

Such a matter is not to be settled by weight of authority, but by reason; but lest any one should suppose that the weight of scientific authority is in fact in favour of accepting indeterminism in the physical world on the strength of experiments on the atom, it may be worth while to quote the words of Einstein, 'that nonsense is not merely nonsense; it is objectionable nonsense',[2] and those of Planck, the discoverer of the facts upon which the theory of indeterminacy has been founded. Planck pronounces with vigour equal to Einstein's against the theory and in favour of the universality of causation: 'In point of fact, statistical laws are dependent upon the assumption of the strict law of causality functioning in each particular case.

---

[1] q, p, $\sim h$ (ibid., p. 175); i.e. the product of the indeterminacy of the position of an electron, multiplied by the indeterminacy of its velocity, is constant.

[2] M. Planck, *Where is Science Going?*, 201.

And the non-fulfilment of the statistical rule in particular cases is not therefore due to the fact that the law of causality is not fulfilled, but rather to the fact that our observations are not sufficiently delicate or accurate to put the law of causality to a direct test in each case.'[1] The truth must surely be this, that the failure of science, so far, to discover causes for certain events is not a fact to be accepted with complacency or with enthusiasm and made the basis of a theory, but should be treated as a challenge to further inquiry in the hope of replacing our ignorance by knowledge. We must regard the principle of indeterminacy as one of the crude theories which are apt to be put forward in the years immediately after the discovery of some startling experimental fact, before the true meaning of the fact has been really digested.

Sir Arthur Eddington's contribution to the symposium is very different from Professor Broad's. The latter contents himself with saying that there may be some very slight element of indeterminacy in physical processes. Sir Arthur Eddington tries to persuade us that the whole doctrine of causal determination has in the current state of physics gone completely by the board and been replaced by that of probability. There is one type of discovery that lends some plausibility to this view. There have been, I suppose, several cases in which an older generation thought it had discovered that all particles of a type P behave under certain circumstances in a certain determinate manner Qd, while later discovery has shown that different instances of P behave in slightly varying ways Qa, Qb, Qc, . . ., and that the truth is only that a large number of P's will have characteristic Q in varying forms grouped closely round the form Qd. From this a hasty thinker may easily draw the conclusion that there are no laws prescribing the precise behaviour of single instances of P, but only laws stating the average behaviour of a large number of P's. And it is often the

---

[1] Ibid. 145; cf. ibid. 210. I may refer also to two contributions in the *Travaux du IXe Congrès International de Philosophie*—those by M. M. Barzin (vii. 15–20) and by Lord Samuel (vii. 21–7).

case that at a certain stage of our knowledge this is the only sort of law about their behaviour that we know. But even to discover such a statistical law as this is to obtain *some* confirmation of the view that being P determines any particular P to have the attribute Q in some form, and leaves us perfectly free to suppose that the particular mode and degree of Q which a particular P has depends on still unknown particularities of its nature or of its environment; which indeed is the only rational conclusion to draw.

There is, however, one line of thought which Sir Arthur works out with some care,[1] which it is worth while to follow. He points out that the majority of the inferences which science draws are inferences about the past. And his view about such inferences amounts, I think, to dividing them into three classes. There are (1) inferences in which from a later event in the history of a substance we infer its previous possession of some attribute or set of attributes whose existence can be verified apart from the inference; e.g. the conclusion, from some test, that a certain salt was silver nitrate—which can be verified by other means than the test in question. There are (2) inferences in which from a later event in the history of a substance we infer its previous possession of some attribute which we cannot verify independently, but can know or reasonably think to belong to some already known class of characteristics. It is an inference of this kind if we infer that the *Iliad* and the *Odyssey* were written by two different though unidentified men; for we already know that difference of personal identity is likely to lead to difference of style. There are (3) inferences in which from observation of some character in a later event we infer that there must have been *something* to cause it, without knowing or even being able to conjecture what it was. To this last class belong the phenomena which have given rise to the new doctrine of indeterminacy. Here we can, if we please, say 'S_1 behaves in one particular way, and S_2 in another; therefore there must have been some difference in the previous character

---

[1] *Indeterminism, Formalism, and Value*, 168–72.

of S_1 and S_2, though we have no idea what it is'. This, because we do not know what the two differing characters of S_1 and S_2 can be and can only describe them at the moment as 'something that will lead S_1 to behave in one way' and 'something that will lead S_2 to behave in another way', Sir Arthur describes as not being genuine inference. 'I am well aware,' he says, 'that our ignorance is immense; but I see no point in attempting to enumerate the things which might exist without our knowing them.'[1]

What exactly is the cash value of the distinction? The position is simply this. (1) In the first case, where we can trace a difference between two results to a difference in the causes which can be independently verified to exist, we have a partial confirmation—if confirmation were needed—of the law of causality. (2) In the second case we think we are on the track of such a confirmation, since we have an inkling of what the difference between the causes will turn out to be. (3) In the third case we have no inkling of how or where the confirmation will occur. But the inference 'since the effects are different the causes must be' is just as sound as it is in the other two cases, though it remains, owing to our ignorance, for the present unverified by experience. The occurrence of such cases throws no doubt whatever on the law of causality; it simply fails to provide fresh confirmation of it. And, to speak for a moment pragmatically, one may surely point out that science would never have made the progress it has made if, whenever men failed to trace different causes for different events, they had been content to suppose that the events just happened to be different for no reason at all. The present failure of science to know why atoms sometimes behave in one way and sometimes in another is not different from many another case in the past history of science in which the momentary failure led people who had a firmer grasp of the causal principle than Sir Arthur has, to some of the greatest triumphs of science.[2]

---

[1] Ibid. 173.
[2] I have not discussed Mr. Braithwaite's contribution to the *Symposium*, because the other two seem to have raised sufficiently the points in dispute.

As regards the physical universe, then, I think we may remain unrepentant determinists; must we be so as regards the universe of moral action? At the outset it must be said that we are much farther, in this region, from the possibility of empirical verification of the law of causation than in the region of physical action. When we conclude from the observation of two physical events that a greater force must have been at work to produce the one effect than to produce the other, we usually can verify by independent means the excess of the one force over the other. When we infer, because a man does the one and not the other of two acts, that he must have desired the one more than the other, we have no delicate instruments of measurement by which we can verify that one desire actually was stronger than the other. Sometimes we can do so by introspection, and then we are so far verifying the law of causation; but often it is only by observing what we proceed to *do* that we can know what we *desired* most. And here we are in the same position as we were in respect to the third of Sir Arthur Eddington's types of inference. We get no empirical verification of the law of causality, but nothing (in the mere fact mentioned) to lead us to doubt it. Those who are interested in the question of *a posteriori* reasons for determinism will find in Professor Broad's article a careful study of the facts which make such verification far less complete in the moral universe than it is in the physical.[1] But it is clear that the essential question is whether we have or have not *a priori* knowledge of the law of causality and of its application to moral action; and the empirical arguments on either side cut very little ice.

The strength of the *a priori* argument for determinism in ethics rests on the consideration that the law of causality does not present itself to our minds as one peculiar to physical events but as one applying to all events as such. An event which escaped its sway would be an event of which no explanation could be given. Suppose some one says that one is here taking one's notion of an event from physical events and applying it

---

[1] *Indeterminism, Formalism, and Value*, 146–9.

without reflection to mental events; my answer would have to be that I at least make no use of the conception of anything physical when I say every event must have a cause; by an event I mean *any* change, *anything* that takes place. And it is surely clear that even for a libertarian the line is drawn not between physical events and mental, but between one special class of mental events and all other events whether mental or physical. No one wants to exempt from the law of causation the occurrence of a sensation on the occasion of a physical stimulus; or the occurrence of an inference on the occasion of the grasping of its premisses. In the one case the event is thought to be completely determined by the physical stimulus +the pre-existent nature and state of the body and of the mind; in the other by the occurrence of the grasping of the two premisses in their connexion. We certainly cannot choose what conclusion we shall draw from the premisses; if we see their truth and notice their relevance to one another we cannot but see the truth which by the laws of logic follows from them. It is only acts where *choice* is involved that can with any plausibility be said to escape the law of causation. And while there might conceivably be some plausibility in making the law of causation apply to all physical and to no mental events, it is very unplausible to make it apply to all physical and some mental but not to other mental events.

The strength of the case for libertarianism, therefore, cannot be said to rest on any ontological ground upon which we could *expect* acts of choice to be free from the law of causation. It rests on two things alone—on the supposed intuition of freedom, and on the thought that morality involves freedom. These are the things at which we must look more closely. I may just say in passing that, if we could believe in occasional or even in universal indeterminacy in the physical world, that view, which is equivalent to a belief in blind chance, would furnish no support either for our intuition of freedom or for our awareness of duty.

In considering the intuition of freedom, we shall do well to consider separately the two questions of freedom to choose, or decide, or resolve, and of freedom to do what we have resolved upon. As regards choice, what is it that we really are aware of? We are aware that a certain kind of activity called choice or resolution takes place, which is different from any other activity—different, in particular, from desiring, and from desiring one thing more than another; and we are aware that it is we and not anything else that performs this activity. We are aware that desires are not like physical forces beating on a physical body from without, to which it is merely passive. They are occurrences happening in the very same being which chooses among them; and they are occurrences such that the mere occurrence of one stronger than all others does not *ipso facto* lead to corresponding action. We are aware that we often reflect on them and come to see that a desire which as it originally presented itself was stronger than another, nevertheless harmonizes less well with the universe of our interests; and we are aware that when we come to see this, it becomes less strong, or some other becomes stronger, and that we then act on what was at first the weaker but is now the stronger desire, or follow the line of what was at first the greater but is now the lesser resistance. Can it be maintained that there is an intuition of freedom to which this account does not do justice? It seems to me that it cannot, and that reflection on the relations between opinion, desire, and choice shows that it cannot. Let us first take, as the simpler case, one in which the thought of duty does not occur, one in which we choose, for instance, between two courses promising different pleasant experiences to ourselves. The suggestion is that at one point in the nexus of events there comes a choice in which some element of the self operates quite freely, independent of the circumstances and also of the self's system of interests as they exist at the moment. Suppose (1) that the act of suspense, whereby we decline to act immediately on the strongest desire and instead subject the desires to reflection, has already taken place. It can hardly be maintained that then we can by an act of free choice (i.e. choice indepen-

dent of the circumstances and of our system of interests) control
the remoulding which the desires undergo as they are brought
into relation with our universe of interests. The existing universe of our interests determines that. Not that we are passive
in this process; it is by the *activity* of thinking about the alternative courses of action that we come to desire one action more
than the other. We are not a field on which desires as independent entities wage their battle. But the I which thinks and desires
is the I which has been moulded by its previous experiences and
opinions and actions.

At the end of the process we are desiring one act more than
the other. Can it be maintained, then, (2) that thereupon we
are conscious of freedom nevertheless to do *either* of the two
acts? Is it not clear that, in a case where the thought of duty
does not come in, we inevitably do that which after reflection
we most wish to do? And incidentally we may ask, 'Would
there be any moral value in a freedom to do, in such a case,
what we do not most wish to do?' It would be a freedom to
act for no reason, and indeed against reason.

Can it be maintained (3) that, while the determinate self,
with its universe of interests, determines what we do, *if* we
perform the act of suspense, an indeterminate element in us
performs the act of suspense? Is it not clear that we perform
this act only if we think, for example, that the greater of two
immediate pleasures may bring more pain in its train than the
lesser of the two? And is it not clear again that we are not free
either to think or not to think this, that whether we do or do not
think it depends on the circumstances and on the determinate
kind of being that we are when we compare the two pleasures?
We cannot choose what opinion we shall form about the situation, and what we do think about it determines us to perform
the act of suspense; or else fails to determine us to perform it,
and then we do not perform it. Freedom to suspend or not to
suspend action irrespective of any reason for doing either
would, again, be a freedom not worth having. To sum up,
then, we do not seem, on reflection, to be conscious either of a

power of thinking what we please in the light of given evidence, or of a power of desiring what we please independently of our opinions, or of a power of doing what we do not most desire to do. Nor, if we had any of these powers, would it be of the slightest value. What would be the moral value of a power of forming opinions not based on the evidence, of desiring not in accordance with our opinion, or of acting to get what we do not desire?

'But', it might be said, 'the situation is altered when we turn to cases in which the thought of duty occurs to us. Then, at least, we do not choose according to the strongest desire; we may choose to do our duty instead of what we desire.' If one has done a conscientious act, and is then asked why one did it, the answer which first comes to one's lips is 'because it was my duty'; and in this there is no mention of desire. Duty tends to be represented as something standing over against all objects of desire. But a little reflection shows that our answer was highly elliptical. It is clear that an act's being our duty is never the reason why we do it. For however much an act may be our duty we shall not be led on that account to do it, unless we *know* or *think* it to be our duty. And again, the thought that an act is our duty will lead us just as much to do it when it is not in fact our duty as when it is. Thus our answer 'I did it because it was my duty' must be changed into the form 'I did it because I knew it, or thought it (as the case may be), to be my duty'. But even this is still elliptical. For it is a familiar fact that people often know or think an act to be their duty and yet do not do it. They will do it only if in addition to knowing or thinking it to be their duty they are impelled with a certain degree of intensity towards the doing of duty—with enough intensity to overcome the urge towards any of the alternative possible acts. Thus the fuller and truer answer would be, 'I did the act because I knew, or thought, it to be my duty, and because I was more powerfully impelled, or attracted, towards it as being my duty than I was towards any alternative act.' Now a question arises as to the nature of the impulsion. The simpler account would consist in saying that all impulsion is desire, and that therefore our answer may be put in the form, 'I did the act because I knew, or thought, it to be my duty, and because I desired to do it, as being my duty, more than I desired to do any other act.' And if this description is true, conscientious action would fall under the same description which we have seen to apply to actions in which the thought of duty does not occur; it would be action in accordance with the strongest desire present at the moment.

The alternative would be the view that what impels us to do our duty is not desire but a certain specific emotion which only the thought of duty arouses—the emotion which Kant calls *Achtung*, respect or reverence. Now I think it is clear that the thought of duty does arouse such a specific emotion. It arouses it in very varying degrees in different people, and in the same person at different times; and in some people the emotion is very weak. Not only do they habitually not do their duty, but they feel little or no shame or remorse at not having done it; while if the emotion in question had any considerable strength, this would at least lead to remorse after the act, even if it were not strong enough to overrule the desires that lead men to do the act. Still, in the ordinary man the clear recognition of a duty undoubtedly arouses to some extent the emotion of respect. Kant represents the choice between doing and not doing our duty as resultant on a struggle between desire and respect, and resists strongly the suggestion that it is resultant on a struggle between desire and desire. But this seems to be due to his tendency to accept too readily the Hobbesian view that all desire is for the agent's pleasure. Since the motive in dutiful action is clearly not that, he infers that it is not desire at all. But it is now generally admitted that Hobbes was wrong; and if we recognize that there is a variety of desires for objects other than one's own pleasure, there seems to be no objection in principle to recognizing a desire to do one's duty; and certainly introspection seems to reveal such a desire. It seems to me, further, that the emotion of respect aroused by the thought that a certain act is one's duty produces, in proportion to its own strength, a desire to do that act, and that duty is done when and only when that desire is stronger than all those with which it has to contend.

But, it might be said, if action is described as following upon the strongest desire, is not resolution or choosing or deciding made completely nugatory? Would not the same act follow if the step called choosing were entirely omitted? The answer to this is in principle contained in what I have said previously. It is the nature of each single desire to be concentrated on a single feature in an imagined future, and if desire were left to itself we should act to get the most desired of these isolated features. But in fact every such desired feature involves, in the getting of it and as a result of the getting of it, many other features which are not desired. To get the single thing which at the moment we desire most of all things, we might involve ourselves in getting many things that will give us pain, or in doing actions to which we have a strong moral repugnance. In the deliberation which precedes choice we set ourselves, more or less thoroughly according to our character, to choose not between isolated objects of desire but between acts each of which is thought to involve a whole set of consequences, and it is one act with all its expected consequences that is chosen in preference to all others with all *their* expected consequences. The choice is thus determined not by the strength of the isolated desires as they were before the process of deliberation, but by the strength of the appeal which one act, with all that it is expected to involve, makes on us, as compared with the appeal which the alternatives make. Thus what is resolved on may be, and often is, very different from what would have been done if deliberation and choice had not intervened. What choice depends upon, and reveals, is not the strength of isolated desires but the trend of the whole character, of the whole system of more or less permanent desires, including of course the desire to do one's duty.

The nature of choice, and its importance, may, it seems to

me, be brought out by contrasting the way in which we actually behave with two accounts of behaviour which might suggest themselves as possible accounts. I assume that every desire must at any one moment be of a perfectly definite intensity, and that all desires must be comparable on a single scale of intensity, even though it must be admitted that we are quite incapable of distinguishing the intensities of two desires which are very much alike in intensity. Now it might be thought in the first place that action would be determined by the strongest single desire. That, however, is not what happens. I take a simple case. If I am attracted to act A by a desire, of intensity $3n$, to get a certain pleasure for myself, and to act B by a desire, of intensity $2n$, to give a certain pleasure to another person, and am attracted to act B also by a desire, of intensity $2n$, to give a certain pleasure to a third person, I shall actually do act B, though the strongest single desire that is affecting me is attracting me towards the other act. That is the truth that is vaguely expressed by saying that it is the universe of my desires that determines my action, and not the strongest single desire. But, on the other hand, it must not be supposed that *all* the desires that are present in me co-operate to determine my action, as the movement of a body is determined, in accordance with the parallelogram of forces, by all the forces that are acting on it. If that were so in human action, our action would be an attempt to get to some extent each and all of the many things we happen to be desiring; and it is clear that such action would be futile in the extreme. What happens, in persons of strong character, is something quite different; they make up their minds that certain of the things they want are incompatible with certain other things that they want more; and they then suppress the desires for the former, so far as concerns their becoming influences affecting their behaviour. They cannot entirely suppress these desires; but they cause them to be, not motives modifying their action, but mere longings for certain objects, which remain even when these objects have been resolutely renounced. This, it seems to me, is the great difference between physical and mental causation, that in the latter there is no law of the composition of all the forces concerned, but some of the forces concerned are, by an act of choice, deprived of any effect on action.

If the line of thought I have tried to present is true, the libertarian belief in its complete form cannot be true. The libertarian belief is the belief that, the circumstances being what they are, and I being what I am, with that whole system of beliefs, desires, and dispositions which compose my nature, it is objectively possible for me here and now to do either of two or more acts. This is *not* possible, because whatever act I do, it must be because there is in me, as I am now, a stronger impulse to do that act than to do any other. Every one would probably agree that this is so when neither of the two acts is being thought of as a duty. It would be agreed that then we must do the act, to do which we have the strongest desire, or rather the act to which the strongest mass of desire leads us. But it is equally true when one of the two acts *is* thought of as a duty, even if we take the view that what impels us to do an act of duty as such is not a desire but a specific emotion of respect or reverence. For even so we shall do the duty if and only if this emotion constitutes an impulse to do the act of duty, stronger than the impulse which moves us towards doing any other act. And if act A can only be done if I have a stronger impulse to do act A than to do act B, and if act B can only be done if I have a stronger impulse to do act B than to do act A, it cannot be the case that I can here and now equally do either act. It must follow from my nature and my present condition that I must do act A, or else that I must do act B.

Not only is it metaphysically impossible that I should be capable of doing either act indifferently, but if I could, the doing of either could have no moral value. It would have no value, because it would not be the result of any thought about the nature of the act, and of any consequent impulsion to do it. It would be an unintelligent and unmotived leap in the dark.

Nevertheless we all, when we are not philosophizing, tend

to hold this opinion, and cannot altogether prevent ourselves from continuing to hold it even when we have come to think it incapable of being true. What then is the truth, if any, which underlies my belief that I can here and now, being what I am, yet do either of two or more acts?

This belief, in the form in which we ordinarily hold it, is the belief that I can cause any one of two or more changes in the state of affairs. In some cases the change we are thinking of is a change in the condition of one's own mind; but far more often a change of something in the physical world is at least part of the change we think we can cause. And such changes can only be caused by first causing a change in the state of one's own body. If I think, for instance, that I can here and now tell either the truth or a lie, there is involved in that the thought that I can cause either of two sets of movements of my vocal chords. And undoubtedly one main source of my sense of freedom to act in either of two ways is the conviction, well based on experience, that my soul or mind has the kind and degree of control over my body which will enable me, if I set myself to tell the truth, to produce certain movements of my vocal organs, and if I set myself to tell a lie, to produce certain other movements of them. This conviction is not, strictly speaking, knowledge; for since I last made the attempt, paralysis may have set in and deprived me of this power. But normally the chances are much against this having happened, and for practical purposes the conviction is justified and is almost as good as knowledge.

The existence of this power has of course sometimes been doubted. It has been thought that mind cannot act on body, and various forms of parallelism of mental and bodily events have been put forward in opposition to the belief in the action of mind on body. But, as several recent discussions of the question have brought out,[1] the theoretical arguments against action of mind on body are really very weak; and the argument for it from experience is very strong; and, to avoid a long

[1] See, for instance, the discussion in Mr. Wisdom's *Mind and Matter*, 65–102.

digression into psychophysics, I am going to assume that common sense is justified in its belief that mind can act on body —provided of course that it is the body which belongs to the mind. Now it seems clear that one great source of our belief in freedom is our conviction—a well-founded conviction, as I think—that there are in any set of circumstances more than one bodily change, any one of which the mind can and will produce if it sets itself to do so.

In saying that mind can produce changes in body, I do not mean merely that a certain change in our mental state is one of the conditions upon which there supervenes, and without which there would not supervene, a certain bodily change. What we naturally think is that, while there are certain static conditions, both of our body and of our mind, without which the bodily change would not take place, a mental act of self-exertion stands out from the background of these static conditions and is that which actually causes the bodily change to take place. To reduce causation to mere necessary sequence is to eviscerate it of a good deal of its natural meaning, and no cogent reason has ever been given for this evisceration.[1]

When I say this, however, I ought to add that I have in the course of this discussion frequently used the word 'causality' in another and wider sense which is also justified by common usage. When I have referred to the law of causality I have meant by this the principle that no change takes place in the absence of conditions upon which it necessarily follows; and in *this* conception of causality there is not necessarily involved the thought of one thing acting on and producing a change in another. And indeed in the causations which we have been mainly considering there is no question of one thing, i.e. one substance, acting on another. When one says that an act of will is caused by the previous desires and thoughts of the willer, there is no question of two substances being involved; for all that happens happens in or to one substance, the individual

---

[1] For a defence of the common-sense view of causality against the criticism of Hume see G. F. Stout, *Mind and Matter*, 15–36.

human being in question. One is then merely asserting a necessary connexion between earlier and later events in the history of this individual. When, on the other hand, one says that a mind by an act of choice produces a change in its own body, one is, I believe, asserting something more than necessary connexion; one is asserting the existence of activity and passivity. To avoid the ambiguity, one ought perhaps to use 'determination' as the more general word to include both what is commonly called transeunt causation and what is commonly called immanent causation, and should restrict the word 'causation' to what is commonly called 'transeunt causation', to the action of one substance on another, whether it be that of body on body, or that of body on mind, or that of mind on body, or (if this occurs) that of mind on mind.

The mind's power of controlling the body has great importance for the moral life. If it did not exist, our moral life, our range of moral activities, would be immensely impoverished. For if a man did not think that his mind can control his body, he would not set himself to make such movements as are involved in telling the truth, in paying his debts, in helping his neighbours, and the like; and if he discovered by experience that he cannot produce such results he would soon cease to set himself to produce them. His moral life would come to be restricted to setting himself to bring about changes in the state of his own character or of his own intellect. He would have a moral life of his own, but he would be cut off from the activities which make up by far the greater part of the moral life of most men.

Yet the question whether the mind can control the body is irrelevant to the question of the freedom of the will. For if we say that the mind can control the body, we are making a statement about the *effect* of an act of will, and are in fact saying that a certain causal nexus exists between acts of will and consequent bodily changes; while what Libertarianism maintains is not anything with regard to the *effects* of acts of will, but that acts of will are not themselves caused by the pre-existing conditions.

Suppose that a man had, without knowing it, lost the power of speech. He could still set himself, or make the effort, to tell the truth, or alternatively set himself to tell a lie. The activity of mind he would be exercising would be the same in the case in which the control over his vocal chords has ceased to exist, as it would be if he still had the control; and the activity of choosing between these two activities would be the same as if the control over the vocal chords still existed. Morally, both the act and the decision to act are just the same as they would be if the control over the body still existed. Thus control over the body, though it is a great part of what we usually think of when we assert our freedom to do this or to do that, is not the morally essential thing that is being claimed. The essential thing that is being claimed is the power to set oneself to do this, or to set oneself to do that, i.e. to perform a mental activity which is just the same whether it is or is not followed by the appropriate bodily movement.

Is there any foundation for the belief that I am free to set myself to produce either of two or more bodily movements? If my previous argument is correct, the belief cannot itself be true. If my nature and condition and the circumstances are such and such, I shall set myself to produce one change; if they are different, I shall set myself to produce another. Yet, if it is not true that I can here and now set myself to produce either indifferently, it is true that in a certain sense I *could* set myself to produce either. For within the total range of my nature there are motives which in certain circumstances would lead me to make the one attempt; and other motives which in certain circumstances would lead me to make the other. Neither act seems to me impossible for me, because neither is clean outside the range of motives which I know to exist in myself. If I knew myself completely, I should know either that the one motive or set of motives is the stronger, in which case I shall set myself to do the one act, or that the other motive or set of motives is the stronger, in which case I shall set myself to do the other. But knowing that both motives are such as I am familiar with, and knowing further that both are present in my mind at the moment, and not knowing which is the stronger, or, if I happen to know which is the stronger now, not knowing which will have emerged as the stronger by the time when I act, the only reasonable belief for me to hold is that I am capable of doing either of the two acts.

Now if in the end I do the right act, then, if the defence of Determinism which I have put forward is sound, my doing the right act implies that, just before I did it, conditions which made it necessary for me to do it were present, and similarly my doing the wrong act, if I do *that*, implies that conditions which made it necessary to do that act were present. If the one act was objectively, in the precise circumstances, possible for me, the other was not; and if the other was possible, the first was not. Yet all the conditions which *ever* justify the assertion of possibility were present justifying the judgement that both acts were possible for me. For what are the conditions that justify the judgement that A may happen? A judgement of possibility may be of three kinds. It may be a judgement of the form 'A may be the case here and now', or of the form 'A may have happened in the past', or of the form 'A may happen in the future'. We need not trouble ourselves with any consideration of the first two types, for it is clearly the third that is relevant to the consideration of free will. Now the one essential condition needed to justify the judgement 'A may happen' is that I do not know of any circumstance which makes the happening of A impossible. If the general argument I have offered for Determinism is true, there is no such thing as possibility *in rerum natura*. If certain conditions are present, certain things will happen, and no alternative to them will happen; if certain other conditions are present, certain other things will happen, and no alternative to *them* will happen. Possibility is always related to a judger, and to say 'so-and-so may happen' is just to say 'I don't know that it won't'. Now it often happens that I don't know that A will happen, and don't know that it won't. Then I am entitled to say that A may happen and may not happen. Now this is actually the position we are in with regard to the acts of any other person. We may have watched him in a hundred similar situations in the past and seen him always behave in one way, and we may therefore think it much more likely that he will behave in way A than in way B; but though the circumstances seem just alike to us, they may seem different to him; or his character may have improved since the last similar situation occurred to him, or it may have got worse; and it is the literal truth that we can neither say that he will do act A nor that he will do act B, but can only say that he may do either. And we are, in principle, in the same situation with regard to our own future acts, and even with regard to our acts in the immediate future. We can see that the situation is never *exactly* like any in which we have been in the past. It may be like in that our relation to one person who forms part of the situation is just like the relation in which we have stood to some person in the past, but it practically never happens that the whole set of people who enter into the situation is related to us just like the whole set of people who entered into previous situations we have been in, and therefore we cannot infer that because we behaved in way A in the past we shall behave in way A now. Again, we may feel convinced that at the moment the motives inclining us to do act A are stronger than any inclining us to do any alternative act. But all motives or desires are subject to a constant alternating weakening and strengthening; we are perfectly familiar with the fact that a desire which at its inception is strong weakens as its novelty wears off. Then so long as *any* interval, however short, separates the present moment from that at which the act will be done, we do not *know* what the relative strength of the different motives will be when the latter moment arrives; and therefore do not *know* what we shall do, though we may of course think it highly probable that we shall do a certain act rather than any other.

Thus the logical precondition of my saying 'I can either do my duty or fail to do it' is always present. But merely not knowing that A will not happen is not a sufficient *psychological* precondition of my judging that A may happen. I should be logically justified in saying, 'Mr. Chamberlain may make Sir Stafford Cripps his next Minister of Labour'. But I should not be likely to form this judgement unless I knew or thought, for instance, that Mr. Chamberlain had socialistic leanings; unless I knew or thought that there was something in Mr. Chamberlain's psychology which might lead to such an act. Such a psychological precondition of the judgement 'I can either do my duty or not do it' is in fact present. For I know that the desire to do my duty is a desire that has a certain strength in me, and I also know that other desires which if followed would lead me not to do my duty have a certain strength in me, so that the possibility of my doing my duty is not (as we sometimes put the matter) a mere logical or abstract possibility, but a very real one, and the possibility of my not doing it is also such a possibility. Thus both the logical and the psychological condition of my making the judgement are present. Or, as we may also put it, it is not merely possible, but has an appreciable probability, that I shall do my duty, and it is not merely possible, but has an appreciable probability, that I shall not do it. Therefore the judgement 'I may either do my duty or not do it' is fully justified.

The thought 'I can do my duty' has also a further justification. The practical utility of a belief is never, indeed, a sufficient reason for holding that belief. If I did not on other grounds think that I can do my duty, the thought that I should be more likely to do my duty if I believed I could do it would not lead me to believe that I could; and if it did, the belief would be unjustifiable, since there would be no logical connexion between the psychological cause of the belief and the belief itself. But if a belief is on other grounds justifiable, the fact that keeping the belief in our minds would have good results is a good reason for keeping the belief in our minds. Now I have tried to show that the belief that we can do our duty is on its own merits justified. I certainly do not know that I shall not do my duty, and I know that there is in me a motive, viz. sense of duty, which makes it appreciably probable that I shall do it. And the keeping of this belief before my mind will in fact make it more likely that I shall do my duty. Consider the effect of holding the opposite belief. Suppose I believed that I could not do my duty; then I should be thinking, in effect, this: 'Though the act is the right one in the circumstances, and one which a better man ought to do, yet since I can't do it there is no use in my trying to do it.' I should resign the struggle, and do the act which most appealed to me on other grounds. But if I keep before me the thought 'that is the right thing to do, and I don't know of anything that makes it impossible for me to do it, and do know of something, viz. the sense of duty in me, which makes it appreciably probable that I shall do it', the wish to do my duty is kept alive and allowed to have its full weight in determining my action.

It is true that the thought 'it is possible for me *not* to do my duty' is equally justified logically, and that this also is not a mere idle or abstract possibility, since I know there are motives in me inclining me to do something other than my duty. And it might at first sight seem that this thought would have as great a tendency to depress us and damp down our moral activity as the complementary thought 'it is possible for me to do my duty' has to intensify our moral activity, and would simply neutralize the effect of the latter. This, however, is far from being the case. The joint thought 'it is possible that I shall, and possible that I shall not, do my duty', which is the thought that the facts of the case justify, is precisely that which is most favourable to the doing of our duty when the time comes. If we felt certain that we should do it, that would simply encourage us to take things too much for granted and to neglect the concentration on the thought of duty which alone will secure our doing it when the time comes. If we felt certain that we should *not* do it, that again would discourage us from paying any attention to the thought of duty. The recognition that we may either do or not do our duty is just that which is needed to induce us to keep our moral armour in the best possible repair.

I may illustrate this by a homely analogy. Of the candidates in an examination, those who are most likely to make the needed effort are neither those who feel sure that they will pass nor those who feel sure that they will fail, but those who know that they do not know whether they will pass or fail. And similarly the thought that it is possible that I shall do what is right and also possible that I shall do what is wrong is precisely that which is most conducive to my exercising that sort of control over my thoughts and desires which is in turn most conducive to my doing what is right, provided of course that a wish to do what is right is also present. This thought, then, is not only true, but one which it is very desirable to keep constantly before one's mind.

What, then, is the difference between the perfectly proper statement which I may make 'it is possible that I may presently do this, and possible that I may presently do that', and the libertarian claim? Possibility is always compossibility. What I am saying when I make the above statement is that there are no existing conditions *known to me* with which my doing A is incompatible, and none with which my doing B is incompatible; and I probably should not make the statement unless I knew some important conditions to be actually present with which each action is compatible. What the libertarian says is that *all* the conditions, known and unknown, are compatible with my doing the one action, and also with my doing the other; and this cannot be true.

But the phrase 'it is possible that I shall do what is right, and possible that I shall do what is wrong' does not do full justice to our actual thought when it takes its usual form 'I can do what is right', though it expresses part of what that thought involves. I could be content with that phrase only if I thought of myself as a mere spectator of the play of forces within my mind, as a looker-on at a game between fairly equal sides may say 'this side may win, or that side may win'. The fact that the spectator is also the agent makes the actual situation different. We say not merely 'I may do right, and I may do wrong', but 'I *can* do right, and I *can* do wrong'. What exactly does this mean?

When I say 'I can do this', which I will now use as a brachylogy for 'I can perform this mental activity of self-exertion',[1] I am not claiming that all the conditions necessary to my doing this are already present. If they were, I should be 'doing this', whereas the claim 'I can do this' is always made about something which one is at least not yet doing, and which perhaps one will never in fact do. If I say 'I can do this', either I am not doing it, or at least I suppose I am not doing it, and if so, I cannot be supposing that *all* the conditions necessary to my doing it are already present. But I am claiming that some of those conditions are present, and present in me. I am in fact saying 'certain of the conditions of my doing this are already present in me, and if certain conditions not yet present are added I shall actually do this'. Now sometimes when I say 'I can do this', I could specify certain external conditions which must be fulfilled if the power is to be translated into act. If I say 'I can walk a mile in thirteen minutes', I should if I wanted to be more precise say 'I can walk a mile in thirteen minutes if the road is not too uphill, if there is not too strong a wind against me, if I am not stopped on the way, if I am not too tired when I start', &c. But when 'doing this' is not the effecting of a certain bodily movement or set of movements, as walking is, but is the purely mental activity of setting oneself to do a certain thing, such external conditions are irrelevant. Yet there must be *some* unfulfilled condition of my performing this activity of 'setting myself'; else I should be doing it, and not merely saying 'I can do it'. The general formula must hold good, that 'I can do this' is really a hypothetical proposition— 'if a certain condition is added to conditions already present

---

[1] This alone is in question, since, as I have pointed out (pp. 231–4), the mind's control over the body is not what is in question when we are discussing the freedom of the will.

in me, I shall do so-and-so'. And it is easy to see what the additional condition must be. It consists of my wishing to do this. 'I can do this' means 'I have such a nature that if I want to perform the activity of setting myself to do this, I shall perform it'; and 'I can refrain from doing this' means 'I have such a nature that if I want to refrain from doing this, I shall refrain from doing it'. Or, putting it briefly, 'I can do this or that' means 'I shall do this if I want, and I shall do that if I want'— 'want' being here a brachylogy for 'want predominantly'. Now this claim is absolutely correct. For we have verified in experience over and over again two things, (1) that we have a faculty of setting ourselves to bring about changes, and (2) that this is exercised when we predominantly want to bring about these changes. Thus the claim which we instinctively make that we can perform either of two (or more) acts of setting ourselves to effect changes, seems to be absolutely correct, when we expand it to bring out what it really means. But what it points to is not the libertarian but the deterministic account; for we clearly imply that if the capacity of setting ourselves to effect changes has added to it a predominant wish to bring about a certain change, the setting oneself to bring it about will necessarily follow.

Suppose it is said that I am whittling away the claim of ordinary common sense, by adding the words 'if I want'. Suppose it is said that the claim is a claim to power not subject to this condition. If this were so, the claim would, I think, have to take one or other of two forms: (1) 'I can do this whether I want or not.' But does any one make this claim? Does any one really think that he could, for instance, set himself to do his duty if he did not wish to do his duty? Suppose that some one suggests that the motive of a dutiful act is not a wish but the emotion of respect or reverence which the thought of duty inspires, he will only be substituting a new condition for the condition 'if I want' which I have suggested. He will be paraphrasing the phrase 'I can do my duty' by the phrase 'I shall do my duty if I am sufficiently under the influence of the motive of reverence'. He cannot think that one who says 'I can do my duty' is claiming that he can or will do it in the absence of this emotion as well as of desire.

(2) The second possible interpretation is 'I have in me already all the necessary conditions of my doing the thing, except that of wanting to do it, and I can produce this condition'. To this interpretation two fatal objections can be made. (*a*) We do not in the least think that we can produce wishes in ourselves by an act of choice, and (*b*) if this were the right analysis of the claim 'I can do act *A*', then the right analysis of the statement 'I can produce the condition of want' would be 'I have in me already all the conditions of producing the condition of want, except the wish to produce this condition, and I can produce this wish'. Thus the claim 'I can do this' would involve the claim 'I can produce the wish to do this'; that would imply the claim 'I can produce the wish to wish to do this'; and so *ad infinitum*—a regress which quite clearly is not involved in our simple claim 'I can do this'.

Thus both the attempts to remove the condition 'if I want' fail, and our analysis of the claim 'I can do this' remains good— that it means 'I have in me a general capacity of setting myself to do things, and if I want to bring about change *A*, this capacity + this desire will lead to my setting myself to produce change *A*'. And if we thus interpret the claim 'I can do act *A*', it is strictly true that I can do act *A* and that I can refrain from doing it. Thus the instinctive feeling that we can either do an act or refrain from doing it (or do some alternative act) is thoroughly justified. But it does not in turn justify the libertarian account. For it involves the assertion of the determined sequence of action on desire. As regards the origin of the desire it says nothing, but it certainly does not claim that desire is originated by an act of free choice, and in fact we never think of our desires as so originated, though we do think of our acts as so originated.

Thus what is claimed in the natural statement 'I can either do act *A* or leave it undone' is that my doing or not doing act *A* depends entirely on myself. And this is in a sense true, because, while my effecting change B in my body, and indirectly change C in something beyond my body, depends on conditions in my body, and in that thing beyond my body, act A, being a purely mental activity of setting myself to effect changes B and C, cannot depend for its occurrence on the extent to which my body happens to be under the control of my mind.

Of course we are not claiming a complete non-dependence of our acts of self-exertion on any conditions outside our mind. Most, at least, of our wants would never arise if they were not suggested to us by the perception of bodies outside us, and this is true even of the desire to do certain things as being our duty. For it is by the use of our bodily senses (though not by that alone) that we become aware of the existence of selves other than our own, and thus of duties to other selves. The independence that is claimed is the non-dependence of our acts on any *immediately preceding* condition except the general capacity of setting ourselves to effect changes, and the wish to effect this or that change—both of which are conditions in our mind and nowhere else.

Thus a great deal of what is claimed in the claim to free will —not only the thought that either issue is still possible, but the thought that the issue will depend on us, our minds, our wishes, not our bodies, nor other minds or bodies, is absolutely true, as well as absolutely vital to the moral life. Again, the thought that the relative strength of our wishes is not already fixed once for all is both true and valuable. But it is a thought which a determinist can admit, as well as a libertarian. A determinist is not in the least bound to say that the effort after self-improvement is fruitless. He can admit quite freely that in a character that is bad on the whole there may yet be an element of desire for better things which, weak at first, may by the influence of example and of teaching, and of the effort after self-improvement which example and teaching may arouse, become the strongest element in the character.

The controversy between Libertarianism and Determinism is

apt to present itself as one in which the metaphysical argument is in favour of Determinism and all the ethical arguments in favour of Libertarianism. This is far from being the case. It seems to me instructive to reflect, in this connexion, on two features of the moral situation. The one is our reliance on the characters of other people, the reliance implied in the use of such words as 'trustworthy'. The other is our attitude when people surprise us by their behaviour. The reliance which we place on the decent behaviour of people whom we know and trust is so much evidence that we think that their actions, when they come to be done, are the result not of a will acting independently of their present character, but of the same continuing character which we have seen at work before. We are in no way detracting from the moral status of our friend if we say 'I knew you could be trusted to do the right thing'. 'Know' is no doubt an exaggeration; for every heart has its secrets which no one knows, and the friends we know best may have their secret weakness which no former situation has revealed but which a new one will. But a confidence amounting almost to certainty is a tribute to our friend's moral worth, not a detraction from it; yet it is not compatible with the libertarian's view that any one may at any moment make a choice which is quite independent of his whole pre-existing character.

Again, if some one behaves, for better or for worse, in a way different from that which we had confidently expected, what is our reaction to this? We do not put down the unexpected act to the credit or discredit of an unmotived choice. We always assume that there must have been, before the act, some existing but hitherto unknown trait of character which has now, perhaps for the first time, manifested itself in act. In our reaction to people's unexpected behaviour, no less than in our expectation of their behaviour, we betray the conviction that action is the result of continuing, even if constantly modified, character.

Another feature of our ordinary moral thought which really harmonizes better with the deterministic than with the libertarian account is the importance for good or evil which we

attach to the formation of habits. We all think that if we repeatedly behave in a certain way we shall make it more likely
that we shall go on behaving in that way, and more difficult for
ourselves to behave otherwise. An attempt may be made to
harmonize this with Libertarianism by saying that habits
'incline without necessitating'. But to describe them thus is to
imply that a habit becomes *one* of the influences which operate
on the will; and this is inconsistent with the thought of a
transcendental will standing apart from the formed character
and free to operate independently of it. The thought that
habits incline without necessitating is in itself perfectly correct.
It is simply one way of expressing the fact that a habitual tendency to behave in a certain way forms one element, and an
important element, in the total character from which future
action will spring, while yet there may coexist with it some
other element which may prove stronger; some long unfulfilled but not extinguished longing after good which,
brought to the surface by some feature of a new situation, may
overcome a bad habit, or some lingering weakness which may
lead us to yield to a new temptation though we have overcome
many others. The thought of habits as inclining without
necessitating, which is the true way of thinking of them, is also
the most salutary, since it frees us from the despair which
would overtake us if we thought of bad habits as completely
necessitating, and from the carelessness that would come over
us if we thought of them as leaving us as free to do well as we
were before their formation.

I may add that the judgements which we make about the
characters of other people (or about our own characters), in
distinction from judgements about particular acts, imply the
view that action is determined by character. For our judgements about character are mostly[1] based on observation of
actions, and we are justified in drawing inferences from people's
actions to their characters only if their actions flow from their

---

[1] Only mostly, because some judgements about character are based on observation
of the expression on people's faces, their gestures, &c.

characters. When we call a man a bad man we do not mean that he is a man who has done more bad acts than good (for that might be equally true of a reformed sinner), but that he still has substantially the same character which was evidenced by bad acts in the past and may be expected to be evidenced by more in the future. In fact Libertarianism is inconsistent with belief in the continuity of human character; but our actual moral judgements are evidence that we do believe in its continuity, though we think it a continuity that admits of modification for better or for worse.

I am far from contending that the whole of our ordinary thought about moral action is reconcilable with the doctrine of Determinism. But it is worth while to point out that it is by no means true that *all* the arguments drawn from the moral consciousness tell in favour of Libertarianism, and only the metaphysical argument tells in favour of Determinism.

If my line of argument is right, we must find the uniqueness of moral behaviour not in freedom from the general law of causation, but in the unique character of the activities which constitute such behaviour—the activity of choosing or deciding, and the activity of setting oneself to do what one has decided to do, to which there is no analogy in the behaviour of any physical thing; and in the further fact, to which there is nothing analogous in the behaviour of a mere animal, that one of the thoughts under whose influence one can choose and set oneself to act is the thought of an action as right.

Besides the 'intuition' of freedom, the other main reason which leads people to believe in the freedom of the will is the thought of responsibility for our acts, which is involved in the facts of remorse, blame, and punishment. These, it might seem, are unjustifiable and indeed unintelligible, unless we are really free to do either of two or more different acts. We must therefore set ourselves to examine the implications of these things. Professor Nicolai Hartmann[1] has argued that of these three phenomena, remorse is the one which is most clearly an evidence

---

[1] *Ethik,*[2] 673–8 (Eng. tr. iii. 172–8).

of free will. Blame and punishment, praise and reward, might, he argues, perhaps be explained as devices adopted for the encouragement of men to future good acts and their restraint from future bad acts, without involving a genuine imputation of freedom; but there can be no such utilitarian explanation of the free assignment by a man to himself of responsibility for his past acts, and of the accompanying remorse.

I think it possible that a society which had ceased to believe in the responsibility of individuals for their acts might retain praise and blame, reward and punishment, as utilitarian devices for the encouragement of virtue and the restraint of vice. But two comments may be made on this. In the first place, I think we should agree that the denial of responsibility is not the assumption on which we actually praise and blame, reward and punish. Our actual assumption is a belief in responsibility. And secondly, we should think it somewhat dishonest to continue to practise praise and blame, reward and punishment, if we had lost the belief in responsibility. We should be treating people as if they were responsible, when we had really ceased to believe that they were.

I think, therefore, that we need not isolate remorse from praise and blame, reward and punishment, but should treat all alike as involving a belief in individual responsibility. The question we must now face is whether this belief is compatible with the Determinism which we have been led on other grounds to believe in, or whether it involves freedom of indifference. I may begin by pointing out that responsibility is always divided. Obviously responsibility for *results of action* can never be assigned to one person alone; there are always circumstances (and these will usually include acts by other people) which co-operate to produce the result, of whose complete cause one person's act is merely the most striking part. But it is also true that responsibility for *acts* is divided. It is never right to assign to one person the sole credit or the sole discredit for any of his acts. Other people by teaching and example, the writers of the books he has read, and so on, have all helped to mould his character into that form of which his action is the expression. But it is equally certain that the sole responsibility for any act can never be assigned to any person or persons *other* than the doer of the act. For acts spring from opinion and desire, and there is no possibility of forcibly implanting either an opinion or a desire in the mind of another. No opinion or desire will find a lodgement in his mind unless his mind accepts it, or rather responds to suggestion with a reaction which is all his own.

To recognize, then, that people and things other than the agent have been part causes of his act may be ground for mitigating the severity of our blame or the enthusiasm of our praise, but it is never in itself sufficient ground for withdrawing praise or blame from him altogether. Other people, and outside circumstances, have never been more than part causes of his act; the act is the reaction of his character to them, and his character is partly responsible.

Mr. Wisdom has suggested[1] that there is one and only one way in which a belief in responsibility can be reconciled with a belief in the law of causation. If the individual soul, he argues, is regarded as having been called into being, at the moment of conception, either by the act of its parents, or by the act of God, then all its subsequent acts are in the long run determined by events entirely beyond its own control, viz. the events that happened before it began to exist. But if it has existed from all eternity, then all its acts may be regarded as determined by previous conditions of which acts of its own formed some part, and its partial responsibility for all it does is thus preserved.

A belief in the eternal pre-existence of the soul no doubt has much to commend it on other grounds. Not only moral considerations, but our whole way of thinking of the soul, involve that the soul is something other than a succession of its states and acts, that it is something that *has* these states and *does* these acts; in other words, that it is a substance. Memory implies the

[1] In *Mind and Matter*, 122–30.

thought, and if it is ever itself a form of knowledge it then implies the knowledge, that the very self which remembers also had the experience which it remembers, and thus establishes the existence of a soul-substance lasting as far back from the present as the earliest experiences we can remember. And if we grant the existence of a soul-substance going so far into the past as this, the belief in its infinite pre-existence is at least no harder to accept than any of its alternatives. The alternatives seem to be (1) the emergence of the soul from purely physical antecedents, or (2) its emergence by emanation or fission from some other soul or souls—either those of the parents or that of God, or (3) its creation by God out of nothing. Can we seriously accept any of these alternatives? Emergence by fission seems to be the only one of the three that is not incredible; and it plainly has difficulties of its own. Furthermore, it should be clear that pre-existence is the hypothesis that goes best with the belief in immortality.

There is thus a great deal to be said, on general grounds, for the belief in the eternal pre-existence of the soul. But it is evident that there are great difficulties in the attempt to understand how and why an eternally existing soul comes to inhabit this or that embryo organism. And, further, it appears to me that, while the doctrine of pre-existence gives a sort of juridical justification of responsibility, in the sense that it leaves the individual with a part-responsibility for all his acts, which he cannot shift on to any one but himself, it is *only* a juridical justification that it gives, and not one that answers to or accounts for our natural thought about responsibility.

What would be the natural reply of one who wants to assert the responsibility of the individual, to the suggestion that an eternally pre-existent soul can be responsible while a non-eternal soul cannot? I think he would say that at two points the suggestion fails to satisfy him. The eternally pre-existing soul had no opportunity of choosing its own character *ab initio*, any more than a non-eternal soul can have had one; there never was a time at which a characterless soul chose to become a soul of a certain character, for the eternally existing soul has always had a character, and its choice of how it should develop must have been limited by the character it already had. It is true that it cannot blame God or its parents for any badness there may be in its character, but will it not instead blame the nature of things, which has prevented it from ever having a completely free choice of character? But further, even if Mr. Wisdom could allow that the eternal soul had sometime in the past had a free choice of character, its character at each moment thereafter is inherited from its past, and its character at each moment determines its action at that moment, while what our natural thought craves for is some element in the self which can at any moment act *contrary* to the character it inherits from its past—can act, as it is sometimes expressed, in the line of greatest resistance. Thus the pre-existence of the soul really does nothing to remove the reluctance which our natural thought has to accepting a deterministic theory. It is not without significance that the Eastern religions which believe in eternal pre-existence are more fatalistic and less inclined to assert individual responsibility than the Christian religion, which, in its orthodox form at least, does not believe in eternal pre-existence.

This attempt to reconcile responsibility with Determinism can, then, hardly be deemed successful. And, holding fast to Determinism, I am inclined to think that the only account we can give of responsibility is this: that bad acts can never be forced on any one in spite of his character; that action is the joint product of character and circumstances and is always therefore to some extent evidence of character; that praise and blame are not (though they serve this purpose also) mere utilitarian devices for the promotion of virtue and the restraint of vice, but are the appropriate reactions to action which is good or is bad in its nature just as much if it is the necessary consequence of its antecedents as it would be if the libertarian account were true; that in blaming bad actions we are also blaming and justifiably blaming the character from which they spring; and that in remorse we are being acutely aware that, whatever our outward circumstances may have been, we have ourselves been to blame for giving way to them where a person of better character would not have done so. I cannot pretend that this satisfies the whole of our natural thought about responsibility, but I think that in claiming more, in claiming that a moral agent can act independently of his character, we should be claiming a metaphysical impossibility.

A philosophical genius may some day arise who will succeed in reconciling our natural thought about freedom and responsibility with acceptance of the law of causality; but I must admit that no existing discussion seems to be very successful in doing so. The most recent elaborate discussion known to me, that by Professor N. Hartmann, while it does justice to the strength of the case for Libertarianism, shows little appreciation of the strength of the case for Determinism.[1]

---

[1] There is in *Mind*, xliii (1934), 1–27, a very persuasive attempt by Mr. R. E. Hobart to show that, quite apart from metaphysical considerations, our natural thought about *moral* questions implies a belief in Determinism. He is, I think, rather sanguine in believing that he has shown the whole controversy about free will to be based on confusions; but I do not know of any better exposition of the extent to which our moral thought involves the belief that actions are the expression of, and flow necessarily from, a definitely characterized and continuing though modifiable self.

XI

THE NATURE OF GOODNESS

THERE are two reasons which make it necessary for any student of ethics to devote attention to the nature of goodness. One is that we habitually think of certain kinds of disposition and action, and of certain persons, as morally good; and we can hardly hope to know clearly what is meant by 'morally good' unless we know both the nature of goodness in general, and what distinguishes moral goodness from any other form of goodness. The other is that a great part of our duty—indeed, according to a widely accepted theory, the whole of our duty—is to bring what is good into existence. Even if we reject that theory it must be admitted that where no special duty such as that of promise-keeping is involved, our duty is just to produce as much good as we can.

The first thing that strikes us in examining the meaning of the word 'good' is the very wide variety of things to which we apply the name. We apply it to persons, to their characters, to their actions, to their dispositions, to tools and machines, to works of art, to states of affairs; and the suspicion naturally arises that we cannot be using the word in the same sense in all this variety of applications. Not that the variety of the things to which we apply it necessarily involves a variation in the meaning in which we use it; for a word like 'animal', for instance, is applicable to very various things, ranging from Julius Caesar and Shakespeare to the amoeba, and yet in calling any of them an animal we are using 'animal' in a single sense, i.e. as standing for a certain very general type of structure and life, which admits of great variety in detail. But there are certain cases in which, on comparing two different applications of a word, we can see that the word *cannot* mean the same in both cases. Thus we may speak of a horse as being fast, and we may also speak of a movement as being fast, but we see that while the horse is fast in the sense that it moves a relatively great distance in a relatively short time, a movement is fast not in this sense (for a movement does not move), but in the sense that it *is the moving* over a great distance in a short time. Aristotle generalized this consideration into the doctrine that when any term is applied to things in more than one category, it must have different meanings in these different categories; and he considered that 'good' is a case in point, since it can be applied to substances, qualities, quantities, relations, actions, passivities, times, and places.[1] It does not seem to me that his general doctrine is justified. It would seem, for instance, that certain times and places might both be good in the single sense that it is useful for certain human purposes that certain events should take place at them. And in any case from the *mere* variety of the things to which a term is applicable, even where the variety amounts to a difference of category, it cannot safely be inferred that the term itself must have different meanings. Yet the example of 'fast' has shown us that *sometimes* the application of a term to things in different categories is possible only in virtue of the term's having two meanings.

When a term is applied to things in different categories, and yet there is some connexion between its meanings in these different applications, and not a mere chance using of the same noise in entirely unconnected meanings, Aristotle suggests that the relation of the different meanings may be either that they are derived from one single central meaning, or that the things called good contribute to one end, or that there is an analogy between the different meanings.[2] He does not expand these alternatives at all, but I think we may take the first alternative as particularly suggestive. In our instance of 'fast', the relation between the two meanings is that both are connected with the covering of a great distance in a short time, a horse being fast because it *does* this, and a movement fast because it *is* this. And it would seem likely that the relation of the meanings of the word 'good' when we apply it to men, to characters, and to

---

[1] *Eth. Nic.* 1096 a 17–29.   [2] Ibid. b 25–9.

actions or emotions, is of the same order. But it is much harder to be sure of this in the case of a term like 'good', which in one of its senses at least seems to be unanalysable, than in the case of a term like 'fast', which is always analysable in terms of an interval covered and of the time taken to cover it. We can analyse the meaning of 'fast' in its two applications, and see that the definitions which unfold its meaning in the two cases are different but connected in a definite way. We cannot do that with 'good', or at least it is not initially clear that we can.

The *Oxford English Dictionary* very judiciously gives as its primary definition of 'good' 'the most general adjective of commendation, implying the existence in a high, or at least satisfactory, degree of characteristic qualities which are either admirable in themselves or useful for some purpose'. Probably no more definite account than this will cover the whole variety of the applications of the word. Probably the only universal precondition of our using the word is the existence of a favourable attitude in ourselves towards the object. And this may give rise in some minds to the thought that what we are asserting of the object is that it is the object of such a favourable attitude—which would at once imply that 'good' is a relational term, signifying that there is a certain relation between the object and him who judges it to be good. To correct this, it may be enough to refer to a point made by Meinong, and thus summarized by one of his expositors:

'Language serves a double function: it *expresses* our states of mind and it *means* or refers to the objects of those states of mind. A man who utters the words "red" or "blue" gives expression to a peculiar inner experience through which he is living, but he is not meaning or referring to this experience. He is talking about certain properties which can only be manifested in extended objects.'[1]

'If I make use of the word "sun", I am, whether I wish it or not, giving expression (*Ausdruck*) to the particular mental process called an idea, to the fact that, either in perception or imagination, some-

[1] J. N. Findlay, *Meinong's Theory of Objects*, 28; cf. Meinong, *Über Annahmen*, ed. 2, 24 f.

thing is being set before my mind. But at the same time, in so far as I express this idea, I also refer to a certain physical object, namely the sun, and this reference to the sun is the meaning (*Bedeutung*) of the word. If a person hears me use the word "sun" he can take this word as a sign of a certain idea in my mind, whose existence he can infer with high probability. But it is perfectly plain, as Meinong points out, that this idea is not what I *mean* when I speak of the sun; unless I am introspecting, and attempting to examine the mental states which accompany my use of words, nothing can be farther from my thoughts than my own ideas. What I am concerned with, what I am referring to, is an extended physical object millions of miles away, which does not resemble my mental processes and stands in no real relation to anything in my mind.'[1]

In the same way what we *express* when we call an object good is our attitude towards it, but what we *mean* is something about the object itself and not about our attitude towards it. When we call an object good we are commending it, but to commend it is not to say that we are commending it, but to say that it has a certain character, which we think it would have whether we were commending it or not.

What then is the characteristic which we ascribe to something when we call it good? I do not think that there is any one characteristic which we are ascribing wherever we call something good. What unites all our applications of the word is not a single connotation of 'good', but this single type of attitude, the favourable attitude, which we are always *expressing*, the meanings of 'good' itself being very various. To bring out this variety, I think it useful first to distinguish the adjective or attributive use of the word from its predicative use, i.e. the usage in which we say 'a good so-and-so' from that in which we say 'so-and-so is good'. When we say 'a good-so-and-so', what we are ascribing to something is 'goodness of its kind'; and this has various meanings according as we are speaking of (1) a person or of (2) a thing. I venture to quote here some sentences from a previous discussion by myself.

---

[1] Findlay, op. cit. 61.

'In case (1) the root idea expressed by "good" seems to be that of success or efficiency. We ascribe to some one a certain endeavour, and describe him as a good so-and-so if we think him comparatively successful in this endeavour. It might be thought that in certain cases (e.g. "a good singer", " a good doctor") another idea is in our minds, viz. that the person in question ministers to our pleasure, or to our health—in general to the satisfaction of some desire of ours. But our pleasure or our health comes in only incidentally in such cases; it comes in just because the endeavour we are imputing to the person in question is the endeavour to give us pleasure or to improve our health. It does not, therefore, it would appear, form part of the general connotation of "good" when thus used. We can in this same sense call a man "a good liar", not because he contributes to the satisfaction of any of our desires, but because we think him successful in what he sets out to do.

'In case (2) there appear to be various elements included in what we mean by "good". We seem to mean in the first place (*a*) "ministering to some particular human interest". A good knife is essentially one that can be successfully used for cutting, a good poem one that arouses aesthetic pleasure in us. But there is also here (*b*) the notion that the thing in question is one in which the maker of it has successfully achieved his purpose—a notion which might be called the "passive" counterpart of the notion explained under (1). As a rule both the notions (*a*) and (*b*) appear to be involved in our application of "good" to anything other than persons; but sometimes the one and sometimes the other predominates. There is, however, (*c*) a third element, less seriously intended, in our application of "good" to non-persons. When we speak of a good lie or of a good sunset we are half-personalizing lies and sunsets and thinking of this particular lie or sunset as succeeding in that which all lies or sunsets are trying to achieve; i.e. we are, not quite seriously, transferring to non-persons the meaning of "good" appropriate to persons.'[1]

I think it is clear that this adjunctive use of 'good' has no importance for ethics. The meanings that are important for ethics are that in which we say 'such-and-such a man is good', meaning 'morally good', and that (or those) in which we say (rightly or wrongly) 'virtue is good', 'knowledge is good',

---

[1] *The Right and the Good*, 65–6.

'pleasure is good'. It is obviously very important for ethics to discover which of such statements as these three are true, because we have agreed that one of our main duties is to produce as much that is good as possible, and we can attach no concrete meaning to this till we have discussed what things are good in this specially important sense. We may agree that what we are ascribing to things when we call them merely good of their kind is something that can be defined in a purely naturalistic way, by reference to human wishes and their fulfilment; the question remains whether 'good' in its predicative sense can be so defined, or indeed can be defined at all.

Of the predicative applications of 'good', it seems to me that we can distinguish three main types. (1) There is first the sense in which a hedonist might say that virtue is good. He does not think that virtue is good in itself, for he thinks that pleasure alone is this. He means that virtue is useful as a means to something that is good in itself. Here we have already come to something that, on the face of it, cannot be defined in a purely naturalistic way. One element of our definition, that in which we use the phrase 'a means' or some equivalent, is naturalistic, since it simply states that there is a causal relation between one thing and another thing which is or may be desired. But in saying that virtue is a means to something *good in itself*, we are including a non-naturalistic element in our definition.

I do not wish to call the usage of 'good' as equivalent to 'a means to good' improper. It is a perfectly sound idiomatic use of the word. But it is clearly to be distinguished from the sense of 'good' as 'good in itself' or 'intrinsically good' or 'good apart from its results', and it will be better, in speaking or writing philosophy, not to say 'good' when we mean 'useful as a means to what is good in itself', but to use this phrase or an equivalent.

But what is good *in itself* may be so in either of two senses. (2) We may call something which has both good elements, and bad or indifferent elements, good in itself, when we think the good elements outweigh the bad ones. Or (3) we may call something good, meaning that it is good through and through. Professor Moore calls things of the first kind intrinsically good, and those of the second both intrinsically and ultimately good.[1] Phrases which would more clearly indicate the difference are the phrases 'good on the whole' and 'good through and through'. Only things that are good through and through will be good in the strictest sense of the word, and the questions I want to address myself to are (1) what is the nature of that which we are ascribing when we say of something that it is good in this sense, and (2) what are the things that *are* good in this sense. These questions have to be to some extent considered together. Under the first question I want to consider in particular what category goodness of this sort comes under. Is it a quality? Is it a relation? Is it a relational property? Or does it form a separate category from any of these? Or does it with any other characteristic or characteristics form a category other than those named?

In my book *The Right and the Good*[2] I have discussed at length the view that goodness is a relation or a relational property, and in particular Professor Perry's view that what we say of a thing when we say that it is good is that it is an object of interest to some one or other. I believe that in its essence the argument I have offered is right. In particular, it seems to me quite clear that there are many things which we know to be objects of interest to many people but yet unhesitatingly describe as bad. And further it seems to me clear that when, for instance, we describe a conscientious or a benevolent action as good we are ascribing to it a characteristic that we think it has in itself, apart from the reaction of any one to it.

Suppose that we deny that certain moral qualities, such as conscientiousness or benevolence, have a characteristic of goodness which is independent of any one's reaction to them, what then are we really affirming about goodness? One or other of three things: (1) that goodness is properly defined as

---

[1] *Ethics*, 73–6.   [2] pp. 75–104.

the being the object of a certain kind of reaction, (2) that things that are good have goodness in *consequence* of being the objects of a certain kind of reaction, or (3) that there is no such thing as goodness at all, the only relevant fact being just the fact that certain things are the objects of a favourable reaction.

On the first view, it is asserted that what we mean when we call certain states of mind good is just that they are the objects of a favourable reaction. Now I think it is clear that we have not this meaning in mind when we normally use the word 'good'. When we call a state of mind good we are thinking of the state of mind itself, and not of our or of any one's reaction to it. Yet it must be admitted that we often use terms not quite unintelligently, and yet without realizing precisely what we are thinking of. This admission seems to me to be required by the fact that we sometimes search for the definition of a term, and accept a certain definition as correct. We should not be searching for the definition if we already knew precisely the meaning of the term; but the fact that we accept a certain definition as correct shows that we think the definition expresses more clearly the very thing that we had in mind when we used the term without knowing its definition. Thus the fact that we have not our own reaction, or any one's reaction, distinctly in mind, when we use the word 'good', is not sufficient evidence that that is not its true definition. The correctness of a definition may be tested by two methods: (i) by asking whether the denotation of the term and that of the proposed definition are the same, whether the definition applies to all things to which the term applies, and to no others. But that is not enough. 'Equilateral triangle' and 'triangle having all its angles equal' have exactly the same denotation, but the one is not a correct definition of the other, since what we *mean* when we call a triangle equilateral is not that its angles are equal but that its sides are equal. We must therefore ask a second question, (ii) 'does the definition express explicitly what we had implicitly in mind when we used the term?' We may apply this double test to any proposed relational definition of goodness. Most of the relational views fail to survive either test. For we may divide them according as they identify goodness with being the object of a favourable reaction (*a*) by some one or other, no matter by whom, (*b*) by the person who judges something to be good, (*c*) by a majority of some class of mankind, (*d*) by the whole of some class of mankind, (*e*) by a majority of men, or (*f*) by all men.[1] Now as regards (*a*), it is clear that we sometimes deny something (say hatred) to be good, or doubt whether it is ever good, when we do not doubt that some one or other has had a favourable reaction to it; so that the definition fails to satisfy the first test, and must therefore fail to satisfy the second as well. As regards (*b*), it may be admitted that this definition satisfies the first test. No one judges anything to be good unless he has a favourable reaction to it, and it might be possible to specify a particular favourable reaction—say approval—which we never have without judging the object to be good. But this definition fails to satisfy the second test. For while the favourable reaction is what the judgement 'this is good' *expresses* (to use Meinong's language), it is not what it *asserts*.[2] That this is so can be most easily seen from the fact that if this were what the judgement asserts, then two people of whom one says 'this is good' and the other says 'this is bad' would not be contradicting each other, since it might be true both that *A* approves of the object and that *B* disapproves of it; whereas it is clear that *A* and *B* do mean to contradict each other. As regards definitions (*c*) to (*f*), they fail to satisfy either test. It is clear that we often judge an object to be good when we do not think that a majority, or the whole, of any class of mankind or of mankind itself is feeling an emotion of approval towards it; and it is further clear that even if we do sometimes think that a majority or the whole of some set of men is approving of object *O*, that is not what we mean to assert when we say that *O* is good.

---

[1] These alternatives, and to a large extent my discussion of them, are borrowed from Professor Moore's discussion of subjectivist views of the meaning of '*right*' (*Ethics*, 87–132). [2] Cf. pp. 254–5, above.

It would be possible to try to avoid this objection by modifying the relational definition of 'good'. We might say that
'good' means not 'arousing an emotion of approval in so-and-
so', but 'such as to arouse such an emotion when attended to'.
This would get over the time-difficulty that attaches to the
original suggestion, viz. that we constantly describe something
as good when we have no reason to suppose that the whole or
a majority of any set of men is even attending to the object in
question, let alone approving of it. But the new suggestion
remains open to *this* objection, that we often call something
good when quite certainly no thought even of what the whole
or a majority of any class of beings *would* feel *if* it attended to
the object is even implicitly in our minds.

Thus it is not in the least plausible to identify goodness
either with being the object of a favourable emotion or with
the power to awake a favourable emotion.[1] That is most
certainly not what we are thinking of either explicitly or even
implicitly when we call a moral action, for instance, good.
Now no one is likely to suggest[2] that the existence of this relation between an object and some mind or minds gives rise to a
quality in the object (distinct from this relation) the name for
which is goodness. The most plausible form in which the
relational view could be expressed would be to say[3] that nothing
possesses the kind of intrinsic characteristic which we ascribe
to things when we call them good; that some things are, however, the actual or possible objects of a favourable emotion,
and that on the strength of this we mistakenly ascribe to them
goodness in themselves. To say that would be more plausible
than trying to persuade us that by 'good' we mean something
which we plainly do not mean.

The fact is, however, that it is impossible to approve of anything without thinking it *worthy* of approval—without thinking
that it has a goodness of its own which makes it fit to be approved. The view that the whole fact is that certain things are

[1] View (1), p. 258 *fin.*   [2] View (2), p. 259.
[3] View (3), p. 259.

approved is one which makes nonsense of approval itself. If things were only approved, without anything being worthy of approval, the act of approval would simply be nonsensical. Approval may be misplaced in detail; the fact that a particular person approves a particular thing does not imply that that thing is actually worthy of approval; but the fact that we approve at all, rightly or wrongly, is the clearest possible evidence of a universal conviction that there are some things that are worthy of being approved. And disagreement about what things are good is just as clear evidence of this conviction as agreement about it would be.

The fact of being approved, then, which the theory we are examining seeks to identify with, or to substitute for, goodness, is a fact which could not exist apart from the thought that the object is worthy of approval, in other words is good in itself. And I believe that attention to our state of mind when we express approval of conscientiousness, say, or of benevolence shows that what we really think about them is that they are good in themselves. No one can *prove* that they are, but then *nothing* could be proved unless there were truths which are apprehended without proof; and we apprehend that conscientiousness or benevolence is good with as complete certainty, directness, and self-evidence as we ever apprehend anything.

But there are other things besides moral dispositions and actions that we habitually think good; notably the exercise of intelligence, and the feeling of pleasure; and the question arises whether these are good in the same perfectly objective and indefinable way in which good moral dispositions and actions are good. I wish to take account in particular of an argument by Professor C. A. Campbell[1] to the effect that only moral virtue is good in this perfectly objective sense of 'good'. The gist of his argument is to suggest that of the goodness of anything other than moral virtue a relational account can be given. He grants, I think, the truth of my criticism of the relational

[1] In *Mind*, xliv (1935), 273-99.

theories which identify goodness with being the object of a
favourable emotion to the person who judges something to be
good, or to the whole or a majority of any set of beings. But
he thinks that a more complicated form of relational account
can be given of the goodness of intellectual or aesthetic activity.
His general view is that 'all value judgements other than those
referring to moral virtue involve an essential reference to
human liking'.[1] He takes as being at least the most important
things, other than virtue, which we judge to be valuable,
knowledge and aesthetic experience—these words being the
more exact way of referring to the truth and beauty that are
named in the familiar trinity of 'goodness, truth, and beauty'.
He starts by considering 'liking'; and 'liking', as it is described
by him, seems to stand for the two facts of desiring a thing
when it is absent, and finding satisfaction or pleasure in it when
it is present; or more strictly for the having of a relatively
permanent disposition which leads us to desire something when
we think of it as a thing we have not got, and to enjoy it when
we have it. But he admits that not *everything* that is liked is
seriously thought of as good for oneself, still less as good for
man or simply as good. He therefore introduces certain distinctions between objects of our liking. The first important
distinction that he draws is between things liked for themselves
and things liked as means to things liked for themselves. It is
obviously only the former that 'have a direct claim to the title
"value",' and we therefore tend 'to identify value-for-self not
with object of *any* liking of the self, but with object of an
independent liking of the self'.[2]

The next distinction is one drawn between different 'end-
values', viz. that between end-values which have also instrumental value and those which have instrumental disvalue;
health and knowledge being instances of the former, idleness
and gluttony of the latter. Now since the self, when it has certain
likings, is conscious that then or at other times it has other
likings, objects of liking which interfere with other objects of

[1] Ibid. 279.   [2] Ibid. 283.

liking, more numerous than themselves or the objects of more intense liking, come to be objects of dislike on the whole. ' "Good-for-self" will now mean object not merely of an independent liking, but of an independent and *integral* liking of the self—an "integral" liking being definable as one which is substantially consistent with the likings of the self as a whole.'[1]

Professor Campbell next points out that a further modification of the meaning of value-for-self arises at the same level of self-consciousness as the modification last considered—viz. that we restrict value-for-self to the objects of likings which are fairly *permanent* as well as independent and integral. But at the same time the self becomes aware of the possibility of its *coming to have* likings which it can foresee to be in a high degree integral and relatively permanent as well as independent; such as a liking for scientific pursuits or for music. The objects of such likings, the things we should like to like, are naturally therefore also recognized as things good for self.

So far, Professor Campbell has offered a very persuasive account of how an individual may naturally organize into an order of importance the objects of his various likings, on the ground of their independence, integralness, and relative permanence; and it is only surprising that he does not assign more weight to a characteristic of likings which he sets aside as of but slight importance, viz. their intensity.[2] One would have thought that that should count for as much, in the establishing of the hierarchy, as the characteristics to which he has attached weight.

He next points out that we are aware that other selves have their likings, as well as ourselves, and suggests that by intersubjective intercourse we discover what things are independent, integral, and relatively permanent objects of liking to other men as well as to ourselves, and come to think of them as not merely good for self, but good for man. And, finally, he holds that, having arrived at the conclusion that certain things are good for man, we drop the qualification and describe them as

[1] Ibid.   [2] Ibid. 283.

simply good, and come to think of them as if their goodness were intrinsic, i.e. flowed from or were consequent upon their own nature, independently of any relation to human likings.

I have already pointed out the difficulty that arises if we identify goodness with the being an object of liking to the whole or a majority of mankind or of any class of mankind. The difficulty is that we often call particular things—particular activities of the intelligence or of the imagination—good, when there is not present, even obscurely in the background of our mind, the thought that these particular activities have ever been contemplated by, still less been liked by, the whole or a majority of mankind or of any class of mankind. Professor Campbell tries to get over the difficulty by saying that they are thought of as objects of liking to *human nature*. But this way of putting the matter cannot be accepted. Human nature is a name for a certain set of powers and dispositions which we think of as common to all men. And no such set of powers and dispositions likes anything. What has likings is a particular man or particular men, and to say that something is an object of liking to human nature is only a loose way of saying that it is an object of liking to all or most men in virtue of their common human nature, or *else* that it is an object of liking to men in so far as they share in a nature which is regarded as *normal* or *ideal* human nature. Now if the first alternative is adopted, we are still faced with the difficulty that many particular things are judged good when we have not the slightest reason to believe that all or most men are even aware of their existence, still less that they like them. And if the second alternative is adopted, we are really falling back on the thought that there are certain things which, whether they are or are not liked by men, are worthy of being liked by them and would be liked by them if they had the ideal human nature in perfection. But as soon as we fall back on the notion that certain things are worthy of being liked, we are deserting the purely naturalistic account of goodness (other than moral goodness) for which Professor Campbell is arguing.

It appears to me that Professor Campbell might have put his case more plausibly if he had adopted a different line from that involved in the use of the phrase 'object of liking to human nature'. The most obvious objection to saying that the statement 'so-and-so is good' means, when made explicit, that so-and-so is liked by all or most men, is that we constantly say of some particular activity of knowledge or of aesthetic imagination that it is good, when we do not think the particular activity in question is even being attended to or ever has been attended to by all or most men. But it might be suggested that in judging it to be good we are really saying that it is an *instance* of a *kind* of thing which we know or think to be an object of liking to all or most men. We know that knowledge, or the successful use of the intelligence, is liked by all or most men, and we therefore express admiration of a particular activity of knowledge or intelligence, though we do not suppose that all or most men have this particular activity before their minds at all. 'Good' in such an application would then mean 'instance of a kind of thing which all or most men like with an independent, integral, and relatively permanent liking'.

The question must be asked, however, whether it is a true account of what we mean when we say that knowledge is good, to say that we mean that it is the object of such a liking to human nature. The alternatives must be pressed: to say that such-and-such a thing is an object of liking to human nature is either a merely historical, statistical statement based on a comparison of the actual likings of particular men, or there is involved in it an appeal to an ideal human nature. Take the first alternative. It must be first remarked that we know nothing either of the likings of man in the earliest stages of his evolution, or of what his likings will be in stages still to come. All that we can say is that there is considerable evidence that all or most men, during the period of human history of which we know something, have liked, for instance, knowledge. And all that we should be justified in saying on the basis of this is that within these limits of time knowledge has been good. We should have to admit that there may have been a time at which people disliked or were indifferent to knowledge, and that if so, knowledge was then bad and ignorance or error was good, or else all three were indifferent—and that such a time may come again in the future.

One might admit for the sake of argument that many of our admirations for particular types of intellectual activity—for the spinning of particular types of theory, for instance—rest upon no better basis than this. The individual finds that certain theories give him pleasure, and he discovers that most of his contemporaries who attend to them also get pleasure from them, and on that basis he judges them to be good. The fashion may change. One generation likes absolutist theories, another likes relativistic theories. One likes monistic theories, another likes dualistic or pluralistic ones. But as to the intrinsic preferability of knowledge to ignorance and error, of that sort of use of the intelligence which notices differences where they exist and identities where *they* exist, which draws from premisses only the conclusions that they warrant, have we not an *a priori* certainty that, whether or not all or most men always have liked and always will like these things—which we cannot possibly know—they are intrinsically better than their opposites, better worth having, more *worthy* of admiration, whether they receive it or not? And it must surely be admitted that, even if we often call one theory or way of thinking better on the ground of the actual preference of ourselves or of our generation, that which makes it really better, if it is so, is not in the least our preference, but its possession of such characteristics as I have suggested, the recognition of differences and of identities where they exist, the drawing of conclusions that are warranted by the premisses; in other words, its being of the nature of knowledge and not of mere opinion whether true or false.

If, on the other hand, we rest our judgement that certain things are good for man not on a historical and statistical study of the actual likings of individual men, but on the notion of a normal or ideal human nature, we are really saying of these things not that they are liked but that they are worthy of being liked, and are worthy of being liked because they are in themselves good.

Professor Campbell makes two claims for his account: (1) that it yields a list of goods for man which in fact agrees with the list of intrinsic goods that is suggested by those who adopt a non-relational view of goodness, and (2) that it accounts better than such a view does for the varieties of opinion that are held in different periods and in different communities as to what things are good.

The first of these claims is, I think, justified, and that it should be so need not surprise any one who holds the non-relational view. For if there are things intrinsically good, and if the human mind has the power of apprehending their goodness, just as it has the power of apprehending other aspects of reality, it will naturally be satisfied by them when present, and attracted by the thought of them when absent, i.e. will 'like' them. And our liking for them will have the characteristics of the liking whose objects Professor Campbell's view identifies with things good for man. The liking for them will of course be an independent liking of them, a liking of them for their own sakes and not as a means to something else. Further, since it depends on an intellectual apprehension of their goodness, it will be a more integral liking than our likings for the pleasures of the senses. And for the same reason it will depend less on accidents of circumstance and will be a relatively permanent liking—not present always with equal strength, nor even present at all when we are absorbed in the pleasures or pains of the moment, but present as a permanent undercurrent of our interests. And further, since it is a liking for certain activities not as being enjoyed by us but as being what they are in themselves, its objects will naturally coincide with the things which Professor Campbell describes as being goods for man and not merely for self. Thus the coincidence between the lists of goods recognized on the relational and on the non-relational view is only what might be expected. In any case it cannot possibly furnish an argument for either view against the other.

The second claim is that the relational account explains better than the non-relational the varieties in the valuation of goods from age to age and from community to community. This claim I must resist. The holder of a non-relational view is not bound to hold that all the intrinsic goods he believes in must always be valued by all men, still less that they must always be placed in their true order of value. Here, as else-where, varieties of opinion are no indication that there is not an objective truth that is there to be apprehended. In the realm of natural science, for example, all sensible people agree that there is a completely objective truth to be apprehended, but we have no difficulty in reconciling this with the fact that different ages and different communities hold very different opinions. Different ages and different communities differ in their degree of mental maturity; each age and each community is liable to have prejudices and erroneous presuppositions of its own. To one age it seems self-evident that nature abhors a vacuum, and that natural species are fixed; to another neither of these pre-suppositions gives any satisfaction. It cannot really, I think, be contended that there is more variation between the opinions of different ages or communities about what things are good, than there is between their opinions about matters of natural science, where the laws of nature are admittedly objective and are unchanging.

In particular, Professor Campbell is on very dangerous ground when he thinks that virtue is intrinsically good and that knowledge is not. For surely the variations in the opinions of different ages about the ranking of the different virtues is more striking than the variations about the ranking of intel-lectual activities; and if variation were an argument against intrinsic goodness in the latter case it would be at least equally so in the former. The truth is that it is not an argument against the objective or non-relational view in either case, and that this view can give as good an account of varieties of opinion as the relational view can; I will not claim that it gives a better.

It seems to me, then, that knowledge, or perhaps we should rather say the activity of the mind which leads to knowledge, is good, *not* in the sense that human nature likes having it (although in fact most men do like having it), but in the sense that it is an admirable activity of the human spirit; that this activity owes its excellence not to our liking it, but to its being conducted according to its own proper principles, i.e. according to the principles discovered by logic; and that different instances of this activity are good in proportion as they are conducted according to these principles.

The main other good which Professor Campbell deals with is aesthetic experience. I think we should here distinguish— not that there is not some affinity between the two—between aesthetic enjoyment and artistic creation. The first is funda- mentally a certain kind of pleasure (though it of course pre- supposes certain intellectual activities). The second is primarily a certain kind of mental *activity* (though no doubt the artist feels pleasure in his own activity). I will therefore reserve any- thing I have to say about the former till I come to discuss pleasure, and will consider now the creative activity of the artist. This, like knowledge, appears to me to be good not in the sense that we like it, but in the sense that it is an admirable activity of the human spirit; and it owes its goodness to its own intrinsic character. The characteristics that are the base or foundation of artistic excellence have not been worked out, and probably cannot be worked out, with anything like the precision with which the conditions of scientific excellence have been worked out by logic. Yet in a vague way we have some knowledge of the intrinsic features of good artistic work— vividness and breadth of imagination, vigour of execution, economy in the use of means, simplicity of plan. We think there is something admirable in these things, and it is for this reason that we honour the great artist. We think there is dis- played in great art an activity of the human spirit which is admirable for its own sake, just as virtuous actions or the triumphs of the scientific mind are.

When we turn to consider whether, and if so in what sense, pleasure is good, we come to what is for me one of the most puzzling problems in the whole of ethics. The first point to which I would draw attention is that, while for the word 'good' when applied to moral dispositions and actions and to intellectual and artistic activities we can fairly substitute 'admirable' or at a lower level 'commendable', we cannot do this in the case of pleasant experiences, taken generally. There is nothing admirable or commendable in the mere feeling of pleasure. Another way in which the difference between good activities and pleasure is revealed is that, while we can call a man good, or at least admirable (for 'good' as applied to men tends to be limited to moral goodness) in respect of his moral actions and dispositions and in respect of his intellectual or artistic activities, any goodness that pleasure may be supposed to have is not in this way reflected on to its enjoyer. A man is not good in respect of the mere fact of feeling pleasure.

These facts suggest that one of two things must be true— either that pleasure as such is not good, or that it is good in some quite different way from that in which good activities are good.

And there is a further consideration which at least seems to point to the first alternative as being the true one. It is often assumed that if anything is good, there is an obligation to set ourselves to produce it, unless by an alternative act we can produce something better; and indeed it is a widely accepted view that productivity of good is the only duty. I have given reasons for holding that this view is not true—that there are other principles of duty, viz. that of fulfilling promises, that of making reparation for injuries done, and that of making a return for goods received. But I accept the principle that if something is good there *is* a *prima facie* obligation to produce it, and an actual obligation unless some more stringent *prima facie* obligation intervenes. Now there are two types of case in which it seems clear that we are under no *prima facie* obligation to produce pleasure. There are (1) pleasures that are themselves the manifestation of a bad moral nature, such as those of cruelty or of lust. It is clear that we not merely feel no *prima facie* obligation to produce them either for ourselves or for others. We feel a positive obligation to improve our own character, and so far as we can that of others, so as to prevent ourselves and them from having such enjoyments.

Now if this were all, it might be possible to modify the statement that pleasure is good, by saying 'pleasures that are not manifestations of a bad moral nature are good'. But against this suggestion a fresh difficulty arises. There are (2) certain pleasures which, even when they are not the manifestations of a bad moral nature, we feel ourselves under no obligation to produce; we feel ourselves under no obligation to produce pleasures of any kind for ourselves. We feel ourselves, of course, under no obligation *not* to produce them, except when they are manifestations of a bad nature. But we feel ourselves under no obligation to produce even innocent pleasures for ourselves. That seems to me one of the clearest facts about our moral consciousness, though it is constantly overlooked by those who maintain both that pleasure as such is good and that there is an obligation to produce what is good.

I should perhaps say something here to substantiate two of the statements I have made or implied: (1) that we are conscious of an obligation to produce pleasure for others, and (2) that we are not conscious of an obligation to get pleasure for ourselves. (1) It is clear that the thought underlying a great many conscientious actions is the thought that by these actions pleasure will be produced for some one other than the agent. Some one might suggest that all that we feel bound to do is to refrain from producing pain for others, or to minimize their pain; and it is true that we feel these duties more acutely than the duty of positively promoting the pleasure of others. But it is surely plain, on reflection, that our sense of duty actually goes beyond this, and that we feel bound in the same sort of way, though not in the same degree, to maximize pleasure, as we feel bound to minimize pain, for others.

It is true again that much of the conscientious action which aims at producing pleasure is not actuated *solely* by the thought that pleasure will be produced for some one else, but also by the thought (*a*) that it will be produced for some one for whose well-being one has assumed a special responsibility (e.g. for one's children), or (*b*) that it will be produced for some one who has at present less than his due share of pleasure (e.g. for badly paid workers, or for sufferers from disease). In such cases there is involved (*a*) the thought of a duty to fulfil a promise, or an implicit promise, or (*b*) the thought of a duty to establish a just distribution of pleasure; and then the sense of a duty to produce the pleasure or remove the pain in question is greatly intensified. But I think it would on reflection be agreed that over and above these special obligations we have the sense of a duty to produce pleasure for others, just because it will be pleasure for them, and that if we had fulfilled all our promises, and if a just distribution of pleasures had already been established, there would still be a duty of going on to increase the amount of pleasure to be distributed.

(2) That we are conscious of no duty to maximize pleasure for ourselves seems to be so clear as not to need argument; and perhaps what is needed is rather some explanation of why the fact has been so much overlooked in ethical theory; it certainly is not overlooked in our natural thinking. The explanation is, I think, to be found in the history of the origin of Utilitarianism. Utilitarianism arose by critical reflection on Egoism. Bentham's sense of justice revolted against the monstrously privileged position which Egoism enjoined each individual to assign to his own pleasure, in his choice of action; but in revolting against a current system he made the mistake which has been repeated over and over again in the history of philosophy, the mistake of not questioning drastically enough the tenets of the current system. While asserting that the individual should aim at the pleasure of others, it seems not

4584   T

to have occurred to him to doubt the genuineness of the one obligation that Egoism had allowed. And the very method which he adopted for converting egoists to Utilitarianism, and which no doubt seemed the most hopeful at a time when Egoism was in the ascendant—that of arguing that it was reasonable for them to seek to achieve for others what they already sought to achieve for themselves—forced him to treat pleasure as something intrinsically good, and to ignore the very different ethical aspects which his own pleasure and any other man's pleasure present to any man. Perhaps only a generation for which the view that we should seek *only* our own pleasure is already out of date can see clearly that we are under no obligation to pursue our own pleasure at all.

Of the two types of case in which we are under no obligation to produce pleasure, an attempt might be made to explain the first without giving up the view that pleasure as such is good. With regard to immoral pleasures, it might be said that they are good *qua* pleasures but bad *qua* immoral, and that their badness *qua* immoral outweighs their goodness *qua* pleasant, and that that is the reason why we are never bound to produce them or aid in their production. To this, one who wishes to deny the goodness of pleasure as such might object, 'Yes, but supposing such a pleasure were intensely pleasant but only slightly immoral, might it not then be our duty, on your show- ing, to produce it, since its goodness *qua* pleasant might well out- weigh its badness *qua* immoral?' But his opponent would have a sound reply. He could say, 'Such a pleasure can be intensely pleasant only when it is intensely immoral; a man can enjoy cruelty intensely only if he intensely wishes to hurt another.' If, however, both parties are agreed (as I think they ought to be) that in fact we are never under an obligation to produce immoral pleasures, they must be agreed that the goodness which springs from pleasantness is never so great as to out- weigh the badness that springs from (or consists in) immo- rality; and this fact, as we shall see presently,[1] constitutes a

[1] p. 275.

difficulty for any one who thinks that pleasures are good in the same sense in which moral dispositions and actions may be good.

What the last paragraph has shown is that we seem quite incapable of equating, in respect of goodness, any amount of pleasure with any amount of morally good action. I suggested in *The Right and the Good*[1] that while both virtue and pleasure have places on the same scale of goodness, virtue begins at a higher point than that at which pleasure leaves off, so that any, even the smallest, amount of virtue is better, and more worth bringing into existence, than any, even the greatest, amount of pleasure. But I now see this (and I should have seen it earlier) to be impossible. If virtue were really on the same scale of goodness as pleasure, then pleasure of a certain intensity, if enjoyed by a sufficiently large number of persons or for a sufficient time, would counterbalance virtue possessed or manifested only by a small number or only for a short time. But I find myself quite unable to think this to be the case; and if I am right in this, it follows that pleasures, if ever good, must be good in a different sense from that in which good activities are so.

Now, however, we must turn to the facts which point to pleasure being under certain limitations a good thing. We do consider the state of pleasure, when the pleasure is not a morally bad pleasure, to be in some sense a better state of affairs than the state of pain; and we feel ourselves under a certain obligation to produce it for other people, when it is not a morally bad pleasure, and still more to prevent or minimize pain, when it is not a morally good pain (such as pain at the misfortune of another). And this is not merely because every one likes pleasure and dislikes pain; for vicious people like vicious pleasures, yet we feel ourselves under no obligation to help them to get these. Besides being liked by the persons who have them, pleasures that are not vicious have the further characteristic of being *worthy objects of satisfaction* for an

[1] p. 150.

observer, and perhaps that is the sense in which we should say that they are good, as we attempted to specify the sense in which good actions are good by saying that they are *worthy objects of admiration.*

The point is not that they are actually objects of satisfaction; for vicious activities may easily be objects of satisfaction to those who engage in them, but we do not for that reason call them good. The point is that we think of our satisfaction in seeing people innocently happy as a justified satisfaction; as we should most certainly think of dissatisfaction at seeing people innocently happy as an unjustified dissatisfaction.

It is worth while to point out that the satisfaction of which the pleasures of other people may be objects, and of which they are worthy to be objects, is quite different in its nature from the satisfaction which a man may feel in his own pleasant experiences. It is a sympathetic satisfaction, and sympathy by its nature must be of one man with another, and cannot be felt by a man for himself. Not only is sympathetic satisfaction different in its object from the other kind of satisfaction; it is different in its whole 'feel'.

If we give as the reason which makes it a duty for a man to produce pleasures for other people, and not a duty to produce pleasures for himself, the fact that the former and not the latter are proper objects of satisfaction to him, we must be careful to avoid two misunderstandings which might arise. (1) We might be thought to mean that he ought to produce pleasures for other people in order to get sympathetic satisfactions for himself. That would of course be a complete misstatement of what we really think about our duty to produce pleasure, or to minimize pain, for other people. It is for their sake that we feel bound to act so, not for our own. That is why I have described the pleasures of other people as *objects* of satisfaction, not as *sources* of satisfaction; if we described them in the latter way, we should be treating them as means to the satisfaction, which is just *not* how we regard them when we feel ourselves bound to produce them.

But (2) the sympathetic satisfactions which we get from increasing other people's pleasure or diminishing their pain are not only satisfactions; they are manifestations of a morally good nature; and it might be suggested that it is our duty to increase the pleasure of others or to diminish their pain, because in or by doing so we bring into being these manifestations of a good nature in ourselves. This is plainly wrong for two reasons. (i) One is that which I have used to refute the former misunderstanding, viz. that it is plainly for the sake of those whose pleasure we increase or whose pain we diminish, and not with a view to bringing about any change in our own state, that we feel bound to act so. (ii) The other is that a morally good nature is just as much manifested in dissatisfaction with the pain, or lack of pleasure, of other people as in the satisfaction which we get from increasing their pleasure or diminishing their pain. When we remove the pain of another, we produce in ourselves merely the substitution of a morally good satisfaction—with his pleasure—for a dissatisfaction with his pain which is of exactly the same moral worth, so that from that point of view nothing is gained by the exchange.

We ought to consider at this point a view which might be put forward with regard to the fact that we are never conscious of a duty to get pleasure or avoid pain for ourselves, as we are conscious of a duty to give pleasure to or prevent pain for others. It might be said that both types of action are right, but that only the latter is obligatory, because in the former case there is no possibility of a moral conflict, since in it our natural desire inevitably prompts us to do that which it is right for us to do—to seek our own pleasure. I do not think that this suggestion can be accepted; for (1) the act of seeking pleasure for oneself is not merely not obligatory, but has not even the specific kind of rightness or fitness which is moral fitness. It seems morally entirely colourless. It is not blameworthy, except when it involves the omission of some duty, and it is never morally praiseworthy. But (2) even if it were, the explanation offered of its not being felt to be obligatory does not seem to meet the case. For it often happens that there is a perfectly natural tendency to seek to give pleasure to some other person, which is just as strong as is in most people the tendency to seek pleasure for themselves. This is noticeably so in maternal love. Yet no one would say that because a mother naturally seeks the happiness of her children she has no duty to seek it. She will very likely be led directly by natural affection to seek their happiness, without stopping to ask whether it is her duty. But any disinterested spectator would say that it is her duty, and she herself would agree if she stopped to ask the question. She would not say, 'it is my pleasure and therefore not my duty', but rather 'it is both my duty and my pleasure'.

What light do these considerations throw on the question whether the goodness of the main things that are commonly called good—let us say virtuous action, intelligent thinking, and pleasure—is a quality intrinsic to them, or a relational characteristic, consisting in their standing in a certain relation to something else? When some entity is commonly referred to by an adjective, there is a certain presumption that it is a quality, just as, when it is commonly referred to by a prepositional phrase, there is a presumption that it is a relation or a relational property. An entity commonly referred to by an adjective may reasonably be supposed to be a quality, unless the adjective can be seen, as many adjectives can be seen, to be replaceable by a prepositional phrase. Now in describing some of the things commonly called good as fit objects of admiration, and others as fit objects of satisfaction, I have used prepositional phrases; and it is proper to inquire whether that amounts to saying that goodness is at bottom a relational property. The phrase 'worthy of admiration', it appears to me, does not justify the conclusion that the goodness which is so described is a relational property. For admiration is not a mere emotion; it is an emotion accompanied by the thought that that which is admired is good. And if we ask on what ground a thing is worthy of being thought to be good, only one answer is possible, namely that it *is* good. It would be absurd to say that a thing is good only in the sense that it is worthy of being thought to be good, for our definition of 'good' would then include the very word 'good' which we were seeking to define. I have tried to call attention to the difference between certain things commonly called good and certain others commonly called good, by calling attention to the fact that admiration is appropriate to the one and not to the other; I have not been trying to *define* the sense in which the one class are good, but to call attention to a fact which implies that their goodness is an intrinsic quality of them.

The same is not true of the phrase 'fit object of satisfaction'. While admiration includes or involves the thought that the thing admired is good independently of our admiring it, satisfaction does not include or involve the thought that that in which we take satisfaction is good independently of our satisfaction. We often take satisfaction in things that we do not think good, but only pleasant. And while it is self-evident that the only ground on which a thing is worthy of admiration is that it is good in itself, it is not self-evident that the only ground on which a thing is worthy of our interest or liking is that it is good in itself.

We may now try to put in a clearer form the fact which has so far been expressed by saying that the innocent pleasures of one man are for any other man a worthy object of satisfaction. This is plainly only another way of saying that satisfaction taken by one man in the innocent pleasure of another is morally suitable, or right; and this is a preferable way of putting the matter because, instead of introducing the new and not altogether clear notion of worthiness, it defines the goodness of innocent pleasures by using a notion which has already been recognized as fundamental in ethics, the notion of rightness.

I suggest, therefore, that the sense in which from the point of view of any man the innocent pleasures of another are good is that it is right for him to feel satisfaction in them.

The account I have given of this sense of 'good', though it

has been suggested to me not by Brentano's doctrine but by direct reflection on the facts, clearly has a close affinity with Brentano's doctrine that 'good' *always* means 'object of a love that is right'; and it is proper that some comment should be offered on Brentano's doctrine. The Brentano school holds that 'good' belongs to a class of merely apparent predicates. The nature of the theory can perhaps best be seen by noting the analogy which they hold to exist between the terms 'good' and 'possible'.[1] That a thing, e.g. a spherical body, is possible is, they maintain, a consequence of its constitutive characteristics, and is not one of them. We call a thing possible when we think it not in itself impossible. And we call a thing impossible when and only when we reject it apodeictically (i.e. when we say 'there cannot be such a thing'); therefore we call a thing possible when and only when we reject apodeictically an apodeictic rejection of it (i.e. when we say 'we cannot say that there cannot be such a thing'); and this is the meaning of 'possible'. The rejection of the rejection of a spherical body is based simply on the consideration of the conception of a sphere; and thus 'possible', while not a real predicate of a spherical body, is a direct consequence of its real predicates. In the same way we see, by attending to the conception of pleasure, that an emotion directed towards it and itself characterized as right cannot be other than love; and to see this is to see that pleasure is good. Thus goodness, while it is an 'irreal determination', is consequent on the real characteristics of that which is good.

With one of the main theses of this theory, viz. with its assertion that goodness is not a constitutive characteristic but is grounded on the real characteristics of that which is good, I am in complete agreement, and I may be allowed to refer to a passage of *The Right and the Good*[2] in which I have argued for this view. But there are other features of the Brentano theory which do not appear to me to be correct.

[1] G. Katkov, *Werttheorie und Theodizee*, 147 f.
[2] pp. 121–3.

In the first place, it seems to be a mistake to suppose that 'good', 'bad', 'possible', 'impossible', 'existent', 'non-existent', form a class of *Scheinqualitäte* consisting in relations to certain mental activities 'characterized as right'. Consider the notion of 'possible' (as applied, for instance, to a square) and of 'impossible' (as applied, for instance, to a round square). It is of course true that the apodeictic rejection of a square (i.e. the statement 'there cannot be a square') is apodeictically rejected by a right act of thought (i.e. if we think rightly we see that we cannot rightly say that there cannot be a square). But the square is not possible because a right act of thought rejects the rejection of it; a right act of thought rejects the rejection of it because the square is possible. Our thought that a square is possible can be right only if and because there is a real relation of compatibility between the attributes of equal-sidedness and equal-angledness in a quadrilateral. Our thought that a round square is *im*possible can be right only if and because there is a real relation of incompatibility between roundness and squareness. The Brentano school is no doubt justified in regarding the judgements '*A* exists', '*A* does not exist', '*A* is possible', '*A* is impossible' as being logically very different from judgements in which some ordinary attribute like 'red' or 'loud' is predicated, but their introduction of acceptance or rejection by right thought as being what the judgements mean seems to me mistaken; and modern logic has found a much more satisfactory account of the meaning of such judgements, when, for instance, it points out that a judgement of possibility is really a judgement of compatibility, and a judgement of impossibility really a judgement of incompatibility.

The theory about the nature of goodness is therefore deprived of any support which it might be supposed to derive from being able to class predications of goodness with other judgements which, while they seem to be about objects, are really about activities of mind directed towards these objects. But it might still be a true theory about goodness, though the corresponding theories about existence and possibility are false. The first criticism I would offer of the theory of goodness is that in defining goodness as 'being the object of a love which is right', it fails to distinguish between the two attitudes which I have called admiration and satisfaction. One has, it seems to me, only to reflect for a very little on one's attitude towards a brave act or a fine intellectual effort, and towards a sensuous pleasure, to see how very different the two attitudes are; or rather, since there is satisfaction in both cases, how completely the element of admiration is lacking in the latter case. And further, while satisfaction at another's pleasure is simply a feeling, not involving the thought that the other's pleasure is good in itself, but only the thought that he is being pleased, admiration involves the thought that that which is admired is good in itself. If I am right in giving this account, nothing can be a worthy object of admiration—it cannot be right to admire it—unless it is also good in itself; while the pleasures of others are good, from the point of view of any man, *simply* in the sense that it is right for him to take satisfaction in them. Thus Brentano's theory seems to be true of 'good' in one of its senses, though not true of it in the other; and in so far as it is true, it is very important.

Finally, however, the theory seems to be wrong in saying that a man's own pleasures are, from the point of view of any man, good in the same sense in which the pleasures of others are. For while we can see the rightness, the moral suitability, of his taking satisfaction in the latter, we can see no moral suitability in his taking satisfaction in the former. Or again, to be glad at the pain of another is wrong; to be glad at one's own pain is either impossible, or if possible merely silly.

If our contentions are right, 'good' in its first sense is a non-relational attribute; 'good' in its second sense is a relational attribute, but while our account of it is a relational one, it is not a naturalistic one, since it defines good in its second sense by reference to 'right'.

To sum up the results we have arrived at: Certain moral dispositions and actions, and certain activities of the intellect and of the creative imagination, appear to be good in a way which depends entirely on their intrinsic nature, on the first being conscientious or benevolent, for instance, or on the second being logical or having the characters, harder to specify, that make artistic activity good. These things are good in a sense which is indefinable, but which may be paraphrased by saying that they are fine or admirable activities of the human spirit, and by adding that they are good in such a way that any one who has them or does them is to that extent being good himself. Pleasure is never good in this, which I should call the most proper sense of 'good' But the pleasures of others (except those which are immoral) are good in a secondary sense, viz. that they are morally worthy or suitable objects of satisfaction. Things that are good in the first and most proper sense we have, by a self-evident necessity, a *prima facie* duty to produce, to the best of our ability, irrespective of whether it is ourselves or others that are going to have or do them. Things that are good in the secondary sense, i.e. the pleasures of others, are also things that we have a duty to produce. It should be added that things which are good in the first sense are also good in the second. Activities that are good in themselves are necessarily worthy objects of satisfaction, and are thus doubly good.

If these are really two different senses of 'good', things that are good in the different senses do not fall on the same scale of goodness and are not comparable in respect of goodness. If they fell on the same scale, and if the duty to produce one rather than the other depended on which was the better, the *prima facie* duty of producing some good activity in another person would always be outweighed by the *prima facie* duty of producing pleasure, if the quantity of pleasure were to be sufficiently great (e.g. if it were to be enjoyed by a sufficient number of people). The natural moral consciousness finds it very hard to believe that any amount of pleasure can thus outweigh a given good activity in goodness;[1] and the recognition of two senses of goodness has vindicated the natural moral conscious-

[1] Cf. p. 275.

ness. We are still free to believe that the *prima facie* duty of producing what is intrinsically good always takes precedence over the *prima facie* duty of producing pleasure for others.

At the same time, things that are good in a single sense *will* be comparable in respect of goodness. It will be a legitimate question whether in any given situation it is rather our duty to promote some good moral activity, or some good intellectual activity, in ourselves or others; and in deciding which we ought to do we have to rely on our very fallible apprehension of the degrees of goodness belonging to each. And if it seems paradoxical to say that a good moral activity is comparable with a good intellectual activity in respect of goodness, it is at least a paradox not peculiar to the view I have put forward; the theory of ideal Utilitarianism also contains it, and adds the greater paradox of regarding pleasure also as falling on the same scale of goodness.

For any man, his own actual pleasures are not good in either of these senses, and his imagined future pleasures are not imagined to be good in either of them; therefore the duty of producing good involves no duty of producing pleasures for himself. Yet it is natural enough, and it has been habitual in most ethical theories, to call them good. It is, however, improper to call them so. For in the proper use of any word (to recur to Meinong's distinction)[1] it is used to *signify* something about that to which it is applied, besides *expressing* a mental attitude towards that thing; while in calling our own pleasures good we are, it would seem, only *expressing* our enjoyment of them when we have them and our attraction towards them when we have not got them.

The two proper kinds of good also have, for any one who recognizes their goodness, this attractive character; and this attractive character, or (as it has sometimes been expressed) the fact that we have a pro-attitude towards them, seems to be all that is common to these three kinds of thing that are habitually called good. Is this, then, the original usage of the word;

[1] Cf. pp. 254-5.

was it originally a mere interjection expressive of attraction, and has it come to have its two significances (as opposed to its expressiveness) as men have by reflection come to see, in some of the things to which they were attracted, that they were more than attractive, that they were worthy objects of admiration, or worthy objects of satisfaction? The suggestion is plausible, but it is opposed by the grammatical form of the word—by its being an adjective. So far as I know, there is no evidence of the origin of the word 'good' from some primitive interjectional form, such as might have been a mere expression of attraction. Unless an inquiry by comparative philologists should discover an interjectional origin of the word, which does not seem at all likely, it seems not improbable that the word started by expressing admiration (which includes the thought that the person or thing admired is good in itself) and that it was by a sort of degeneration that it has come to have its other types of application.

This leads naturally on to a further inquiry. One of the great puzzles of ethical theory lies in the sense we have of obligations to do certain things which do not seem likely to bring into being the greatest possible amount of any of the generally recognized *personal* goods, either in the way of good moral or intellectual activities or in the way of pleasure. We feel an obligation to do a promised service to another, far greater than the obligation we feel to do him an unpromised service, and that even when we cannot foresee any more distant personal goods which will be brought into being by our action. Similarly, we feel an obligation to make reparation for wrongs we have done, and return for benefits we have received, even when we do not think we shall be bringing more good into being for the person we have wronged or the person whose services we have accepted, than we could bring into being for some other person by an alternative act. And we feel an obligation to do justice as between different people, even when we do not think the sum of goods either moral or intellectual or hedonistic will be increased thereby. The force of this last consideration can be most easily seen by noting the facts that even the most convinced utilitarians have recognized the duty of dividing pleasure justly between man and man, even when the sum of pleasures to be produced is not increased thereby, and that some of them have recognized the duty of doing so even when the sum of pleasures to be produced in this way is less than that which would be produced by an unjust distribution.

The question that faces us is whether we may not be able to account for these facts consistently with Utilitarianism by supposing that in all these cases there is some *different* kind of good that is created by our action, and that that is why we ought to do the action. These other goods might in general be called *situational* goods.[1] They would not be activities or enjoyments resident in individuals, but would involve relations between individuals. Their nature will be seen more clearly by pointing to the several instances. The suggestion would be that I ought to fulfil promises because the receipt of a service by a person to whom it has been promised is a situational good which I can bring into being by fulfilling my promise and shall fail to bring into being if I do not fulfil it; that I ought to make reparation for injuries I have done because the receiving of reparation by one who has been wronged is a similar situational good; that I ought to make a return for services I have received because the enjoyment of services in return for services is again a situational good; that I ought to do justice as between man and man because the enjoyment of happiness in proportion to merit is a situational good, over and above the good which consists in the meritorious character or its activities, and that which consists in the happiness. All of these situational goods would be goods not in the sense of being worthy objects of admiration, but in the sense of being worthy objects of satisfaction, just as for any man the pleasures of other people are.

It is to be observed that initially quite a different account of the matter might be given. It might be said that the suggestion just made in every case puts the cart before the horse—that it

---

[1] I take the phrase from N. Hartmann, *Ethik*², 236 (Eng. tr. ii. 31). The German is *Sachverhaltswerten* (state-of-affairs values).

is not true that we ought to produce pleasure for other people because the pleasure of other people is a worthy object of satisfaction, but rather that it is a worthy object of satisfaction because we ought to produce it; that it is not true that promises should be kept because the reception of promised services is a worthy object of satisfaction, but that the reception of promised services is a worthy object of satisfaction because promises ought to be kept; and so on in the other cases. To decide between the two views, we must consider each of these branches of duty on its own merits. The question seems to me a difficult one, but I will answer it to the best of my ability.

Let us start with the duty of promoting the pleasure of other people, and the still more obvious duties of not causing pain to other people, and of diminishing their pain; for brevity I will use the phrase 'the duty of promoting the pleasure of others' as covering all these duties. It seems to me clear that the pleasure of other people is a worthy object of satisfaction to any man. And it is to be observed that a good man takes satisfaction in the pleasure of others quite independently of any judgement that any one has done his duty in causing that pleasure, and is dissatisfied at the pain of other people quite independently of any judgement that any one has done wrong in causing this pain. He feels a satisfaction at the mere existence of the pleasure, a dissatisfaction at the mere existence of the pain, however it has been caused, apart from any satisfaction or dissatisfaction he may feel at the way it has been caused. And again, a good man's satisfaction at the pleasure of others, or dissatisfaction at their pain, is independent of the thought that he ought to increase the pleasure or diminish the pain of others; he may feel the satisfaction or dissatisfaction before he becomes conscious of the duty, and if there is no obvious means by which he could increase their pleasure or diminish their pain, he may feel the satisfaction or dissatisfaction without coming to be aware of the duty at all. Thus it may, I think, certainly be said that a good man's taking of satisfaction in the pleasure of others is independent of any thought of duty. Two questions, however, remain: (1) Is the fact that the pleasure of others is a worthy object of satisfaction the objective basis of our duty to bring it into being? and (2) Is the thought that the pleasure of others is a worthy object of satisfaction the subjective ground of our *thinking* we have a duty to bring it into being? The answer to the first question seems to me to be Yes. And if so, the duty of trying to produce pleasure for others will fall under the same general principle as the duty of trying to promote good activities; it will be grounded on the goodness of the result to be produced—though the two results are good in different senses.[1] The answer to the second question must be more qualified. I do not think that a good man formulates explicitly the dictum 'the pleasure of others is a worthy object of satisfaction' before he feels the duty to bring it into being. The position rather is that he in fact feels satisfaction at their pleasure or dissatisfaction at their pain, and feels, rather obscurely, that his interest in the pleasure of others is something that he can with moral safety follow—a feeling which he never has about his interest in his own pleasures. If this be so, it is an implicit awareness that the pleasure of others is good, in the sense of being a worthy object of interest, that becomes the ground of the sense of a duty to produce it.

Let me turn now to the duty of distributing pleasures among others in proportion to their goodness. Here, again, it seems that a good man takes satisfaction in finding goodness rewarded, independently of the thought that it was any one's duty to produce this situation, and independently of the thought that he ought to do what he can to effect in other cases the rewarding of goodness. He will take satisfaction in the happiness of the virtuous, and dissatisfaction in their unhappiness, even when he thinks this has been produced as the result of natural laws and not of moral action. And as with his interest in the pleasure of others in general, so with his special interest in the happiness of the virtuous, he feels obscurely that this interest is one that can be trusted. His sense of a duty to act

---

[1] Viz. those pointed out on pp. 271–6, 278–9.

justly seems, I think, to be properly said to rest on an obscure sense that the happiness of the virtuous is a good in the sense of being a morally worthy object of interest.

Turn next to the duties of making reparation for wrongs we have done, and of making a return for benefits we have received. Here again, a morally good spectator will find satisfaction in seeing these things take place; but in this case the satisfaction seems to me to depend on the previous thought that it was A's duty to make such compensation to B. It is not simply B's acquiring of a certain advantage or pleasure that a morally good spectator feels to be a worthy object of satisfaction; if this were so, we might say that A's duty to make compensation arises from the fact that what he thereby produces is good, in the sense of being a worthy object of satisfaction. What a morally good spectator thinks to be a worthy object of satisfaction is B's getting the advantage or pleasure *by A's action*, by A's giving it to him; and that thought rests upon the prior thought that B has a right to get it from A, or in other words that A has a duty to give it to him. The spectator's primary thought is that A by doing an injury to B or by accepting a benefit from him has by his own act put himself under a moral obligation to B, and any satisfaction the spectator feels at A's fulfilling the obligation presupposes the thought that there is an obligation, and is not presupposed by it.

And similarly it seems clear to me that, while a good man will feel satisfaction at a second man's fulfilling his promise to a third, that satisfaction presupposes the thought that the promiser has, by making the promise, put himself under an obligation to the promisee. In this case also, therefore, it appears that the rightness of the act does not depend on the goodness of the result produced, even if we admit that the result produced *is* good, in the sense of being a worthy object of satisfaction. The rightness of the act will, as in the cases of reparation for wrongs and return for benefits, depend on the *nature* of the result to be produced, but not on its *goodness*, since it is good only because there is a duty to produce it.

XII

MORAL GOODNESS

I HAVE suggested that things that are good in the predicative as opposed to the adjunctive sense fall into two classes: (1) those that are good in the sense of being worthy objects of admiration, and (2) those that are good in the sense of being worthy objects of satisfaction. Both of these come, from one point of view, within the scope of ethics; for a thing's being good in either of these ways brings into being a *prima facie* obligation to produce that thing; we feel under an obligation not only to promote good activities, but also to promote the pleasure and diminish the pain of others. But goods of the second type are not themselves, as such,[1] morally good. Nor, again, are all goods of the *first* type themselves as such morally good; excellent scientific or artistic activity is good but not morally good. I wish now to consider that part of class (1) which *is* morally good. What we are apt to think of first, when we ask ourselves what kinds of thing are morally good, is certain types of voluntary action, proceeding from certain motives, such as the wish to do one's duty or the wish to diminish the pain of others; and we might be disposed therefore to identify moral goodness with goodness of will. But this would be a mistake. For if we hold that actions are morally good when and because they proceed from certain motives, we can hardly fail to ascribe moral goodness to those same desires when they do not lead to action. They may not lead to action either because the circumstances fail to suggest any action by which we might produce what we desire, or because some other desire is stronger; but in either case the desire itself may be of the same kind and of the same intensity when it is not followed by action as when it is; and if it is what

[1] Though of course *some* of the pleasures of other people which may be promoted are manifestations of a good character and themselves morally good.

makes the action good when action follows, it is also good when action does not follow. And if we widen our conception of what is morally good to include certain desires, we cannot refuse to include also certain emotions. If desire for another's pleasure is good, so also is satisfaction at his actual pleasure; if desire to relieve another's pain is good, so also is sorrow at his actual pain. In fact satisfaction or dissatisfaction at an existing state of affairs is of exactly the same value, morally, as desire to bring such a state of affairs into existence, or to prevent it from coming to exist. And if we may group desires and satisfactions together under the heading of 'interests', interests, no less than actions inspired by interests, may be morally good.

But there is something further that has to be included among the things that are morally good. So far I have spoken of actual felt desires and emotions, or satisfactions. Take now the case of a man who habitually, when he attends to (for instance) the pleasures of other people, takes an interest in them, but who is not at the moment attending to them, either because he is asleep or because he is attending to something else. There is no means of knowing directly how his state differs from that of a man who is habitually indifferent to the pleasures of others; for it is only the physical effects of actions that can be perceived, and only *actual* desires, emotions, and the like that can be discovered by introspection. But we may feel certain by inference that the state of a man who is habitually unselfish differs somehow from the state of one who is habitually selfish, when both men are asleep or otherwise engaged; for if their state during the period of inattention were exactly alike it would be unintelligible that their behaviour afterwards should be different. It is, indeed, conceivable that the only difference between them, during the interval, should be a difference in the state of their bodies; and if that were so, there would be nothing that is morally good existing through the interval, but only morally neutral conditions which lead to morally unneutral results. But not only our whole moral life, with its accompaniments of repentance and remorse for the past, but even the ordinary facts of memory, are witness to the continued existence of the self through intervals such as those of sleep; and the soul's nature and state in sleep must be just as definite as its nature and state in waking life, though it is in some respects different; for nothing individual that exists can be in any respect indefinite. Answering to the difference that there is between the behaviour of a selfish and that of an unselfish man, it is reasonable to suppose that there is a difference between their characters when they are not behaving at all.

But, it may be said, all that exists when the two men are not behaving is potentialities of behaving, or tendencies to behave. The answer to that is that there is no such thing as potentiality that is not rooted in actuality. That which potentially has the characteristic a can have it only by actually having some other characteristic b. We have, as I have said, no means of knowing what is the actual characteristic that distinguishes the selfish from the unselfish man, when neither is behaving selfishly or unselfishly; we can only say that there must be some difference between the two characters which actually exists, and becomes the cause of their different behaviour when the occasion arises. The man who habitually behaves bravely is in some sense really brave even when he is asleep, or when no occasion for bravery is present; and his bravery has moral goodness when it is dormant no less than when it is being exercised.

We may say, then, that what is morally good is acts of will, desires, and emotions, and finally relatively permanent modifications of character even when these are not being exercised. Some might think that we are coming nearer to what is most truly good as we proceed thus 'inwards', from what is perceived to what can only be discovered by introspection, and then to what can only be divined by inference. But that would be quite a mistake. What is perceived by the senses has, indeed, no moral value, for all that the senses perceive is a man's body performing certain movements. But then that was not what we meant by a moral action; a moral action was the setting oneself, from a certain motive, to effect a certain change, and this is as truly inward as anything can be. What *can* be said, however, is that a character is a larger and grander bearer of moral goodness than any single manifestation of character— whether it be an action, a desire, or an emotion—can be.

But if a character is the grandest bearer of moral value, it is also true that we can build up our conception of an ideal character only by considering first the various elements, the various interests, that would compose it, and by adding that in the ideal character these various interests would be present with intensities proportioned to their goodness. We must begin by asking what are the various interests that are morally good.

It is generally agreed among moralists that action owes its goodness, and the measure of its goodness, to the motive from which it springs. The most noteworthy exception to this is Kant, who maintains that an action is good only when it is done not from a motive, but from a maxim. But this is due to his using the word 'motive' in an unusually narrow sense, a sense such that the sense of duty is not reckoned as a motive. The limitation is contrary to the natural meaning of the word, and in the natural meaning of the word Kant is at one with other moralists in saying that moral goodness depends on the motive from which the act is done. Any attempt, then, to decide the measure in which different kinds of action possess moral goodness involves as a preliminary some attempt to state the various kinds of motive from which action can spring.

It has been in the past a widely held view that all action springs from the desire for pleasure, and the first modern philosopher who seriously sought, by an account and classification of motives, to set this view aside, was Bishop Butler. Butler's account was that besides self-love there are two other general motives, benevolence and conscience, and two groups of highly particular motives, 'terminating upon objects peculiar to themselves'; one of these groups consisting of desires for such things as food, drink, water, and shelter, each such desire tending primarily to the good of the individual, and the other group consisting of desires for such things as esteem, each such desire tending primarily to conduce to the general good; these latter desires are related to general benevolence very much as the first group of particular desires is related to general self-love.[1]

In its general lines Butler's attack on the description of human nature as being actuated only by selfish motives is thoroughly justified. But his account needs some revision if it is to be made to agree with the facts. Take, for instance, his view that hunger is distinct from self-love, not a desire for pleasure but a desire for food. This is clearly correct in so far as it says that a hungry man is not necessarily a deliberate hedonist, coolly and calmly seeking his own greatest pleasure, or greatest sum of pleasures. Such an account is obviously untrue both of many of the least worthy and of all the most worthy of our actions. It is untrue of the man who 'sells his birthright for a mess of pottage', who under the sway of some strong instinctive impulse like hunger or lust does actions which he knows are bound to destroy his prospects of a life of happiness; and it is untrue of the man who acts from a sense of duty regardless of his personal happiness. It is with the former opposition that we are here concerned. It is obviously an inadequate answer to the question what hunger is, to say that it is the desire for food. Desire is always for something not yet existent, but the food exists already. We shall at least have to say that hunger is the desire to eat or to be eating food. But then we may go on to ask what it is about the eating of food that attracts us. Can we not be more definite in our statement? Why is it, really, that we eat our breakfast and our dinner? To a large extent it is true that we eat our meals to make and keep ourselves fit for the reaching of some ulterior end, whether that be the doing of our duty or the attainment of success, or whatever it be. But if we ask ourselves what are the more immediate reasons that make the eating of food attractive, it seems to me that we

[1] Butler's Works, ed. Gladstone, ii. 33–6.

are left with only two. There is, on the one hand—and this is
what is dominant in any case of extreme hunger—the desire to
get rid of a present gnawing discomfort; and there is, on the
other hand—and this is dominant when we get our meals at
their accustomed times and in sufficient plenty—the desire for
the sensuous pleasures of taste. Suppose that a man were
anaesthetized, so that he felt none of the discomfort of hunger,
and that he were conscious of chewing and swallowing but felt
no pleasure in these processes. It seems to me clear that in
such a case the eating of food would not attract him at all,
except for one of the ulterior causes which I have mentioned
only to set them aside as irrelevant to the question: What is the
intrinsic motive for eating? It would seem then that our desire
for food is a desire to eat food (1) as freeing us from a certain
pain, and (2) as giving us a certain pleasure, the one element or
the other predominating as the hunger is more or less acute.
And if so, the hedonist will be entitled to reckon the desire for
food as an illustration of his general thesis. But it is an instance
of self-love not in the sense of desire for pleasure in general,
but of desire for a particular pleasure or for relief from a
particular pain, or for a combination of the two.

In principle, this account seems to cover a great part of the
life of most human beings—that it is a search, not for pleasure
in the abstract, but for particular pleasures. It is often thought
that hedonism can be refuted by urging that it erroneously con-
cludes, from the fact that pleasure is felt in anticipating our
action or its results, or again from the fact that pleasure normally accompanies the fulfilment of desire, that pleasure is the
object of desire. And that is a true criticism of the arguments
offered by some hedonists. But it should not lead us to over-
state the case and say that it is normally just certain activities
and not certain pleasures that are the object of desire. Would
men seek riches if it were not for the pleasure they have experienced in the past, and hope to have again, from having
riches at their command? Would they seek fame if they had
not experienced the pleasure of hearing men speak well of them

and were not looking forward to experiencing it again? Would they play games if they had not enjoyed the thrill of the successful control of their muscles and of the triumph over their adversary?

I start, then, with desires for particular pleasures, as being probably the commonest of all the types of desire. Secondly, out of these desires there arises in some people, and actuates them in some of their actions, a desire for their own pleasure on the whole. In so far as people are actuated by this, they become capable of giving up some particular pleasure towards which they are strongly attracted, because they think it will interfere with their attainment of the greatest amount of pleasure on the whole. Both this type of life and that previously described are selfish lives, but the former—to use the language I have used previously[1]—is a suggestible and the latter a planned selfishness. The latter is a sort of rationalization of the former.

Thirdly, there are desires for some particular good activity, or for the attainment of some particular virtue, or knowledge, or skill. These desires are closely bound up with desires for particular pleasures. For in general the exercise of any good activity, and even the possession of technical skill, is a pleasant thing, and is known to be such, and we can hardly be desiring the good activity or the skill without desiring the pleasure that accompanies them. Yet we can at least distinguish between the two desires as two distinct elements in our total mental state, and can say that in some cases the one desire and in others the other predominates. The skilled workman desires both to do his job well and to have the pleasure of doing it well, but one workman will be thinking more of the one and another more of the other. And some of our desires for pleasure are unaccompanied by any thought that the activities on which the pleasures supervene are good. This is true, for instance, of desires for such pleasures as those of eating and drinking, in contrast with those of virtuous or scientific or artistic activity.

Fourthly, in some people there arises out of these desires for

---

[1] p. 200.

particular forms of perfection or good activity a generalized wish for good activity. This is the motive which Aristotle describes as dominating the good man, and it is also the motive in what T. H. Green describes as the life of self-realization. In Green's account self-satisfaction, which is a particular form of pleasure, sometimes *seems* to predominate over self-realization; I think we may take it, however, that at bottom self-realization and not self-satisfaction is Green's ideal.

Fifthly, there are desires that particular people other than oneself should have particular pleasures. It is often difficult for an observer to know whether an act of apparent benevolence to another person proceeds from this motive, or from the wish to engage in the good activity of conferring pleasure on another, or again from the wish to have the pleasure of conferring it. But from time to time the difference between the other-regarding motive and these two self-regarding ones betrays itself even to an observer. For the person whose motive is the other-regarding one will sometimes rather stand aside and let a greater benefit be conferred on the object of his love by some one else than confer a lesser benefit himself; while one whose motive is either of the self-regarding ones will behave in the opposite way. And apart from such cases I think it is possible by introspection to distinguish the three motives, and after, when two of them or all three are present, to say which is the predominant one.

It is noteworthy that such desire for the pleasure of an individual may coexist with almost complete selfishness towards others. A mother who is capable of the greatest self-sacrifice to spare her child any pain may be at the same time quite callous to the pain of children not her own. And further, such restricted altruism is, I suppose, always accompanied by some egoism. A mother desires not only the happiness of her child, but also the happiness she herself will get from seeing her child happy and from her child's companionship and affection. Nevertheless, it is a mistake to describe the motive of her action as *égoïsme à deux*. There may be much egoism in it, but one, and often the predominant, element in it is an altruism, very restricted in its scope, but very strong and in itself quite disinterested. And the same is to be said of other restricted altruisms.

Sixthly, in some people there supervenes on this restricted altruism a generalized altruism in which the pleasure or happiness of all human beings, or even of all sentient beings, becomes an object of desire.

Seventhly, there are desires for the exercise of good activities by, or the improvement of character or intellect in, some particular person or persons other than the desirer. Clearly this is an additional component in the total attitude of most parents towards their children, and of many men towards their fellow countrymen. And eighthly, there is a generalized form of this, which is the desire for the perfection of all human beings. And each of these can obviously become a motive to action.

Ninthly, it seems to me that we must recognize as a distinct motive the desire that some one else should suffer. It might be suggested that what is at work here is the desire to have the pleasure of making him suffer, or of seeing him suffer. But that would be putting the cart before the horse; we should not anticipate pleasure from making a man suffer or from seeing him suffer, unless we first desired him to suffer.

Tenthly, there is at least possible a generalized desire that every one except oneself should suffer. But, to the credit of human nature be it said, it is far more doubtful whether such a desire ever really exists than it is that a generalized desire for the happiness of other people exists.

Eleventh, there is the wish to make another person's character worse in some respect. This is not a common motive; for in most cases, where a man seems to an observer to be setting himself to corrupt the character of another man for the sake of doing so, he is really not attracted by the thought of the other person's becoming worse, but is using the corruption of his victim's character as a means to his own pleasure or his own gain. Yet it seems to me difficult to deny that in some cases there is a real wish to corrupt the character of another, and that this is sometimes at least a component in the motive to action.

Twelfth, we can conceive of a generalized form of the last-named motive, in which the agent wishes all other men to be as bad as possible, and to be made so by his agency so far as he can make it effective. But it may be doubted if this motive has ever operated in a human heart. It would be the motive not of a man but of a devil.

So far I have spoken of motivation in which there is no thought of claims or of duties. But we must now take account of the wish to fulfil some particular claim thought of as morally binding. And finally there is the generalized form of this, in which the wish is, not to do that which is the fulfilment of a particular claim (or which is *prima facie* obligatory), but to do the act which is the maximum fulfilment of claims and is in the strict sense obligatory.

I have not thought it necessary to offer any proof of the existence of these several motives. I think I have found them all (with the exception of the tenth, eleventh, and twelfth) at work in myself, and I venture to think that, with these same exceptions, they all exist from time to time in many people's minds—though some of them perhaps only very occasionally. The only ground on which I think objection would be likely to be made would be the assumption of psychological Hedonism, or of the more general view of which psychological Hedonism is one form, that only states or activities of the desirer himself can be the object of desire; and that is a belief which rests on confusions which have often been pointed out, and will not stand the test of a scrutiny into the motives from which we actually act.

Perhaps the main ground on which it might be urged that only imagined future states of the desirer can be desired is this: If what is desired, it might be said, were a state of any one other than the desirer, then the desire should be satisfied by the mere coming into existence of the desired state; but in fact no one's desire is satisfied merely by the coming into existence of a state of some one else; the desirer must come to know or think that it has come into existence; and indeed the desire will be satisfied if the other person's state does not come into existence at all, but the desirer merely thinks that it has. Therefore, it might be urged, what is desired is not the other person's state, but the desirer's own state of confidence that the other person's state has come into existence. What a mother desires, it might be said, is not that her child should be happy, but that she should know or think it to be happy; and that is proved by the fact that she will be satisfied if she thinks it is happy, even if it is not happy in fact, and will not be satisfied if it is happy but she does not know or think that it is.

This argument rests on a confusion between the fulfilment of desire and the satisfaction of the desirer. The fulfilment of desire is simply the coming into existence of that which is desired; the satisfaction is a new mental experience in the mind of the desirer. The latter naturally does not arise unless the desirer knows or thinks that the desire has been fulfilled, whether or not in fact it has been fulfilled; it naturally arises if the desirer thinks with confidence that the desire has been fulfilled, whether or not it has. The fact that the satisfaction of the desirer depends not on the occurrence of the external event but on the desirer's opinion about it has no tendency to show that what was desired was a state of the desirer's own mind. In fact, there is no general ground on which we can rule out any imaginable state of affairs from being desired; we can only attempt to discover, by reflection on our own desires and by inference from the behaviour of other people round us, and from the facts of history, what types of imagined states of affairs in fact are desired; and this is what I have been trying to do.

It will be noticed that throughout this catalogue of motives I have distinguished a more particularized, instinctive form and a more generalized and rationalized form. In some cases one or more intermediate forms might be recognized. For instance, there may be a man in whom conscientiousness with regard to the fulfilment of all promises is strong, but conscientiousness with regard to benefiting others weak. Such a man will have a generalized sense of duty to do, out of the alternative acts which would be fulfilments of particular promises, the act which would be the maximum fulfilment of promise; but he has not reached the stage of wishing to do that which is the maximum fulfilment of *all* obligations, including those of beneficence as well as those of promise-fulfilment. And similarly intermediate forms might be interpolated between the particularized and the generalized motives which I have distinguished in other cases. But it would be tedious to attempt what one could certainly not complete, a minute account of all the possible intermediate forms.

It is, in general, possible to range these motives in order of excellence. We may leave out of account the generalized wish to cause pain and the generalized wish to cause moral evil, as falling below the level of human nature. Of the other motives I have mentioned, we must surely rank lowest the wish to produce moral evil in some other person. Just as we saw[1] good activities to be good in a fuller sense than pleasure, being worthy objects not only of satisfaction but also of admiration, moral evil is bad in a fuller sense than pain, being a worthy object not only of dissatisfaction but also of condemnation; as is evidenced by the fact that a good man will fear it more, whether in himself or in others who are dear to him. If this is so, it is natural that the wish to produce moral evil is a worse motive than the wish to produce pain. The wish to produce pain comes, however, next to it in the scale of demerit.

The complete generalization of this wish, the wish to produce as much pain as possible for all human beings, probably does not exist as a human motive. But the partial generalization of the wish to produce pain, the wish to produce and to go on producing a maximum of pain for some individual, the wish involved in hatred, is plainly worse than the wish to produce a particular temporary pain, the wish involved in anger.

[1] pp. 282–3.

When we come to consider whether any moral value attaches to the wish to procure some particular pleasure for oneself, the question is rather complicated and difficult. I will set down what appears to me to be true about it. Pleasures themselves may be divided into three classes—those which are marks of a good nature, and themselves morally good, such as the pleasure of helping another; those which are morally indifferent, such as the sensuous pleasures; and those which are marks of a bad nature, and themselves morally bad, such as the pleasure of hurting another. The desire to get an indifferent pleasure is itself indifferent. The desire to get a morally good pleasure, as being morally good, is itself morally good; the desire to get it, as being a pleasure, is morally indifferent. The desire to get a morally bad pleasure, as being morally bad (if such a desire exists, which is doubtful), is morally bad; the desire to get it, as being a pleasure, seems morally neutral, though the accompanying indifference to the badness of the pleasure is morally bad.

The generalized wish to get a maximum of pleasure for oneself is also morally neutral (though the indifference which may accompany it as to whether the pleasures to be got are or are not the pleasures of engaging in bad activities, is morally bad). Prudence, the tendency to act on such a wish, is therefore not a virtue, but only a characteristic useful to its possessor.

The wish to promote some good activity, or some improvement of character or of intellect, in another, appears to be as certainly better than the wish to produce pleasure for another, as the wish to corrupt a character is worse than the wish to produce pain. And again, the generalized wish to promote the moral and intellectual improvement of all human beings is better than the wish to produce pleasure for them, as the wish to promote their deterioration, if such a wish existed, would be worse than the wish to make them all suffer pain.

When we compare the wish to promote perfection or good activity in another person with the wish to achieve it for oneself, I can find no ground for regarding either as better or less good than the other. Suppose I wish to bring about in myself some good activity, moral or scientific or artistic, or some moral or intellectual improvement which will lead to such activities; and abstract from any thought of the pleasure or credit or gain I can get by such activity or such improvement. What is left is an attraction towards a certain activity or change of character or of intellectual state as being good, and this is seen to be, not the same thing as, but of the same moral worth as, the wish to produce a similar activity or change in another person. I may, owing to particular circumstances, be wishing for the one when I am not wishing for the other, just as owing to particular circumstances I may be desiring the moral improvement of my children when I am not desiring the moral improvement of any one else, and may on another occasion be desiring the moral improvement of a pupil when I am not even thinking of that of my children. But in all three cases we are desiring something to come into being because it is good, and all three desires seem therefore to be of the same moral worth.

Finally, we must compare the desire to do one's duty, both in its particularized and in its generalized form, with all the other motives I have named. It seems to me clear that in either form it ranks above all other motives. For suppose that a person is attracted towards one act as being the fulfilment of a moral claim, and to another act without having this thought about it. Suppose, for instance, that he thinks of a certain use of his money as being the fulfilment of a moral claim which a creditor has on him, and is at the same time attracted towards bestowing it in charity. So long as he thinks of one act as being an act he ought to do, and of the other not as being something he ought to do, we are bound to say that he will be acting better in doing what he thinks he ought than in doing what he does not think of as something that he ought to do. It is only if he thinks of the possible object of his charity as himself having a moral claim on him, that he can be acting better in bestowing the charity than in paying the debt; and then we are no longer contrasting action from the sense of duty with action from a different motive, but action from the sense of one *prima facie* obligation with action from the sense of another. Or again, suppose he is attracted towards some scientific activity by the thought that it is a fine activity of the human spirit, and towards some philanthropic activity by the thought that he ought to engage in it; and suppose that he cannot do both things; we should say he was acting better in doing what he thought he ought than in doing the alternative action; we should say that only if the scientific activity also presented itself as a *prima facie* obligation (as it well might) could he possibly be acting morally better in preferring it to the alternative.

It might be suggested that that argument is not conclusive—that, though action from the sense of duty is better than action from any other motive when the two motives conflict, action is still better when it proceeds from the motive of love without the thought of duty occurring at all. But I do not think this can seriously be maintained. The motive of love which we now are supposing to arise unaccompanied by any thought of duty is the same in kind with the love which in the case of conflict of motives we judged to be inferior to the sense of duty; and the imagined though non-existent sense of duty which according to this suggestion is inferior to love is of the same kind as the sense of duty which we judged to be higher than love when the two conflicted; so that if the sense of duty was the better when the two conflicted, it would still be the better if it existed in the case in which it actually does not.

It is not as if the sense of duty could fairly be described as a hard impersonal devotion to an abstract principle in contrast with the warm outflow of love towards another person. In its typical manifestation, the sense of duty is a particularly keen sensitiveness to the rights and interests of other people, coupled with a determination to do what is fair as between them; and it is by no means the case that it tends to be divorced from warm personal feeling; it tends rather to be something superadded to that.

But, finally, the desire to do the act which is genuinely obligatory is better than the desire to do the act which is the fulfilment of a particular *prima facie* obligation. Suppose a man thinks act A to be *prima facie* obligatory in some respect, but act B to be actually his duty; he is obviously acting better in doing the latter act than in doing the former.

We seem to have been able to establish an order of worth among the various motives from which human action flows. But it is clear that action often flows from a combination of motives. (In such a case we may call the combination of motives the resultant motive, and the simple motives the component motives.) What are we to say of the worth of such combinations of motives? Suppose we agree that motive A is better than motive B. Is an action from motives A and B better than, or worse than, or morally equal to, one done from the better motive A? It was Kant's view, and it is probably often held, that the addition of a lower to a higher motive always involves that the action has less moral worth. Let us suppose that M does an act from the better motive A simply, and that N does it from a combination of motives A and B. There appear to be two quite different possibilities, not distinguished by Kant. The strength of motive A in N may not be great enough, without the co-operation of the other motive, to induce him to do the act, while in M it is *ex hypothesi* strong enough by itself to induce him to do the similar act. Then we should have to say, with Kant, that M's act is better than N's. But there is another possibility—that motive A, love of duty for instance, is equally strong in both, and that in N motive B only serves as an additional but not necessary inducement to do the act. Then we must say that the additional presence in N of motive B makes his action better than M's if motive B is itself a good one (e.g. desire to produce pleasure for another), and leaves it equally good with M's if motive B is a morally indifferent one (i.e. desire to get pleasure for himself). It will only be if the additional motive B is a positively bad one that we shall think N's action less good than M's.

There is another doctrine of Kant's, quite distinct from that just mentioned, but co-operating with it in producing his very rigoristic moral view. This is the doctrine that no motive other than sense of duty has any moral value at all, that desire to produce pleasure for another, for instance, is no better than desire to produce pain for another. This might be justified if we could regard action from any desire as simply flowing from heredity and environment, and action from sense of duty as a perfectly free undetermined action for which alone we could give the agent credit, since in it he springs quite clear of the influence of heredity and environment. But unless we can maintain this extreme libertarian position, we need not agree with Kant's denial of moral value to all desires. And plainly great violence is done to what we really think, when we are asked to believe that ordinary kindness when not dictated by the sense of duty is no better than cruelty.

Kant's picture of the ideally good man as going through life never animated by natural kindness but only by the sense of duty has always been felt by most readers to be unduly narrow and rigoristic, and if I am right, it rests on two mistakes. If we avoid these mistakes, we can think of the ideally good man as having many good motives in addition to the sense of duty, but with a sense of duty strong enough to induce him to do his duty even if the other motives were absent.

So far I have spoken of the goodness of *motives*. I have still to ask whether the goodness of action depends entirely on the goodness of its motives. It is plain enough that the two are connected. If a man exerted himself to bring about the very same changes which an ideally good man in the same circumstances would set himself to bring about, but in doing so was actuated only by the thought that in doing so he would be acquiring credit for himself, no one would assign any moral goodness to his action. And if he did so, actuated only by the thought that in doing so he would be hurting some one else, we should call his action morally bad. Yet to say that the goodness of actions depends *solely* on the goodness of their motives would be to simplify matters far too much. Suppose *A* does an action whereby he thinks he will produce pleasure, for instance, for *B*, and pain for *C* and *D*, and does it attracted only by the desire to produce pleasure for *B*, with comparative indifference to the pains of *C* and *D*, his motive is purely good but his action is not purely good. No bad motive has been at work, but a good motive, the wish to spare pain to *C* and *D*, has not been at work or has not been at work as strongly as it would have been in an ideal character. The way in which we judge of the goodness of an action is, I think, somewhat as follows. If *A* does an act which he foresees to be likely to have certain characteristics, we ask ourselves what attractions an ideally good man would have towards the act in virtue of certain of its characteristics, and what aversions he would have in virtue of others. We judge, perhaps, that an ideally good man would be more deterred from the act because it would hurt *C* and *D* than he would be attracted towards it because it would give pleasure to *B*; and we judge *A*'s action bad on the whole not because of its actual motive, which is good, but because in doing it *A* is failing to have a strong aversion which an ideally good man would have. We judge the action by comparing the agent's set of attractions and aversions with the set of attractions and aversions which would ideally arise in face of the foreseen changes to be produced by the action.

It is easy to illustrate the point. Suppose that *A* out of nepotism bestows a job on *B*, in whom he is interested, ignoring the much stronger claims of *C*, *D*, &c., but wishing them no ill. His motive is good, so far as it goes, though it does not rank very high in the list of motives. But his action is definitely bad, because he is not being deterred as an ideally good man would be by the thought of the injustice to *C*, *D*, and the rest.

Even action done from a sense of duty may for this reason fail to have moral goodness, may *perhaps* even be morally bad. The nepotist may act from the thought that he *ought* to bestow the job on *B*; and so far there is an element of goodness in his action. But in so far as he is failing to be influenced by the thought that he ought to do justice to *C, D,* and the rest, his action is a bad one; and it is easy to imagine a case in which the *prima facie* obligations he is failing to be influenced by are much more weighty than those he is being influenced by; and in such a case his action will be on the whole positively bad.

An alternative way of considering the matter should, however, be considered. It may be said that such an action, in which the effective motive is a good one, and the agent merely fails to be affected by morally more weighty considerations, is not bad, but merely of a low degree of goodness. But I think this answer can be seen not to agree with what we really think. Imagine a man who is never influenced by the wish to harm any one, but . who is completely selfish, never acting even from a narrow sense of duty, nor from a wish to make any one other than himself better or happier, regardless both of the rights and of the interests of every one else. We should not hesitate to call such a man a bad man. We might feel more certain of his badness than of the badness of a man who sometimes acted from the desire to hurt another, but also sometimes from the desire to help another. Yet on the view we are now considering none of his actions would be bad, since none of them would proceed from a positively bad motive, but all from the neutral motive of desire to further his own interests or his own pleasure. We should have a very bad man who never did a bad deed. But a bad character is a character from which bad acts tend to flow, and if we are clear that the character is bad, we ought to be clear that the actions which are the typical manifestations of the character are bad. We should be clear, then, that the lack of good motivation as well as the presence of bad motivation may make an action bad.

If this argument be correct, we are now in a position to see that rightness and goodness do not fall so much apart as we should think them to do if we held that goodness depends entirely on the motive present, while rightness depends not at all on motive, but on intention, or, more strictly, on the nature of that which we set ourselves to do. For an action will be completely good only if it manifests the whole range of motivation by which an ideally good man would be affected in the circumstances, a sensitiveness to every result for good or for evil that the act is foreseen as likely to have, as well as to any special *prima facie* obligations or disobligations that may be involved; and only if it manifests sensitiveness to all these considerations in their right proportions. But if the agent is responsive to all the morally relevant considerations in their right proportions, he will in fact do the *right* act. Thus no action will have the utmost moral excellence which an action in the circumstances can have, unless it is also the right action.

But if we have shown that in its limiting case a morally good action must be the right action in the circumstances, we have still left moral goodness and rightness in some very important ways independent. To begin with, a right act need not be a completely or even a partially good act. Take a case in which we should have no doubt what is the right act to do. Suppose that *A* owes money to another man who in addition to being his creditor is very poor and very deserving. We should agree that he ought to pay the debt, that that is the right act. But suppose that the debtor is a candidate for Parliament and the creditor one of his constituents. It might easily happen then that the debtor paid the debt, i.e. did the right act, merely to escape discredit in his constituency, and in such a case the act would be morally quite neutral. Again, he might conceivably pay the debt to encourage the creditor to some extravagance which he could not afford. Then he would be doing the right act but his action would be morally bad.

Again, an act may have a high degree of moral goodness and yet be entirely different from the right act. A man may be alive to almost all the morally significant features of alternative acts, but may (from prejudice against some individual, for instance, or from lack of imagination) fail to be attracted by just that feature of one of the alternative acts which to a person of ideal moral goodness would be the decisive feature; and in such a case he will do an act completely different from the right act.

Yet, as might be expected, goodness of character is the only condition that with even the slightest degree of probability tends to make for the doing of right acts. If a man is not morally good, it is only by the merest accident that he ever does what he ought. The act to which he is attracted by one feature of it, itself morally indifferent or bad, may be the act towards which a good man would be attracted by its whole system of morally significant features, but if it is so, the coincidence is accidental. Thus a theory which insists on the difference and mutual independence of rightness and goodness is by no means precluded from recognizing those connexions between the two which are well known to common sense.

XIII

SUMMARY

IT is proper that I should now attempt some summary, with a few fresh elucidations, of the line of thought which I have tried to present. I have, following a phrase of Lord Gifford's will, taken as my theme the foundations of ethics. I have not tried to discuss by any means all the subjects that are usually included in a text-book of ethics, but to restrict myself to the foundations. Not that I can flatter myself that the foundations have always been well and truly laid by me. The whole subject is so difficult—in some respects indeed it is the hardest branch of philosophy—that one must just do one's best, and hope that where one's suggestions do not commend themselves, they may lead to some modified view which will be nearer to the truth, and that where they are flatly wrong, they may by re-action against them help some one to see more clearly what is true. I have, at least, tried to stick to my task by avoiding the discussion of theories which are of merely historical interest, and by confining myself to problems which are in the forefront of ethical interest to-day. At the same time, there are, of course, many recent theories which I have not dealt with. I have tried to stick to my own line of thought, and to deal only with theories which lay on or near it.

The general conception of ethics on which I have worked is this: Ethics is often described as a normative science, as laying down norms or rules of right or of good behaviour. That seems to me to be in a sense true, and in a sense untrue. In a sense, ethics would be guilty of great officiousness in undertaking this task. There are many plain men who already know as well as any moral philosopher could tell them, how they ought to behave. Not only do they see their concrete duty, in the difficult situations of life, with admirable clearness and correctness, but they have principles, of a certain degree of generality, on which no moral philosopher can improve—tell the truth, keep your promises, aim at the happiness of those round you, and so on. But these general principles, while perfectly sound when properly understood, are apt to lead to difficulties, familiar even to the plain man, when their nature is not properly understood; for they are apt to conflict, at least in appearance, with one another. What is the plain man to do when he cannot tell the truth to *A* without breaking a promise to *B*, or when he cannot give pleasure to *C* without hurting *D*? Moral philosophy cannot relieve his *practical* difficulty by telling him in advance what he ought to do in such a case. What he ought to do will depend on the precise circumstances, including his precise state of knowledge and opinion, and some of these circumstances he must know better than any one could tell him; if he can get help in his practical difficulty anywhere, it will be not by reading a treatise on moral philosophy, but by stating his case to some one in whose goodness and wisdom he has confidence, a good and wise 'plain man'. But besides his practical difficulty, he is apt to be plunged in a more deep-seated perplexity. 'What can be the authority of moral rules', he is apt to say, 'if, when we try to apply them to the problems of daily life, they are found to contradict one another?' And there is another source of perplexity for him. He finds that some of the moral rules he habitually accepts—not the very general ones of which I have given instances, but rules such as those which prescribe monogamous marriage and forbid unchastity—have been and are by no means accepted even as an ideal among all races of mankind; and this, again, is apt to lead to doubts of the authoritativeness of *any* of the accepted rules.

These two difficulties, at least, moral philosophy can do something to remove.

The first difficulty it relieves in this way. Rules such as 'tell the truth', 'injure no man', cannot survive if they continue to be taken as absolute rules of such a kind that any and every act which is an instance of telling the truth is thereby rendered right, and any act which is an instance of injuring another man is thereby rendered wrong. The rules cannot *both* be true, when thus understood, if there is a single case in which one cannot tell the truth without inflicting pain. And we find, further, that we cannot believe that there is any *one* of them which is universally true, as thus understood. At any rate we all feel sure that it is sometimes right to say what is not true, that it is sometimes right to break a promise, and so on with any one of such rules. The only way to save the authority of such rules is to recognize them not as rules guaranteeing the rightness of any act that falls under them, but as rules guaranteeing that any act which falls under them tends, so far as that aspect of its nature goes, to be right, and can be rendered wrong only if in virtue of another aspect of its nature it comes under another rule by reason of which it tends more decidedly to be wrong. Kant overshot the mark when he tried to vindicate for such rules absolute authority admitting of no exception; but he would have been right if he had confined himself to insisting that any act which violates such a rule must be viewed with suspicion until it can justify itself by appeal to some other rule of the same type.

The second difficulty moral philosophy can relieve by an examination of the moral rules current in a given society, with a view to dividing them into their different classes. Of these, it seems that four may be distinguished. There are, or may be, some whose correctness is self-evident (as, for instance, the rule that we should produce as much good as we can); some whose rightness can be deduced from a self-evident rule by applying the rule to the universal conditions of human nature; some which can be derived from a self-evident rule by applying the rule to the actual conditions of the particular society; and some which cannot be justified even on that basis and must be discarded as based on incorrect views about human nature or physical nature, or on views which were true in past conditions of society but have ceased to be true to-day.

These two perplexities, one arising from conflict between the rules current in a single society, the other arising from conflict between the rules accepted in different societies—the pointing out of the conflicts, and the attempt to reconcile them—lay at the origin of ethics in western lands, as we can see from studying the Greek sophists, Socrates, and Plato; and we may conjecture that they lie at the basis of all ethical inquiry. If ethics does in fact relieve these perplexities, it to that extent has a practical value, by removing a great discouragement from the moral life. But it is essential that it should be pursued in a purely theoretical spirit, guided only by the wish to discover what is true; the cause of morality has really been hindered, as Kant pointed out with great force,[1] by cheap and easy defences of the accepted moral code. And of course the study has great theoretical interest, quite apart from any practical value that it may be found to have.

Thus ethics has grown up, as an attempt to attain greater clearness in our thinking about questions of conduct. A little reflection shows that two kinds of judgement play the chief parts in this department of our thought, those in which we judge certain acts, or kinds of act, to be right, and those in which we judge certain kinds of things other than acts, such things as virtue or knowledge or pleasure, to be good or worth aiming at; and it becomes one of the chief tasks of ethics to reach clarity as to the meaning of the predicates of these judgements. In the inquiry into the meaning of such terms there are two stages. At the first we content ourselves with pointing out any ambiguities there may be in the usage of the terms, and distinguishing what seems to be the primary meaning in moral thought, as distinguished from any meanings of lesser moral importance and any which are not moral at all but, for instance, logical or aesthetic. At the second stage we try to inquire into the nature of that thing which we primarily mean by the term in question, in ethical thought—whether it falls under any more general category such as that of quality or relation, whether it can be defined by the use of simpler terms, and if so whether its definition involves the use of some other ethical term (as it would if right could only be defined in terms of

---

[1] *Grundlegung*, Akad. Ausgabe, iv. 410-11 (Abbott's translation, pp. 32-3).

good, or good in terms of right) or whether it can be defined by the use of purely non-ethical or naturalistic terms. The first stage of the inquiry is an inquiry into the use of language, and reaches results such as might properly be stated in a dictionary; the second inquiry is an inquiry into the nature of certain characteristics; but of course it should not be assumed without inquiry that characteristics such as we have in mind in our use of terms really exist. The last-named inquiry should precede the second-named inquiry. For unless we are satisfied that these characteristics—rightness and goodness—exist, there would be little point in inquiring what would be their nature if they did exist. Now, taking rightness first, I think we can satisfy ourselves that it exists; i.e. I think we can see that in many situations that occur there is an action possible which because it would be of a certain type—for instance, because it would produce more that is good than any other act possible in the circumstances—would be *in that respect* suitable to the circumstances (in the particular way which we describe by the words 'morally suitable');[1] and further, that there is at least one possible action than which no other, *in view of its whole character*, would be *more* suitable morally. The first of these facts seems to me to be apprehended as self-evident; the second naturally follows from it. That seems to me the proper order; when we face a moral situation, what we see first is the existence of component suitabilities, or responsibilities, or claims, or *prima facie* obligations—whichever language we prefer. And because we see the existence of these we see that there must be some action (or possibly several alternative actions) which would have a higher degree of resultant suitability than any of the other actions that could be done in the circumstances, though we may have no certainty as to which action (or actions) would have this characteristic.

The next step is to reflect on the nature of this characteristic which we call rightness; and this involves the inquiry whether it is definable or not, and if so, in what sort of terms it is definable.

[1] Cf. pp. 51–5.

One may inquire first whether it is definable in non-ethical terms. I have examined, I believe, the most important attempts to define it in such a way, and have, I hope, given sufficient reasons for holding that no combination of non-ethical terms expresses the nature of what we *mean* by rightness, however much we may think that actions having such-and-such a non-ethical characteristic must necessarily *be* right. And then, passing to attempts to define rightness by the use of another *ethical* term, e.g. as productivity of what is good, I have tried to show that this does not express what we *mean* by 'right', even if we were to think that all acts having this character *are* right, and that no others are so. If these contentions are correct, moral rightness is an indefinable characteristic, and even if it be a species of a wider relation, such as suitability, its differentia cannot be stated except by repeating the phrase 'morally right' or a synonym; just as, while red is a species of colour, what distinguishes it from other colours can be indicated only by saying that it is the colour that is red.

From this it is natural to pass to asking what are the proper *subjects* of the predicate 'right'. Now here, even within the moral sphere, we find that 'right' is applied to a variety of kinds of thing. We can say that certain emotions and desires are the right emotions and desires to have in certain situations, and it seems clear that 'right' here has a moral meaning, not reducible to non-ethical terms. But 'right' is used mainly, and 'obligatory' is used only, of *actions*; and 'obligatory' is used only of them, because they and they alone, in distinction from emotions and desires, are what is directly willed. We should be justified, then, in treating actions as the most important subjects of the predicate 'right'. It seems, further, that actions can be called right for a variety of reasons, so long as 'right' is used in a rather wide sense as equivalent to 'morally suitable'; for an action is in one respect morally suitable if it proceeds from good motives, in another respect morally suitable if it (whatever motive it proceeds from) in fact produces results which are the maximum possible fulfilment of the various moral claims that exist against the agent. But if we use 'right' in the narrower sense in which a 'right' action is an obligatory action, we can, I think, see that neither of these is the proper subject of rightness. The *former* cannot be obligatory, because only that is obligatory which can be chosen, or which, at least, the agent could choose if he were a better man; but however good a man he were, he could never choose his immediate motive, since what we choose is acts and never anything else. And the *latter* cannot be obligatory, for the same reason, viz. that we cannot choose to produce results, but only to exert ourselves to do so. We are apt to be misled here, because we usually describe our duties as duties to do such things as paying our debts, relieving distress, and so on, where the phrases we use seem to refer simply to the achievement of certain results; but on reflection we see that such a phrase as 'paying one's debts' includes a reference to two different though connected things—an activity of setting oneself to pay one's debts and the receipt of money by our creditor which normally results. Of these two things only the first is an activity of ours at all; and therefore it alone can be that which is obligatory.

It is quite natural that both the view which includes the motive, and that which includes the achievement of a certain result, in that to which we are obliged, should have received much support among moral philosophers; for both the well-motivated action and the action in which we not only exert ourselves in the right way but achieve what we set ourselves to do, have undoubtedly a certain moral suitability on that account. But it is not moral suitability of the special kind which can alone involve obligatoriness, since neither the desire to be felt by us here and now, nor the result to be achieved by us, can be chosen, and only what is capable of being chosen can be obligatory.

I need hardly add that in saying that motives are not an element in what is obligatory, I am not suggesting that a man who never acted from a good motive could do the whole duty of man. That this could not be so follows from two reasons.

If a bad or indifferent motive ever leads to a right act, it can only be by accident, and therefore in a succession of acts from such motives very few are likely to be the right acts in the circumstances. And secondly, good desires being the most essential element in a good character, and one of our main duties being that of producing what is good wherever we can, and the betterment of our own character being one of the good things that are most under our own control, it is one of our main duties to set ourselves to improve our own character, and that will almost inevitably lead to our later acts being to some extent well motivated.

In saying that it is setting oneself to produce this or that change that is obligatory, I may seem to have come perilously near to saying what I have expressly disavowed, that it is by its motive that an act is made right or wrong. It is, of course, always from some motive or other that we set ourselves to bring about changes. But the setting oneself is quite different from the doing so from any particular motive. If I set myself to produce a state of affairs in which one thing will be in the state A and another thing in the state B, I may do so either from the wish to effect the first of these changes, accepting the other indifferently or even unwillingly as a necessary accompaniment of the first, or from the wish to effect the second of them, accepting the other indifferently or even unwillingly as a necessary accompaniment of the second; then my self-exertion is the same in the two cases, but the motives are quite different. And further, in deciding what I ought to do, it is evident that I must consider equally *all* the elements, so far as I can foresee them, in the state of affairs I shall be bringing about. If I see that my act is likely to help M, for instance, and to hurt N, I am not justified in ignoring the bad effect, or even in treating it as less important than the good effect, merely because it is the good effect and not the bad one that I *wish* to bring about. It is the whole nature of that which I set myself to bring about, not that part of it which I happen to desire, that makes my act right or wrong.

If we are right in holding that the *general* nature of the things that are obligatory is that they are activities of self-exertion, what can we say about their *particular* character? Perhaps the most widely current view on this question is that the special character of all the acts that are right, and that which makes them right, is that they are acts of setting oneself to produce a maximum of what is good. This seems to me far from being, as it is often supposed to be, self-evident, and to be in fact a great over-simplification of the ground of rightness. There is no more reason, after all, to suppose that there is one single reason which makes all acts right that *are* right, than there is for supposing (what I fancy no one who considers the matter will suppose) that there is a single reason which makes all things good that *are* good. And in fact there are several branches of duty which apparently cannot be grounded on productivity of the greatest good. There appears to be a duty, for instance, of fulfilling promises, a duty of making compensation for wrongs we have done, a duty of rendering a return for services we have received, and these cannot be explained as forms of the duty of producing the greatest good; we are conscious of duties to behave in these ways even when we have no conviction that the greatest sum of good will be thus produced, and this is so even when we take account of more distant results such as the increase in general mutual confidence which the keeping of a single promise is likely to produce; for we are conscious of the duty even when owing to the secrecy of the promise this result is not likely to happen. Again, we are conscious of a duty to do what is just, and this refers not to the production of a maximum of good, but to the right distribution of it. *This* may perhaps be brought within the formula of 'producing the maximum good' by recognizing enjoyment of happiness in proportion to merit as a more complex good to be distinguished from the merit and the happiness; but it seems impossible to explain the other duties just referred to by similar hypotheses, because the results to be produced, if good at all, are good only because there is a duty to set oneself to produce them. We seem to be driven to conclude that there is not one single ground of the rightness of all right acts; but the number of separate grounds appears to be quite small. And the ultimate propositions at which we arrive seem not to express mere brute facts, but facts which are self-evidently necessary. For instance, the very object of a promise being to encourage some one to believe that one will act in a certain way, it is self-evident that he has a moral claim to our behaving in that way if he wants us to do so.

If we now turn to ask how we come to know these fundamental moral principles, the answer seems to be that it is in the same way in which we come to know the axioms of mathematics. Both alike seem to be both synthetic and *a priori*; that is to say, we see the predicate, though not included in the definition of the subject, to belong necessarily to anything which satisfies that definition. And as in mathematics, it is by intuitive induction that we grasp the general truths. We see first, for instance, that a particular imagined act, as being productive of pleasure to another, has a claim on us, and it is a very short and inevitable step from this to seeing that *any* act, as possessing the same constitutive character, must have the same resultant character of *prima facie* rightness. But we are perhaps in one respect better off than we are in geometry, at least; for while in geometry the diagrams by whose aid we come to see the general truths merely approximate to having the two characteristics which we see to be necessarily united, we have before us in ethics acts already done, in which we can recognize the two characteristics to be actually present and necessarily united— the characteristic, for instance, of being productive of pleasure to another person and that of being *prima facie* right.

On the other hand, we cannot, in general, claim intuitive or any other kind of certainty as to the actual (or resultant) rightness of particular acts. For *prima facie* obligations differ in the degree of their obligatoriness, and we often cannot say which of two or more *prima facie* obligations involved in a particular situation is the more or the most obligatory. When we are dealing with obligations of the same kind, we have certain criteria for measuring their obligatoriness; we can see that, *ceteris paribus*, there is a greater *prima facie* obligation to produce a great good than to produce a small one, and a greater *prima facie* obligation to fulfil a very explicit and deliberate promise, than to fulfil one which is casually made and not taken very seriously by the promisee, or again to fulfil a prior promise rather than a later one inconsistent with it. But if we try to balance an obligation to produce a certain good against an obligation to fulfil a certain promise, we move in a region of uncertainty. In some such cases, all or almost all conscientious men agree in their answer, and then we may hope that the judgement they agree in is true. In others they would be pretty evenly divided, and then all that any of them can say is 'this *seems* to me to be the right course'. And one who does what seems to him to be right is doing what in another sense *is* right,[1] and is doing an action of moral worth.

This is the gist of what I have been trying to say about judgements of which the predicate is 'right'; I turn now to those of which the predicate is 'good'. Here too we have to recognize the existence of various senses in which the word is used. We must recognize that 'good' is often used merely in the sense of 'good of its kind'. We must recognize that it is often used in the sense of 'a means to something good', the sense in which a hedonist who thought pleasure the only thing good in itself might nevertheless call virtue good if he thought it a useful means to pleasure. We must recognize that it is often used of whole states of affairs in which good is thought to predominate over evil. But there is clearly another sense in which 'good' is used as meaning 'good absolutely' and not merely 'good of its kind', as meaning 'good in itself' and not as a means, as meaning 'good through and through' and not merely predominantly. And it is this sense that is the most important for ethics; for it is things that are good in this sense that are involved in what is the widest of all our duties, the duty of

---

[1] pp. 161–5.

producing as much that is good as we can. But, within this sense, it seems that we can distinguish two sub-senses. Suppose we take three things which we think it incumbent upon us to produce, to the best of our ability—virtuous activity, the use of the intelligence, and the happiness of other people—we find that they fall into two classes. We can distinguish them first by noting the difference between the mental states of which they are worthy objects. All alike are worthy objects of interest—of satisfaction when they are present, of desire when they are absent, of regret when they are lost. But the first two are also worthy objects of admiration; they are fine activities of the spirit; and no one would say that of pleasures just as pleasures. Or again, we may distinguish them by noting that whereas the first two confer goodness on their possessors, pleasure as such confers no goodness on its possessor. And finally, we may note that while virtuous activity and the use of the intelligence are morally worthy objects of interest for any one, no matter who is to exercise them, it is only the pleasures of other people and not his own pleasures that are morally worthy objects of interest to any one, his own pleasures being completely neutral in this respect—natural objects of interest, but morally neither worthy objects of satisfaction nor worthy objects of dissatisfaction. It seems, then, that there are two senses in which things good in themselves are good, and that virtuous activity and the use of the intelligence are good in both senses, pleasures are good only in one, and for any man only the pleasures of other people are good in that one sense.

Have we, in describing things good in themselves as worthy objects of interest or as worthy objects of admiration, made their goodness consist in certain relations to those who take interest in them, or admire them? I think not, in the latter case; for admiration includes not only a certain emotion, but also the thought that the object of that emotion is good, and therefore only that which is already good in itself can be a worthy object of admiration. On the other hand, the fact that only the pleasures of others, and not his own, are a morally worthy object of interest to any one, at once indicates that their goodness consists in a certain relation to him, which they have not to their owners and which his pleasures have not to him. This relation is not one which can be stated in purely non-ethical terms, as the relation of *being* an object of interest can be stated; it involves the ethical or non-naturalistic term 'worthy' or 'suitable'. And we can get further light on its nature by noting that to be an object worthy of interest is the same—not as being the object of a right interest, for a thing worthy of interest is worthy of interest even when no interest is taken in it, but as being a thing, interest in which, if such interest exists, is right or morally suitable. Thus this secondary type of goodness is defined by reference to rightness.

And now that we have recognized in the pleasures of others things that are good in this secondary and relative sense, we may perhaps recognize other things that are good in the same sense. I suggest that the complex good which consists in the proportionment of happiness to moral worth is good in this sense. It is obviously not in itself a worthy object of *admiration*; our admiration would be only for him who had effected it. But it is a worthy object of *interest*. And the relativity of this good, in contrast with the absoluteness of the goodness of virtuous activity and of the use of the intelligence, betrays itself in the fact that, just as his own pleasure is not a morally worthy object of interest to any man, so the right proportioning of pleasure between himself and others is not a morally worthy object of interest to him, but only the right proportioning of pleasure between others. There is clearly nothing morally right in desiring happiness proportioned to one's own merits—though of course there is nothing morally wrong either; for rightness and wrongness are not contradictories but contraries.

In discussing rightness or obligatoriness, I attempted, after considering the nature of this characteristic itself, to throw some light on the nature of the things which possess this characteristic. Similarly, after discussing the nature of goodness, I tried next to answer the question, what kinds of thing are good. A first answer to this question was indeed given in the consideration of the *meanings* of 'good'; for we found that the two main meanings of good which I have indicated—'good as worthy object of admiration' and 'good as worthy object of interest'—were applicable to two different sets of things, the first to certain moral and intellectual activities, the second to certain pleasures. I did not attempt to indicate more precisely which intellectual activities are good; those which are good are good because of their intrinsic characteristics, and it is the business of two other branches of philosophy, logic and aesthetics, to specify these characteristics. But it is part of our business to indicate which kinds of *moral* activities are good. It is usually to activities of *will* that we apply the description 'morally good', but it would be a mistake to limit moral goodness to these; for emotions, such as delight at the good fortune of another, and desires which do not lead to action, can be morally good, no less than actions; and actions themselves are good, in the main, by reason of the desires from which they spring. We may perhaps generalize by saying that what is morally good, besides certain actions, is *interests* of certain kinds, and that these owe their goodness, and their degree of goodness, to what they are interests in. With one exception, to be mentioned later, the highest interest is the interest in something that is good in the strictest sense, i.e. in the bringing into being, in oneself or in another, of good moral or intellectual activity or disposition or capacity. Next to that comes the interest in the pleasure of others. Interest in pleasure to be enjoyed by oneself is neutral in respect of goodness or badness, except where the pleasure is itself the proper pleasure of a good or of a bad activity. Interest in inflicting pain on others is itself morally bad, but less bad than interest in the bringing into being of bad activities in oneself or in others. Interests falling within any one of these classes tend to be better or worse according to their generality, a wide altruism being, for instance, better than a narrow, and a wide malevolence being worse than a narrow. They also tend to be better or worse according to their intensity, an intense altruism being better than a tepid, and an intense malevolence being worse than a tepid.

When we consider interests as forming *motives to action*, we have to recognize that there is a better motive than any of these, the wish to do one's duty; for it is clear that it is always morally better to act from the sense of duty than to do an alternative act from any other motive, however good, and if the sense of duty is the best motive when it is in conflict with others, it is also the best motive when it conspires with others in pointing to the same action. It is the best because, while the other good desires are desires to bring into being this or that good thing, without considering whether it is the greatest good one could bring about, in conscientious action an attempt, at least, has been made to do this.

While the desire to do one's duty is thus different in kind from all other motives, it seems true to say, not, with Kant, that it alone has moral value, but that it has the highest moral value. Certain other motives also have moral value, because of the affinity of nature that there is between them and the sense of duty, since they include a part of the thought which is included in the sense of duty. The other good motives are attractions towards certain actions *as being of a certain character*; the sense of duty is an attraction towards them *as being right as being possessed of that same character*.

Again, it does not seem to be correct to say, with Kant, that the addition of any other motive to the sense of duty necessarily makes the motivation of an act less good than it would be without that addition. So long as the strength of the sense of duty is equal in both cases, the addition of another good motive improves the motivation, and the addition of a neutral motive, i.e. of the desire for one's own happiness, does nothing to make the motivation worse.

Motive is the main factor that makes an action good or bad, but it is not the only one. The motive of the great majority of bad actions is one which is not bad at all, the desire for pleasures which are themselves morally neutral—such as the pleasures of eating and drinking, of warmth and shelter. Theft, for instance, rarely proceeds from any form of malevolence; it springs from the wish to get easily such comforts as money will buy; yet theft is bad. It is bad, not because it has a bad motive, which it has not, but because it lacks a good motive which a man of ideally good character would have in the same situation. It is bad because of a moral insensitivity which it manifests, an insensitivity to the rights of others to what they own. Again, many acts which we think bad are bad not by reason of springing from a desire to inflict pain on others, but by reason of the insensitivity to their pain which they manifest. Thus an action is judged good or bad not by reference merely to its motive, but by a comparison of that with the whole range of motives that would ideally be present. If a man is not repelled by some feature of a proposed action that an ideally good man would be repelled by, his action is to that extent bad. In other words, intention as well as motive plays a part in fixing the degree of goodness of an action. But it plays a smaller part; for if we intend by an action to help A, for instance, and to hurt B, our action is a better one if what we *want* is to help A, than if it is to hurt B. The fact, however, that intention plays some part in fixing the goodness of an action implies that only the doing of what is the right action in the circumstances can have the greatest moral value that an action in the circumstances can have. At this point, then, the right and the good converge. But of course the doing of the right action will be the best action only if it is done from the best motive to which the circumstances could give rise. Further, the rightness of actions is not, in general, proportional to their goodness; for the rightness of an action necessarily depends equally on the nature of *all* that is intended in it, while its goodness depends primarily on what is desired, and only in a lesser degree on what is intended but not desired.

It is further to be noted that the admission of intention as well as motive in what makes an action good helps to explain

the high esteem in which self-sacrifice is held. The motive of
an act of self-sacrifice may be no better than that of another
in which no self-sacrifice is involved; but the former action
includes also the intention to accept pain to ourselves as the
price we are ready to pay to bring about the good we desire to
bring about; and, our own pleasure being morally neutral,
willingness to give it up in a good cause is a component which
has moral worth and gives additional worth to the action that
involves it.

Lord Gifford directed that his Lectureships should be used
for 'Promoting, Advancing, Teaching, and Diffusing the study
of Natural Theology', but he added 'in the widest sense of that
term', and he expressly included as part of what he meant by it
'the Knowledge of the Nature and Foundation of Ethics or
Morals, and of all Obligations and Duties thence arising'. I
have confined myself to this part of the whole subject, as being
that to which I have devoted a good many years of reflection.
Perhaps the parts of this course of lectures which correspond
most closely to what Lord Gifford had in mind are those in
which I have examined whether what may broadly be called the
objective or what may be called the subjective view of obligations and values is the true one—whether they are rooted in
the nature of things or are names expressive merely of human
preferences, emotions, or opinions. This inquiry is certainly
germane to natural theology proper; for if the subjective view
were true, man in investing God with moral attributes would
indeed be making God in his own image, while if the objective
view is true, the way is left open for a further inquiry whether
morality involves a religious basis.

At the same time, the consideration I have attempted of a
number of difficult questions of detail with regard to the moral
judgements we habitually make is also germane to the subject
of natural theology. The objectivity of the moral system
would be impossible to maintain if we were to find that in passing particular moral judgements we were necessarily involved

in self-contradictions; just as it would be impossible to maintain the truth of our apparent intuitions into the nature of number and of space, if our particular intuitive judgements on these subjects led to self-contradiction. It is therefore a necessary preliminary to any natural theology which is going to ascribe any moral attributes to God—and a natural theology which did not do this would not interest us much—to examine the whole field of our moral judgements in search of apparent contradictions, and then to examine these to see if clearer thinking removes them or is powerless to do so. How far I have been successful in this search I am unable to say, but at one point at least I have to admit failure. It seems to me that something like half of our ordinary thinking on moral questions implies a belief in the indetermination of the will, and something like half a belief in its determination; and I have neither found elsewhere nor discovered by my own reflections any adequate solution of this difficulty. But the truth can never be inconsistent with itself, and we may hope that better thinking will in the long run remove this apparent contradiction, as sound thinking has already removed many others.

INDEX OF PROPER NAMES

PRINTED IN GREAT BRITAIN
AT THE UNIVERSITY PRESS, OXFORD
BY VIVIAN RIDLER
PRINTER TO THE UNIVERSITY